Mindfulness In The Classroom

An Evidence-Based Program To Reduce Disruptive Behavior And Increase Academic Engagement

Joshua C. Felver, PhD
Nirbhay N. Singh, PhD

16pt

Copyright Page from the Original Book

Publisher's Note

This publication is designed to provide accurate and authoritative information in regard to the subject matter covered. It is sold with the understanding that the publisher is not engaged in rendering psychological, financial, legal, or other professional services. If expert assistance or counseling is needed, the services of a competent professional should be sought.

Distributed in Canada by Raincoast Books

Copyright © 2020 by Joshua C. Felver and Nirbhay N. Singh
New Harbinger Publications, Inc.
5674 Shattuck Avenue
Oakland, CA 94609
www.newharbinger.com

Cover design by Amy Daniel; Acquired by Tesilya Hanauer;
Edited by Ken Knabb; Indexed by James Minkin

All Rights Reserved

Library of Congress Cataloging-in-Publication Data

Names: Felver, Joshua C., author. | Singh, Nirbhay N., author. | Horner, Robert H., author.
Title: Mindfulness in the classroom : an evidence-based program to reduce disruptive behavior and increase academic engagement / Joshua C. Felver, Nirbhay N. Singh, Robert Horner.
Description: Oakland, CA : New Harbinger Publications, [2020] | Includes bibliographical references and index.

Subjects: LCSH: Affective education. | Mindfulness (Psychology) | Classroom management. | Educational psychology.
Classification: LCC LB1072 .F45 2020 (print) | LCC LB1072 (ebook) | DDC 371.102/4--dc23
LC record available at https://lccn.loc.gov/2020004761
LC ebook record available at https://lccn.loc.gov/2020004762

Printed in the United States of America

22 21 20
10 9 8 7 6 5 4 3 2 1   First Printing

TABLE OF CONTENTS

Foreword vii
Acknowledgments xiv
Introduction xv
    CHAPTER 1: Preparation for Using Soles of the Feet 1

PART I: Soles of the Feet for Students: Classroom Curriculum

    CHAPTER 2: Class 1: Introducing Soles of the Feet 35
    CHAPTER 3: Class 2: Practicing with a Pleasant Feeling 58
    CHAPTER 4: Class 3: Practicing with an Unpleasant Feeling 83
    CHAPTER 5: Class 4: Practicing with the Triggers to an Unpleasant Feeling 110
    CHAPTER 6: Class 5: Planning to Use Soles of the Feet in Daily Life 132
    CHAPTER 7: Follow-up Booster Session 150

PART II: Soles of the Feet for Students: Individual Program

    CHAPTER 8: Session 1: Introducing Soles of the Feet 175
    CHAPTER 9: Session 2: Practicing with a Pleasant Feeling 198
    CHAPTER 10: Session 3: Practicing with an Unpleasant Feeling 219
    CHAPTER 11: Session 4: Practicing with the Triggers to an Unpleasant Feeling 245
    CHAPTER 12: Session 5: Planning to Use Soles of the Feet in Daily Life 266
    CHAPTER 13: Follow-up Booster Session 284

PART III: Supplementary Materials

    CHAPTER 14: Instructional Tips and Strategies 309
APPENDIX 1: Worksheets and Handouts 375
APPENDIX 1A: Handout—Knowing Your Feet 376
APPENDIX 1B: Worksheet—Knowing Your Feet 378

APPENDIX 1C: Belly Breathing Handout   380
APPENDIX 1D: My Soles of the Feet Routine   381
APPENDIX 1E: Eliciting Emotions Support Sheet 383
APPENDIX 1F: Identifying Triggers Worksheet   385
APPENDIX 1G: Using Soles of the Feet in Daily Life 387
APPENDIX 2: Soles of the Feet–Fidelity Monitoring Forms   389
APPENDIX 3: Soles of the Feet Research   392
APPENDIX 4: Supplementary Resources   411
References   418
Back Cover Material   435
Index   439

"This book has a hugely important message for all who wish to understand and help children and young people, particularly those whose feelings easily spiral out of control. The simple but powerful set of proven strategies, laid out in a clear syllabus for class or individual teaching, promises to be a game changer."

—**Mark Williams, DPhil,** emeritus professor of clinical psychology at the University of Oxford, and coauthor of *Mindfulness-Based Cognitive Therapy for Depression*

"Soles of the Feet is a portable, easy-to-use mindfulness practice for students of all ages, with and without disabilities, to self-manage disruptive behavior. The program, firmly grounded in theory and research, is easy to deliver by teachers after limited training. The book is as simple and clear as the program, containing all you need to try it out: first for yourself, and only if it works for you, with your students!"

—**Susan Bögels, PhD,** professor of family mental health and mindfulness at the University of

Amsterdam, and author of *Mindful Parenting*

"There is so much I appreciate about this user-friendly book. Felver and Singh cover all the important details practitioners need to consider in implementing the Soles of the Feet intervention in their schools. The directions for each lesson are explicit and clear; the appendices include ready-to-use handouts. Assisting students in developing self-regulation is an important educational goal—in this book, readers will find a toolbox for achieving this objective."

—**Andrew Roach, PhD,** associate professor of school psychology, and doctoral program coordinator in the department of counseling and psychological services at Georgia State University

"Beautifully written and full of practical wisdom, *Mindfulness in the Classroom* offers a well-researched way to help students cultivate self-regulation skills. It provides a strong theoretical explanation for why this simple and usable mindfulness practice works, and includes clear class outlines and

teacher-friendly supplementals. Highlighting the pitfalls of using mindfulness as a classroom management technique, the authors offer a powerful way for students (and teachers) to break free of coercive discipline, manage strong emotions, and practice self-management routines that will help them in every aspect of their lives."
—**Patricia C. Broderick, PhD,** research associate at Penn State University; and author of *Learning to Breathe, Mindfulness in the Secondary Classroom,* and *The Life Span*

"Felver and Singh have produced a practical book that ensures teachers can teach children in schools an evidence-based mindfulness strategy: Soles of the Feet. The resource is well thought through, offering advice from school experience and expertise in teaching mindfulness. Everything you need to help students to manage their strong emotions in school, and to reduce disruptive behavior as a result, is included in this fully complete manual."

—**Richard Hastings, PhD, CPsychol, FBPS, FIASSIDD, FAcSS,** professor of education and psychology at the University of Warwick, England

"Teachers will find this book remarkably lucid and practical in its aim to empower students to self-regulate their behavior using the mindfulness practice of Soles of the Feet. The authors have uniquely integrated the teaching of Soles of the Feet with evidence-based practices in behavioral and instructional support, and have embodied the qualities of mindfulness throughout the book, including nonjudgmental awareness, acceptance, and the patience and repetition necessary for mastery by students."

—**Joseph Lucyshyn, PhD, BCBA-D,** associate professor of special education at the University of British Columbia, and coeditor of *Families and Positive Behavior Support*

"Based on a solid foundation of theory and research, *Mindfulness in the Classroom* illustrates how a simple yet powerful practice can help children and youth develop psychological skills for meaningful and long-lasting positive change. There is no need for readers to fill any gaps with additional reading as it is all contained here—necessary background, clear and detailed outline of different practices, and easy-to-use supplementary material."

—**Chris Krägeloh, PhD,** associate professor of psychology at Auckland University of Technology in New Zealand, and coauthor of *Mindfulness-Based Intervention Research*

"Never have children needed to be resourced more than now with skills to navigate the myriad challenges in their lives. *Mindfulness in the Classroom* is not only timely, but it stands out from the field of other such programs because it is steeped in solid psychological theory, has been extensively researched, and was developed by two of the leading figures in this field."

—**Willem Kuyken, PhD,** Ritblat Professor of Mindfulness and Psychological Science at the University of Oxford, and coauthor (with Christina Feldman) of *Mindfulness*

Foreword

"Soles of the Feet" (SoF) is a mindfulness program designed specifically for children and youth in school settings. It incorporates ideas, procedures, and logic (breathing, cognitive focus, acceptance) that draw from an array of mindfulness approaches. In this text, however, the material is organized with specific attention on improving the ability of school adults to support at-risk students. This is done first by providing the reader with the logic and core elements of SoF as a clinical intervention. The reader is then asked to both master the breathing/thinking routine at the heart of the practice and to appreciate the mechanisms by which mindfulness facilitates self-regulation. As with any new skill, the teacher is first asked to assume the role of learner, build fluency and confidence, and then move to the role of instructor. The goal is to use the materials and curricular steps as they are described in the book, but to enliven that content with personal experience. The book provides instructional elements for (a) introducing SoF to an adult reader, (b) guiding the reader through classroomwide instruction of SoF, and (c) tailoring the five instructional SoF sessions for use with individual students who may need more intensive support. The scripted materials make the text a formal curriculum for delivering SoF (both for whole classes and for individual students) and a primer on mindfulness approaches.

Readers will appreciate the efforts made to make the content accessible, practical, and relevant. Procedures are described with precision, but with repeated encouragement for adaptation to fit local contexts, students, and community expectations. While the value of the text lies in the details, there are four overarching messages that readers are encouraged to appreciate:

The first is the fundamental assumption throughout the book that our goal as teachers and educators should be the empowerment of students, not just the establishment of instructional control. This is not just a book about reducing disruptive behavior, it is a book about teaching core self-regulation skills that allow students to be academically and socially successful in schools. This is not a book about tricks that teachers can use to manage behavior, but a book about building self-managed routines that will benefit students in their school, home, work, and community. The clear emphasis given to building the capacity of students to move beyond anger and disruption is a wonderful foundation. The practical message is that while adults must be able to set limits and expectations, the real gift is providing students with the competence to manage their own behavior.

The second message from the book is the need to explicitly teach SoF as a behavioral routine. The initial sessions/classes introduce the student to the rationale for SoF and then provide a tutorial on key skills. These key behaviors (e.g., breathing, attending, accepting) are first taught as individual elements then chained together into a fluent and functioning routine. It is a routine that interrupts existing dysfunctional chains of behavior, redirects the student toward calming and self-controlling behaviors, and transforms vulnerable situations into successful situations. The authors clearly present the SoF routine as a skill to be taught, and practiced. The SoF logic is not about ephemeral change but about overt mastery of physical and cognitive skills. This is a book about building self-regulation as a personal competency, not an aspiration.

The third message from the book is the most subtle. It is critical that students both understand the rationale for SoF and master the SoF routine. But the real impact of SoF training comes from teaching the students *when* to use their self-regulation ability. A key distinction in the SoF instruction is that "disruption" and "anger" are not characteristics of people but responses to certain types of situations. All students act with grace, kindness, and consideration in some situations. Some students also act with anger and aggression, but they do this in certain types of situations, typically due to their learning histories in these situations.

Within SoF, students learn both to anticipate and recognize when they are entering or engaged in a vulnerable situation. It is in these situations that the SoF routine becomes most valuable. Understanding how to follow the SoF routine is important, but the real value of the approach is when a student recognizes that certain kinds of situations are difficult or dangerous and "signal" the need to use their SoF skills. The authors offer a curriculum that starts by practicing the SoF routine, then using the SoF routine with "easy," pleasant situations. Only when students are fluent with this level of use do the authors introduce more difficult and challenging situations. A central skill of any adult using this book will be judging when and how to introduce SoF routines with more emotionally charged contexts. The success of the SoF approach, however, depends on students leaving Session 5 not only with competence in how to follow the SoF routine, but also with a personal understanding of *when* that skill should be applied.

The fourth broad message provided by the authors is to treat SoF as a *piece* of any behavioral solution, not the whole answer. Self-regulation is an undervalued part of American education, and programs like SoF provide much-needed guidance. At the same time, all educators must recognize that educational success has many components, and the skills related to SoF, while important, are only a part of the puzzle. Building social networks, developing academic competence, learning not just how to avoid anger and disruption but how to achieve social goals through positive behavioral routines are all part of effective education. The authors encourage us to give SoF a sufficient "try" so that we experience the success and efficiency of the approach. But they also offer the caveat that students with more intense behavioral and mental health needs will require more comprehensive support. It is left to each reader to determine the niche in their school where SoF best fits. Clear guidance is given for classwide SoF training and for use of SoF as part of individual student support efforts. Determining how these fit with broader schoolwide and clinical supports will be an important consideration for both educators and researchers.

In conclusion, I recommend the reader take the authors' encouragement to take the core elements of SoF seriously and implement SoF with thoughtful attention to the fidelity tool provided in Appendix 2 but also with continuous commitment to having fun. In many ways, SoF is a program that only starts students down a path of self-regulation. Success with SoF may well be a central part of not just getting through a rough patch in school, but of shifting behavioral and academic trajectories. The empirical evidence provided in Appendix 3 is encouraging, but as the authors note, there remains much we do not understand. Both clinical and scholarly efforts are needed to move SoF from an enchanting self-regulation program to an embedded part of the self-regulation training regularly provided to all American children.

—Robert H. Horner, PhD
University of Oregon

Acknowledgments

We would like to express our gratitude to the teachers who have dedicated their lives to helping youth learn and grow, and to the children and adolescents who have trusted us in our guidance to look inward and meet challenges with courage. It is our sincerest intention and highest aspiration that this work reduce the suffering of others.

Introduction

This book presents a simple program called "Soles of the Feet" (SoF), a basic mindfulness practice that students learn to use when they notice that they are becoming upset and would like to remain calm and make decisions that don't have negative consequences. Students like learning SoF because it gives them a sense of self-control over their experience, and teachers like it when students are more self-regulated because they are less disruptive in the classroom and more academically engaged in school.

This book was written explicitly for the benefit of students who are struggling in school settings. No student wants to fail academically (not even the surly teenager who may emphatically declare the exact opposite sentiment!). No student wants to get in trouble with their teacher. No student enjoys losing control of their behavior in front of their friends and peers. This book was written for these students so that they may be more successful in school, by which we mean that students will be less disruptive in the classroom, more academically engaged, and more likely to succeed academically, and thus meet with more long-term success as an adult. A corollary process is that teachers of these students may find that it is easier to teach when students are less disruptive. However, this outcome (although critically important) is secondary to the benefits students experience directly through learning SoF. It is with this intention that this work was conducted, and it is our sincerest hope that those who work with challenging students will find SoF to be helpful in ensuring the success of the youth in their charge.

Why Does Disruptive Student Behavior Matter?

A quality education during childhood and adolescence is one of the most important experiences of one's lifetime. Decades worth of research has indicated that academic achievement (i.e., successfully meeting academic goals such as completing high school) predicts numerous outcomes not only during childhood and adolescence, but also throughout one's adult life. Those who successfully finish high school are much more likely to be steadily employed, to continue on to post-secondary education, to earn more income, and to have stable social lives. Conversely, academic underachievement is associated with a host of negative long-term consequences such as poverty, incarceration, and other psychosocial challenges. Succeeding academically is clearly of paramount importance to individuals, and also to any society as a whole that aspires to have a high quality of life for all of its members.

There are numerous reasons why youth do not achieve academically, and disentangling the relations of these variables for groups of youth over time poses a daunting task for social and educational scientists, as well as for clinicians working with individual youth and families. Among these variables, it is no surprise that the degree to which students are fully attending to and participating with classroom content, also referred to as *academic engagement,* strongly predicts their long-term academic achievement. Given the strength of the relation between academic engagement and academic achievement, it is extremely important that those working with students be equipped with skills to promote academically engaged behavior in all of the students whom they serve.

There are any number of reasons why a student may not be academically engaged. Students may be uninterested in the content or preoccupied with other thoughts and daydreaming. This is referred to as *passive off-task behavior.* Far more commonly, however, students are exhibiting disruptive behaviors that prevent their being able to attend to instructional content and also distract other students and disrupt the teacher's ability to effectively teach. This is referred to as *active off-task behavior.* Active off-task behavior can take numerous forms, such as verbal outbursts (e.g., impulsively shouting out answers to questions, talking to a peer when the expectation is to work silently at one's desk, or insulting a school staff person), getting out of one's seat and walking around or leaving the classroom, or physical aggression (e.g., kicking a peer in the chair in front of a student, hitting a teacher, or throwing a chair). These active off-task behaviors often create a coercive cycle of interactions between the student and the teacher that, over time, can escalate into more serious responses from the school (e.g., detentions, suspensions, or expulsions), which are often ineffective at reducing the problematic behavior and which further prevent the student from learning in the classroom and achieving academically. Clearly, effective interventions to reduce the occurrence of off-task behaviors are necessary to support the needs of these at-risk students.

Similarly, there are also many reasons why students exhibit disruptive behavior in the classroom. Some students may be frustrated with the difficulty of the classroom assignment. Others may be struggling with peer challenges that spill over into the classroom and make them more likely to act out. Others may be struggling with situations outside of the classroom, such as parents going through a divorce. Regardless of the reasons why a student may exhibit disruptive behavior in the classroom, the short-term patterns of student behavior that occur prior to a student becoming disruptive are fairly predictable. First, an event occurs, either in the student's immediate environment (e.g., a teacher tells students to take out their silent reading books, or a peer covertly taunts a student) or in the student's mind (e.g., a student remembers that they were yelled at and grounded by their father the previous night, or a student begins to worry about facing a bully on the bus ride home). Second, a student has an intense emotional or physiological response to the event (e.g., feelings of frustration, worry, or anger, or the heart rate increases and muscles begin to tense). Third, the emotional and physiological responses increase the likelihood of the student's thinking about, and elaborating upon, the event that made them upset in the first place (e.g., "I hate doing math sheets! This isn't fair!" or "I can't believe she called me that this morning, what a jerk!"), and these thinking patterns in turn increase the emotional and physiological responses in an escalating cycle. This pattern of escalation then increases until the student becomes so upset that they effectively lose control of their ability to regulate their behavior and they act out in a disruptive manner in the classroom.

Disruptive behavior is the end result of a chain of events that may have occurred minutes or hours earlier, during which time the student is likely not academically engaged and learning. Further, it is extremely difficult to coach students through strategies to calm themselves down and return to the classroom activity once they are at such an emotionally upset and physiologically escalated level: the disruptive behavior is now already occurring and the proverbial "horse is out of the barn." Strategies that target the very beginnings of this escalating pattern of disruptive behavior are therefore critical to preventing the occurrence of disruptive behaviors from occurring in the first place.

Soles of the Feet Teaches Students to Self-Manage Their Disruptive Behavior

The impetus for developing SoF was to help children and youth with intellectual disabilities or autism spectrum disorder to manage their aggressive and disruptive behavior without external control by their caregivers. While one of us was working as a behavior analyst with parents of an adolescent who functioned at a mild level of intellectual disability, the mother mentioned that her son absolutely hated being told what to do. This made it almost impossible for her to successfully implement the behavior intervention plan. When the adolescent was asked why he did not want to be told what to do, he said, "I want to be in control," and then requested that he be taught a way to control his own behavior instead of his mother implementing the behavior intervention plan. This request resulted in the development of the Soles of the Feet routine, a simple practice that required the adolescent to pause and shift the focus of his attention from an emotionally arousing situation to a neutral part of his body: the bottom (the soles) of his feet. The adolescent was taught an early precursor of the current SoF program to manage his emotional arousal that often resulted in aggressive and disruptive behavior. When his enthusiasm for using SoF lagged, his values statement ("I want to be in control") was used to remind him why he might wish to continue. After several weeks of practice, he learned to use the SoF routine with fluency at the first indication of emotional arousal and was able to manage his aggressive and disruptive behavior without reminders from his parents.

We then used variations of the early SoF procedure to perfect a series of task-analyzed steps to teach individuals to manage their aggressive and disruptive behaviors. The SoF practice was developed as a mindfulness practice that is portable, that is easy to use, that requires no equipment, that needs no continuous instructions from others, and that assists with self-management of socially undesirable behavior. It teaches the individual to shift from an automatic reaction to an internal event (e.g., when a negative thought arises) or an external event (e.g., when someone says something that is hurtful) to a mindful response. The time it takes the individual to shift his or her attention from the arising emotional thoughts to a neutral place provides a pause, which enables the arising of a mindful response from a state of calmness. Consistent practice enables the development of an inhibitory response to emotionally negative arousal situations. The SoF practice has been effectively used by children as young as three years to adults with early stage Alzheimer's disease and by people with or without disabilities. (For more on the research, development, and contexts in which SoF has been applied, and for more information concerning mindfulness-based programs more generally, please see Appendix 3.)

After several years of highly successful implementations of SoF in both clinical and research contexts, we began to consider if SoF could be applied to other contexts where individuals display high rates of challenging behavior. At that time, one of us was working as a school psychologist and serving on behavior-support teams and realized that not only did schools have an abundance of children with challenging behaviors, but that there was a great need for effective, time-limited, and simple interventions. The decision was made to pilot test the SoF protocol with students in need of additional support in school settings. These initial implementations and pilot studies (Felver et al., 2017; Felver, Frank, & McEachern, 2014) demonstrated that not only was SoF highly successful at reducing disruptive behavior in schools, but that students were more academically engaged and reported liking the SoF practice. We have used what we learned from these pilot studies and from our own clinical experience directly teaching SoF to youth, and training teachers to use SoF with students, to create the present book.

Soles of the Feet: A Unique Mindfulness-Based Program

Mindfulness as an applied topic of scientific inquiry has become increasingly popular during the past thirty years (Baer, 2003; Brown, Ryan, & Creswell, 2007; Khoury, Sharma, Rush, & Fournier, 2015). Emerging research suggests that mindfulness practices can reduce stress and improve well-being in adults, and clinicians and researchers have also become more interested in exploring the utility of mindfulness-based programs (MBPs) with youth and in school settings. As examples of this surge of research activity, there have been several entire peer-reviewed journal special issues devoted to the topic of MBP in school settings, including *Psychology in the Schools* (Renshaw & Cook, 2017) and *Mindfulness* (Felver & Jennings, 2016), as well as entire books devoted to the topic, such as the *Handbook of*

Mindfulness in Education (Schonert-Reichl & Roeser, 2016) and *The Mindful School* (Jennings, 2019).

Despite the promise of MBPs, there are several impediments to the widespread adoption of these practices. Among these limitations is the fact that MBPs are usually six to eight weeks in duration and are recommended to be implemented by an "expert" mindfulness practitioner. Given the increasing demands on school schedules and the limited resources to provide extensive and expensive trainings, most MBPs are simply not feasible in contemporary public school settings. However, among the vast array of diverse MBPs, SoF stands out as an outlier in these regards. It is very brief, taking only five sessions of about thirty to forty minutes each, which can fit into a typical class period. It is basic, by which we mean that it does not intend to deliver comprehensive instruction on the applications of mindfulness practice to life, but that it focuses on a single pragmatic adaptation of using a simple practice to keep calm when becoming upset. Part of the utility of SoF, then, is that it is easy to use. We have found that most people who have experience working with youth (such as teachers or school psychologists) and are willing to practice a few simple mindfulness activities for a couple weeks can deliver SoF with fidelity after limited training. Another advantage of SoF is that it is quite feasible to use in busy school environments. Lastly, teachers and students like using SoF because it is very effective in supporting struggling students.

It is also worth noting that the rate at which new and highly varied MBPs have been developed has outpaced replication of existing MBPs. Without replicating an intervention, it is difficult to conclude whether the evidence base supporting an intervention's efficacy is truly there or merely a one-off research finding. Unlike many other new MBPs, SoF has been scientifically replicated over a dozen times. It is one of the most researched MBPs in existence.

Mechanisms of Action in Soles of the Feet

Before utilizing any intervention modality, it is useful to understand the theoretical mechanisms of action. That is, it is important to know how something works before you use it, and this is particularly true when working with vulnerable populations such as youth. The question of exactly how mindfulness-based programs produce their beneficial effects has not been definitively answered in the scientific field; however, scientists all over the world are actively studying this very topic and several theories have emerged that are useful to consider.

A first model that is worth considering is to understand mindfulness-based programs through the lens of behavioral theory, and more specifically via operant conditioning. This theory defines behavior as any observable response by an organism, which includes responses that can only be self-observed such as thoughts and feelings. There are two underlying assumptions that are important to consider in behavioral theory and that are also critical to understanding how SoF operates. The first assumption is that all behavior is the result of a preceding event, also called an antecedent. With this assumption in mind, all behavior is thus predictable if one knows what antecedent is "triggering" the behavior to occur. The second assumption is that all behavior is learned, and this learning is produced by how the environment responds after a behavior occurs, also known as the consequences that follow a behavior. If these consequences result in the behavior happening more frequently over time, the behavior has been "reinforced" by the consequences. If the behavior occurs less frequently over time, it has been "punished" by the consequences. (Note that the terms "reinforcement" and "punishment" are technical behavior analytic terms and that they do not mean that the consequences are (or are not) pleasant or aversive; they simply refer to the frequency of occurrence of a given behavior.)

Interventions developed with behavioral theory in mind are typically categorized as being consequence-or antecedent-based strategies. Most of the behavioral strategies used in school settings are consequence-based. As an example, suppose a teacher hands out independent seatwork involving the completion of math worksheets. If a teacher provides verbal praise after a student completes this assignment well (for example: "Johnny, excellent job on this math worksheet, keep up the good work!") and the student continues to do well (or does even better) on these assignments, then one can conclude that the completion of math worksheets is being reinforced by the teacher's praise and attention. In contrast, suppose a student is talking out and being disruptive during a whole-class instructional period. If a teacher responds by verbally reprimanding the student (for example: "Sharonne! Stop talking to other students or you will get a detention!") and the student over time talks out less during these class periods, then one can assume that the talking out behavior was discouraged by the teacher's scolding.

Of course, individuals respond to consequences and antecedents differently, and it is precisely for this reason that consequence-based strategies that are effective for some students may not be for others. For instance, some students do not like all of the attention that they gain by being singled out in class, and in fact verbally praising a student for any desired behavior may actually result in the given behavior occurring *less* often (i.e., being discouraged). On the other hand, some students receive so little adult attention that any form of interaction is a powerful incentive, and verbally reprimanding these students can result in the undesired behavior occurring *more* often (i.e., being reinforced). What's more, there are two major limitations to any consequence-based strategy for addressing school behavior, particularly with regard to undesired and disruptive behavior. The first is that the behavior has to occur *before* the strategy can be implemented. This is problematic, because by their very nature, these behaviors are disruptive to the individual student's learning and also to other students in the classroom. It is therefore much more desirable to *prevent* the behavior from happening in the first place, rather than responding to every occurrence. The second problem is that, for most student problem behavior, the consequences needed to reduce the occurrences of the disruptive behavior must be delivered by the teacher. Self-directed consequence strategies (e.g., giving oneself a reward for doing a desired behavior, or praising oneself for behaving differently) typically require much more developed adult thinking and self-regulating abilities that are largely not possible for youth due to their stage in human development. It is much more desirable for a student to be able to self-deliver a strategy to reduce a problem behavior because this fosters the student's independence and ability to self-regulate their actions, thereby freeing up limited teacher resources to focus on teaching rather than responding to problem behavior.

Antecedent-based strategies target the conditions that occur *before* a given behavior. Although less typically employed in a school context, these strategies can be very effective in school contexts because they aim to prevent a behavior from occurring in the first place, thus eliminating the numerous problems that result from the occurrence of problem behaviors. But however useful they may be, antecedent-based strategies do have one crucial limitation: there must be a clearly observable "warning" that the problem behavior is likely to occur in the near future. Without this warning signal (which is technically a more proximal antecedent to the problem behavior; see the "Escalating Behavior Sequence" diagram), there is no clear indication that the antecedent strategy should be utilized.

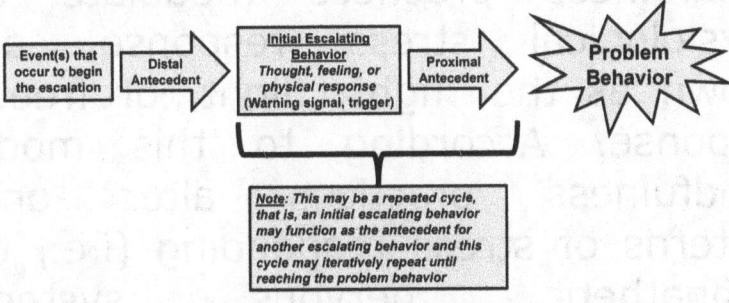

Another leading theoretical conceptualization describes how through mindfulness practice one gains enhanced ability to control attention, regulate emotions, and increase self-awareness (Hölzel et al., 2011). This model, also referred to as the "top-down" control model (Chiesa & Serretti, 2013; Tang, Hölzel, & Posner, 2015), theorizes that mindfulness practices specifically target these higher-order cognitive processes. The benefit of these enhanced processes is that individuals are better able to self-regulate (i.e., to intentionally act in a way congruent with their goals and objectives), and that this enhanced self-regulation underlies all other benefits gained through mindfulness practice.

A final theory states that mindfulness practices modulate the physiological stress response, also known as the "fight, flight, or freeze" response. According to this model, mindfulness practices alter one's patterns of stress responding (i.e., the sympathetic nervous system's hypothalamic-pituitary-adrenal axis) by enhancing the competing parasympathetic nervous system activity during states of low arousal. Said simply, mindfulness practices directly enhance a physiological state of relaxation and low arousal, which over time reduces habitual stress and high arousal responding to everyday challenges. Changes to this underlying physiological stress responding in turn produce many other benefits (e.g., not becoming highly agitated and upset when confronted with a day-to-day challenge), and this model is thus referred to as the "bottom-up" pathway, because change is produced through alteration to basic physiological activity (see Tang et al., 2015, for a review).

It is worth noting that the aforementioned top-down and bottom-up theories both have strong empirical evidence in support of the models, including research from the fields of psychology, neuroscience, and endocrinology. It is also worth noting that these models are not necessarily competing, and that many believe that both theories could be in fact true and operating in concert. As an example, Chiesa and Serretti (2013) suggested that in following mindfulness training, individuals initially develop enhanced cognitive abilities that produce benefits to their daily lives (the top-down model), and that, over time and with sustained practice, these less reactive "mindful" patterns of behavior produce alterations to one's physiological responses to stress (the bottom-up model). Given that there is mounting evidence to support both theories, it does stand to reason that such a longitudinal pattern of change would seem inevitable, underscoring the importance of sustained practice over time.

The SoF procedure described in detail in this book is explicitly designed to prevent the occurrence of problem behavior and can best be conceptualized as an antecedent-based strategy. The basic premise of SoF is that students learn to identify *the earliest warning signals* (which are referred to as "triggers") that begin an escalating cycle of behavior that will likely culminate in problem behavior (such as physical aggression or off-task academic behavior). Once they become aware, or mindful, of these warning signals, they engage in a simple activity of redirecting their attention to a neutral part of their body: their feet. By shifting attention to their feet, students learn to effectively interrupt the escalating cycle that results in problem behavior. Over time, this leads to more well regulated students. This being said, it is equally as accurate to think about SoF as a "top-down" cognitive control strategy (i.e., students develop a different way to think about problems, and this helps them regulate their behavior) and as a "bottom up" rehabitualization of physiological stress responses (i.e., students become physically less reactive to things that used to upset them). How you choose to think about the mechanisms of SoF is up to you; both conceptualizations are valid and have strong scientific support.

Mindfulness is commonly defined as "paying attention in a particular way: on purpose, in the present moment, and nonjudgmentally" (Kabat-Zinn, 1990) or "The self-regulation of attention so that it is maintained on immediate experience ... an orientation that is characterized by curiosity, openness, and acceptance (Bishop et al., 2004). Inherent in these definitions are two core concepts: paying attention and an attitude of acceptance or simply observing things as they are. These concepts are important to SoF, as this sequenced curriculum explicitly encourages students to simply notice their thoughts, feelings, and actions that are triggering their escalating pattern of problem behavior. This is critical: the instructions are *not* to change or stop these triggering thoughts, feelings, and actions, but rather to simply notice them as they are. For many students (and adults), trying to change or stop a thought, feeling, or behavior is at best impossible and at worst can make the thought, feeling, or behavior *worse*. Thus, applying this concept of mindfulness to the awareness of our thoughts, feelings, and behaviors can by itself prevent further escalation. The second concept is also essential to SoF, and to all mindfulness-based programs: using one's attention to regulate behavior. In SoF, the instructions are not to try to change the unpleasant thoughts, feelings, and behaviors that lead to further behavioral challenges; rather, students are taught to move attention to the neutral physical sensations of their feet. In these ways, SoF is considered a mindfulness intervention as it embodies these core elements of regulating attention and accepting experience simply as it is. As previously mentioned, from a behavioral perspective, SoF is also an antecedent-based strategy to disrupt the "chained" behavioral events (see the "Escalating Behavior Sequence" diagram).

Combining both the behavioral and mindfulness theoretical orientations, we argue that the benefits of SoF are best explained from a *mindful-behavioral theoretical* perspective. We believe that SoF involves simply bringing more attention to one's full array of experience and to the relation between these events (thoughts, feelings, and actions), accepting these experiences as they are (i.e., with acceptance), and then intentionally choosing a different response (i.e., redirecting attention to another source of awareness). This being said, SoF is also in line with the top-down and bottom-up theories previously described. Certainly, there is an intentional cognitive process at play when one decides to move attention to one's feet, and thus, SoF is certainly targeting one's ability to self-regulate attention, in line with top-down theory. Over time and with repeated practice, if one applies SoF to times when one would normally become dysregulated and exhibit disruptive behavior, one will naturally have fewer instances of disruptive behavior and lower physiological arousal. As with any practice, if done consistently enough, eventually these activities become habits and it is logical that with fewer instances of disruptive behavior, one is naturally less stressed and overall physiologically calmer, in line with bottom-up theory.

How to Use This Book

This book was specifically developed for ease of implementation. We have attempted to anticipate all the questions that may arise, drawing from our years of experience delivering SoF and teaching others how to deliver the curriculum. We strongly recommend that readers first read chapter 1, in which we explicate many of the preliminary steps that one should consider undertaking prior to delivering SoF, such as gaining experience with mindfulness practice and conceptualizing how this curriculum will fit within your school.

Part 1 of this book details the SoF curriculum for a group of students in a classroom. Part 2 does the same for working with individual students. Full details on each of the five sessions and an optional booster session are provided, including sample scripts. It should be noted that the sample scripts provided are only examples. We do *not* recommend simply reading these scripts to your students. As with any mindfulness curriculum, it is critically important that you as the instructor *embody* the qualities of mindfulness that you are trying to engender in your students. We recommend that you look at the sample scripts to give yourself some ideas for how to present the material, but the elements provided should come from your own words and experience.

Part 3 of this book contains all the supplementary materials you need to implement SoF. In chapter 14, we have provided answers to the most commonly encountered questions we are asked by those who are learning to use SoF. We recommend that you read through this chapter carefully in preparation for delivering SoF so that you are prepared for the challenges you may encounter and are best able to respond. The remainder of this part includes other materials you will need to deliver this curriculum (worksheets and handouts, Appendix 1), research tools for monitoring program fidelity (Appendix 2), and a few other resources that others have found helpful for developing their own knowledge and skills related to teaching mindfulness and supporting students with challenging behaviors (Appendices 3 and 4). The materials found in Appendix 1 are designed for printable replication and are available for download at http://www.newharbinger.com/44741.

It is our sincerest hope that you find these materials helpful in your work. Our intention is to support students who are struggling with challenging feelings and behaviors in school settings, and we believe that SoF offers an effective strategy for such students. We would also like to express our gratitude to you as a teacher or school staff person for your very important work. We hope that this book supports your career in educating and supporting your students.

CHAPTER 1

Preparation for Using Soles of the Feet

Overview Description of Soles of the Feet for Students

Soles of the Feet (SoF) was developed as a basic curriculum to teach a single mindfulness activity, the SoF routine, that can be used effectively during periods of intense emotions. More information on the development of SoF can be found in the Introduction to this book and in Appendix 3, where we describe some of the research and development that went into the protocol. We also strongly recommend that you read through chapter 14 before you start working with any student, as preparing yourself for common challenges (and reading solutions to these challenges) can be most helpful.

SoF is designed to be taught over five classes (or sessions, if you're working with an individual student), although some students may need longer to move through the curriculum than others. Class 1 is designed to introduce the students to the material and to provide direct instruction on some of the components of the full SoF routine, such as identifying parts of the foot and mindful breathing. Classes 2, 3, and 4 include an activity whereby students recall a powerful emotional memory and try to vividly imagine this memory in order to create an *in vivo* e motional experience. Once that emotional experience is felt, students practice the full SoF routine in which they move their attention to the neutral somatic experience of their feet. Class 2 uses a powerful pleasant emotional memory, usually a very happy memory.

Class 3 uses a powerful unpleasant emotional memory, such as an angry memory. Class 4 focuses on using SoF again with an unpleasant emotional memory, but this time, they focus on the earliest point in the recalled experience, deploying the SoF routine at the first point when they notice the emotion. Class 5 involves making an explicit plan for generalization, meaning a plan for when the students will use SoF in their day-to-day lives at school and outside of school. The curriculum describes all the steps with a scaffolded level of instruction so that it can be accessible to any student, including those with disabilities.

The majority of this book focuses on providing very detailed instructions for how to deliver SoF to a classroom of students or one-on-one to individual students. This chapter is meant to describe the planning steps that we suggest you undertake before you begin using the SoF curriculum with students. The order in which these preparatory steps are presented is not intended to be linear; indeed, you may find that you'll need to develop fluency with SoF concurrently with your preparing the school and colleagues for delivering it. This being said, we *strongly* suggest that you prioritize the development of your own mindfulness practice before you begin teaching others any mindfulness practice.

Preparing Yourself to Use Soles of the Feet

Obtain basic training in mindfulness practice. Every mindfulness training curriculum that we are aware of emphasizes the necessity of developing one's own mindfulness practice before teaching mindfulness to others, and we recommend this as well. We cannot emphasize enough that you should develop a basic mindfulness practice before you begin to teach others. The rationale for this recommendation is simple, and is best explained with an example.

Imagine that you are going to teach a student a new skill, say playing the guitar, but you have never played a guitar in your life. Now, you might be able to read a book about playing the guitar, watch videos, and even attend a workshop, and this could give you some insight into how to play. Indeed, you might be able to walk a student though the basic motions of holding a guitar a certain way, plucking strings using a pick, and pressing down certain frets to make a chord, and you may be met with some success. However, there will invariably come a point where the student will ask you a more subtle question that you can only answer from experience, such as the quickest and most efficient way of transitioning your fingers between specific chords, and you will not be able to provide the best instruction. Furthermore, the student will undoubtedly come to the realization at some point that you actually don't know how to play yourself, and this will further undermine your teaching.

Instructing mindfulness programs, such as SoF, is not different from teaching someone how to play the guitar: you must have experience before you can teach it well. Students will ask questions that you have to be able to answer from your own experience (for example: "When you say accept things as they are, do you mean just give in?"). Your depth of experience will allow you to answer these types of questions with knowledge and integrity. Students will also be looking to you to provide a model of mindfulness, and if you are not "walking the walk," they will know. Imagine if you are teaching students a behavior regulation strategy for angry emotions (such as SoF) and you fly off the handle and start screaming at the class every time a student speaks when they're not supposed to. You'd lose credibility, to say the least! Students know if you are genuine and authentic, and to teach mindfulness genuinely, you must have a basic practice. Period.

Now, this is not to say you have to join a monastery or enroll in a three-month silent retreat to be able to teach SoF (indeed, there is no evidence in the scientific literature suggesting that any length of mindfulness practice necessarily makes one a better instructor). Rather, it's just that you have to have a basic understanding of the core practices, concepts, and ideas that support mindfulness. Fortunately, with the widespread popularity of mindfulness activities, there are many options, probably including many in your immediate community. Suggestions for how to seek out mindfulness practice resources in person, or via remote learning and self-instruction, are provided in Appendix 4 ("Supplementary Resources").

Lastly, with regard to personal practice, we want to stress that mindfulness is a practice, and not an intellectual activity. It's more akin to exercise: you have to do it, not read about it, to actually learn it. From our experience, we suggest that people practice basic mindfulness breathing exercises for about twenty to thirty minutes a day for a few weeks, and then meet with a seasoned instructor to ask questions, as a good starting point. Basic guided mindful breathing instructions can be readily found online from well-regarded resources (again, see Appendix 4). Taking a few minutes every day to sit still, notice the sensations of breathing, and simply observe thoughts and experience entering and leaving awareness can be very interesting, and many people report significant health benefits simply from doing just this. We suggest doing this consistently for a few weeks and debriefing with a seasoned practitioner to make sure that you are not developing any unhelpful habits. This should suffice to enable you to teach SoF, and the more you practice, the more experienced you'll become at the activities (just like anything else!). Note that you cannot ever be "good" at mindfulness, nor can you be "bad" at it. Rather, you can either do it and know what it is or not.

Developing a basic mindful breathing exercise is the very minimum recommendation for familiarity with a foundational mindfulness practice, but it does not address the core aspects of what mindfulness is, nor does it ensure that one understands what mindfulness is as a practice. We suggest that practitioners pursue additional training to understand mindfulness as a practice and not merely a cognitive construct. Appendix 4 provides resources for further reading and practice that may be helpful.

Develop fluency with Soles of the Feet practice. You also need to become fluent specifically with SoF to be able to deliver SoF to students. You need to understand the activity fully before you can teach it, as there will invariably be questions about the procedure that students will ask you that you can only answer from your own experience. Also, after you build some fluency with SoF yourself, you'll probably become a stronger advocate for its use in schools. This is best illustrated with a personal anecdote.

When I (Dr. Felver) was a graduate student at the University of Oregon, I contacted Dr. Singh to gain access to the SoF materials in order to conduct a research study with local elementary school students as part of my master's degree in special education. After reading the material and sharing it with my collaborators, I honestly had some reservations. The curriculum seemed too simple and too good to be true, since it basically just provided a structured learning sequence for noticing when you become upset and paying attention to your feet. That's it. My collaborators and I decided to do a self-experiment before putting the effort into conducting a clinical research trial of SoF. We decided we'd practice SoF ourselves every day for a week at least a couple of times a day and try to use it when we became upset or angry in our normal lives. We came back a week later with the same exact experience—it was really effective, and we concluded that it was actually its simplicity that made it so useful. Since that time, I've continued to use SoF myself and taught it to many students in multiple settings, and I'm still amazed by how effective the procedure can be.

The short of it is that you need to practice SoF yourself before you teach it to others. You'll be a better instructor, and our suspicion is that you might find it to be more useful than you suspected. But don't take our word for it, give it a shot and see what happens.

Preparing Your School for Soles of the Feet

In addition to developing your own personal mindfulness practice and fluency with SoF, it is also important that you begin to lay the foundational groundwork so that SoF can be delivered effectively in your school context. Following are some suggestions we've found helpful in ensuring that SoF is implemented as smoothly as possible.

Introducing a mindfulness practices into public school settings. The last decade has borne witness to a dramatic transition in contemplative practices' integration into mainstream culture. It is increasingly common to see yoga being practiced during physical education, and in our own research, we find that schools are generally willing to incorporate mindfulness into the general education curriculum. The very fact that you are reading this book probably means that you are interested in bringing this particular mindfulness practice, SoF, into your school, and that you've already had preliminary conversations with your peers about your intentions to do so. This all being said, we want to sound a few notes of caution, because although it is increasingly common for mindfulness practices to be welcome in public school settings, there are still instances when this is not the case.

The primary barrier that we've encountered comes from communities being justifiably concerned about maintaining secularity in public schools. As you are no doubt aware, public schools in the United States of America are explicitly secular by law, and religion cannot be taught as a mandatory general education requirement. Some people who are unfamiliar with mindfulness practices may see your intentions of bringing these activities into school as a version of bringing religion to a place where it does not belong, and these fears may go so far as deep concerns that you are trying to change student's religions or have them join a cult.

We suggest that you take a direct and explicit stance in your community when bringing any mindfulness practice into a school setting. Specifically, we've found that repeatedly communicating to school staff during staff meetings and professional developmental seminars, and to parents via newsletters, is an effective means of sharing information about SoF and mindfulness training generally. We suggest that you be direct and succinct with the information. Explain that SoF is a mindfulness practice that teaches students how to pay attention and self-regulate their emotions when they become upset. The practices are secular and are done in numerous public schools across the country, and anyone who wishes to see the materials may do so. If the context allows, we suggest you actually demonstrate SoF with the people with whom you are sharing this information (e.g., at a school staff meeting) by walking them through the SoF routine for a couple of minutes. Once they see the activity, they will probably feel more comfortable about it. We have found that once people know exactly what you are doing and see that you are being totally open and trying to share this information, their defenses go down and they do not have reservations, whereas not being so vocal and explicit can lead to misunderstandings that can cause problems. So we suggest being proactive in these communications at the onset of beginning to bring SoF into your school community.

Placing Soles of the Feet into the context of your school's behavior supports. Many schools have adopted formal systems for providing behavioral interventions to students based on their need. Some examples of such frameworks include the Response to Intervention (RTI), the Multi-Tiered System of Support (MTSS), and Positive Behavior Interventions and Supports (PBIS). A detailed explication of these systems is outside the context of this chapter, but the general idea is that more intensive services should be provided to students with more intensive needs, and less intensive (or preventive) services should be provided to students with less intensive needs. Considering how you can use SoF in your school within a multitiered system will be useful before you begin to deliver the intervention.

At the classroom level, SoF can be considered either a preventive low-tier support (Tier 1) or as a mid-tier indicated level of support (Tier 2). By this we mean that teachers find that SoF can be taught to students who have typical levels of off-task and disruptive behavior (i.e., low-tier) as a way of enhancing expected classroom behavior or reducing any minor problems during more contentious school times (e.g., transitioning from recess to seated desk work). At the mid-tier level, SoF can be useful for classrooms that are struggling with higher rates of disruptive behavior. We've found that either approach is useful, but it is useful to plan ahead of time how you consider you will use SoF before you start delivering it, so that the process is thought out and highly structured.

At the high-tier level of support, SoF is best considered as an individual one-on-one intervention for students who are struggling with high rates of off-task disruptive behavior (Tier 3). These students may already be identified by an existing behavior-support team or receiving special education services for behavioral problems. If this is the context, we suggest that the person working with the student be prepared for this student's individual needs and perhaps be a trained mental health counselor for optimal effectiveness.

Identifying a classroom or student in need of additional support. There are multiple pathways that could connect a given teacher or classroom with SoF. Some teachers seek out SoF themselves and plan to use it in their classroom for their own purposes. Other teachers are referred to the school's behavior-support specialist or school psychologist to receive training in SoF or to have an outside behavior-support specialist come into the classroom to deliver SoF. All of these approaches are appropriate.

If you are in a position where you are considering the use of SoF, we would just like to reiterate one important point—that SoF is one of many excellent behavior-support interventions available. Appendix 4 provides a list of resources where you can find other evidence-based strategies.

It is possible that SoF is not the best fit for your context; thus, you should consider other non-mindfulness strategies. In our experience, well-meaning teachers who personally find mindfulness practices to be effective are often highly interested in bringing these technologies into school settings, which is wonderful. However, we would also sound a note of caution: SoF or any other mindfulness-based program is not a panacea. The most effective intervention to support students should be selected, and such intervention may or may not be aligned with practices that are one's personal preference.

As an illustrative example, in our clinical work as psychologists working in the context as individual therapists with youth, we often use mindfulness-based strategies with our clients given our expertise with these technologies. However, sometimes there are certain clinical presentations for which mindfulness programs do not have the best evidence base. For instance, if an adolescent client presents with severe anxiety that is so impairing that they haven't been able to attend school for over a week and can barely focus well enough to maintain a conversation, we would not opt to jump right in with mindfulness practices. A referral to a child psychiatrist for a medication trial and basic cognitive-behavioral therapy are indicated in this situation, although we might eventually begin to offer mindfulness training as a supplementary intervention later in the course of treatment. As professionals working with youth, it is our obligation to provide the best possible interventions to support the children and adolescents who are in our charge, and this may or may not warrant mindfulness-based programs.

Recruiting other adults to support the delivery of SoF. One aspect of delivering manualized interventions such as SoF that is often overlooked is the importance of recruiting other adults to support the program delivery. In the context of SoF, this typically includes other school staff who work closely with the students to whom you are teaching SoF.

At the most basic level, we strongly recommend that all other school staff who spend a significant amount of time with the students to whom you are delivering SoF be informed of what you are doing. This includes the aforementioned points of describing what SoF is (a secular mindfulness strategy) and explaining that SoF is used to teach youth a skill for self-regulating intense emotions and resulting behaviors.

At a more intermediate level, we've found it very effective to have other school staff, if they are willing, directly support students' use of SoF. Encouraging teachers to prompt students to use SoF when they are upset can be very effective if done skillfully (see chapter 14 for a more thorough discussion). Bridging SoF with other existing behavior-support strategies (such as behavioral point charts) can also be effective if done correctly.

Lastly, if you are in close communication with the students' parents, this can also offer a great opportunity to recruit additional adult support. Letting parents know you are doing SoF and providing some direct information about how they can support the student in developing this skill (e.g., by gently reminding the student to use SoF when they are frustrated at home) can be highly effective.

Identifying a student in need of additional support. If you are considering using SoF with a single student, there are some additional considerations to bear in mind. First, we would *strongly* suggest that you work in collaboration with your school's behavior-support team to make sure that any work you do with the student is in line with the overall strategies already in place, so that you are working together as a team and not in isolation. Before working with the student, you should also consider a thorough evaluation of whether the student is a good candidate for SoF. Sometimes this may entail a full functional behavioral assessment (FBA) to shed light onto the antecedents and consequences of the student's disruptive behavior. Remember that SoF is an antecedent-based strategy (see the Introduction), and thus, if a student's behavioral concerns are more driven by consequences in the environment (e.g., attracting adult attention), then SoF may not be the most effective strategy to employ. Consultation with your school's team is highly recommended to make a thorough plan that considers all available strategies and supports.

Before working with a student, we suggest meeting with the teacher who knows the student best (if that is not yourself). During this meeting, we recommend that you describe what SoF is, demonstrate the strategy, describe ways that they can support the student in using SoF in the classroom once they've developed some initial fluency with it, and gather some background information on the student's behavior. This background information includes identifying specific times and locations where the student has disruptive behavior and identifying what the possible triggers are for their intense unpleasant moods that we hypothesize may be causing the disruptive behavior. Being equipped with this information makes for a much more effective intervention once you meet with the student, as you'll know exactly how to tailor your suggestions for practicing SoF with the student.

Although SoF is a relatively low-resource intervention (usually only five thirty-minute sessions), school practitioners should consider if there are other low-cost solutions for disruptive behavior in the classroom. This underscores the importance of gathering background information and direct observation. For example, there may be a conflict in the home that is not being resolved that may be better addressed by individual outpatient services. Or perhaps simply moving the student's desk to a different part of the classroom would help resolve an issue.

Logistical and classroom space considerations for delivering Soles of the Feet. Whether working with a classroom of students or an individual student, one of the first considerations you need to make is planning for all the logistics of delivering SoF.

Identifying a location for where you will be teaching SoF is an initial consideration. Because SoF does involve periods of silence to practice SoF, we recommend that the location and time selected be as quiet and free of distractions as possible. This is not to say that SoF must only be practiced in dead silence without any distractions. (Of course such a school location rarely, if ever, exists!) But every effort should be made to select an environment that is as conducive to practice as possible.

It is worth considering the frequency of SoF delivery. There is no rule for how frequently this intervention should be delivered, as this varies based on logistical considerations and the students with whom you are working. We typically find that delivering SoF to students once or twice a week is a good rate, provided that students have enough time between sessions to engage with the activities assigned for home practice. Ideally, you as the teacher have the flexibility to adjust the rate of delivery of sessions so that students do not move through the curriculum too quickly and aren't given the time to fully develop fluency, nor move through the materials so slowly that they lose track of their personal progress.

Understanding the Structure and Process of Soles of the Feet

Applied scientists frequently discuss the critical importance of maintaining fidelity of implementation, that is, preserving the integrity of manualized intervention procedures when they are delivered. There are two key elements to fidelity of implementation: structure and process (Century, Rudnick, & Freeman, 2010; Feagans Gould, Dariotis, Greenberg, & Mendelson, 2016). *Structural fidelity* refers to the actual intervention material or lesson content (i.e., *what* is being delivered). *Process fidelity* refers to the manner or pedagogical approaches used when delivering interventions or lessons (i.e., *how* the material is being delivered). Both of these elements are important to bear in mind when delivering SoF in order to maintain the curriculum's integrity and fidelity of implementation.

The structural elements of SoF are straightforward. You have a set of materials and lesson plans to deliver and core concepts for students to learn. Each lesson follows a similar format based on generic best practices of instructional design. Lessons begin by reviewing the previous lesson's material to activate prior knowledge. Then you review the assigned between-lesson practice and troubleshoot any barriers to practice. An outline for the upcoming new content is next provided so that students know what to expect from the lesson that day. Each session begins with a practice of the Soles of the Feet routine. New session content is then delivered, ending with a recap of the new material presented and how it fits into the overall SoF curriculum. The between-lesson practice assignment is detailed, and the session concludes with another practice of the SoF routine.

The process elements of SoF are more nuanced and are specific to mindfulness programs. Following are several examples of how you can do this in your work with students. Many of the concepts introduced will be new to students and may be new to you as an instructor. It is therefore extremely important that you are fluent with the concepts (nonjudgment, acceptance, attention regulation) before you deliver so that you can both teach it well and model these skills for your students. It is critically important to embody this mindful attitude you are trying to engender in your students because you are serving as the example! Encourage an attitude of mindfulness with all activities and remember that nothing is "good" or "bad"—some behaviors lead to more or less desirable consequences, but judging behaviors does not fix anything and is antithetical to a mindfulness perspective. Similarly, there is no such thing as good or bad practice, just practice! Encourage the Nike school of thought—Just Do It!

Everything that students notice is interesting and should be embraced with openness and curiosity. Nothing should be discounted or invalidated, and teaching nonjudgmental awareness is key. For example, if students report that they feel "nothing" in their feet, then this is interesting—what does nothing feel like?

Acceptance of negative emotional states (e.g., anger or frustration) is also very important. In contemporary Western culture, these unpleasant emotional states are often condemned as being wrong and bad. From the perspective we are trying to engender in mindfulness, unpleasant emotions are simply that—unpleasant (as opposed to pleasant or neutral experiences). By labeling emotions (or any experience) as bad, more problems and ultimately suffering will be created.

Using gerunds or present participles for verbs (verbs ending in-ing) to engender an active present-moment action—for example, encouraging student "breathing" rather than asking students "to breathe"—can help to orient students toward a present-moment experience.

Please see Appendix 2 for a fidelity monitoring form that was developed specifically for SoF. If you are using this curriculum for research purposes, please consider utilizing this form to monitor fidelity of implementation. If you are using this curriculum to support your students outside of the context of research, we recommend you read this form carefully and self-evaluate whether you are implementing the curriculum with fidelity to both the structural elements (what you are delivering to your students) and the process elements (how you are delivering content).

Providing Sufficient Scaffolding Across Sessions

This book is intended to provide a structured curriculum for teaching students a simple self-regulation strategy for addressing aggressive and disruptive behavior. Lessons are sequenced iteratively such that by the end of the five classes or sessions (depending on whether you are working with a class of students or an individual student), the students should be fluent in identifying the proximal antecedents for their anger and then be able to use the SoF routine to make their feelings of anger disappear or diminish and thus, prevent aggression. Their fluency with the actual SoF routine is also scaffolded through these sessions, beginning with mastery of the component steps (Class/Session 1), to being able to use the entire routine with verbal and visual support (Classes/Sessions 2 and 3), and then finally being able to use the entire routine without any external supports (Classes/Sessions 4 and 5).

Throughout the curriculum, there are several boxes that signal to you to STOP and CHECK for understanding. They look like this:

> ### STOP and CHECK for understanding
>
> Before delivering the curriculum, make sure you understand the function of these "STOP and CHECK for understanding" boxes.

These boxes are reminders for you as the instructor to stop whatever you are doing in the curriculum and take stock of where your students are at. Remember—it's a scaffolded and iteratively sequenced curriculum. Your students will not become experts at using SoF if they do not complete earlier elements. We recommend using these provided stop points to assess your students' progress and evaluate if you need to slow down and cover some earlier material before proceeding in order to make sure that the student meets with success. The table below details the skills that should be mastered before the student continues in the curriculum, corresponding to the "STOP and CHECK for understanding" boxes you will come across to help you gain a sense of the scaffolded steps to mastering SoF.

Class or session	Criterion for advancing to the next class or session
1. Introducing Soles of the Feet	• Able to use Soles of the Feet routine by following verbal instructions
2. Practicing with a Pleasant Feeling	• Fluency with mindful breathing • Memorization of vocabulary describing anatomy of the foot • Able to identify the feeling of happiness • Experience of making the feeling of happiness disappear or diminish
3. Practicing with an Unpleasant Feeling	• Able to verbally recite the full Soles of the Feet routine with or without reading from their sheets • Able to identify the feeling of anger • Experience of making the feeling of anger disappear or diminish
4. Practicing with the Triggers to an Unpleasant Feeling	• Able to use Soles of the Feet routine between lessons • Able to identify triggers to feeling of anger • Experience applying Soles of the Feet routine to triggers of anger, thus preventing the feeling of anger from arising, or making it disappear or diminish
5. Planning to Use Soles of the Feet in Daily Life	• Fluency with using Soles of the Feet routine outside of session with minimal or no external supports • Fluency with using Soles of the Feet during proximal antecedents of anger and while feeling angry • Able to identify settings and times when they can use Soles of the Feet

Final Comments on Preparation to Use Soles of the Feet

This chapter has provided some preliminary suggestions for how to prepare for using SoF. In conjunction with this chapter, we suggest that you read chapter 14 before teaching SoF for the first time. It is useful if you encounter problems to have at least a sense of what to do, and we've provided a detailed list of the most commonly encountered challenges with this curriculum.

Lastly, in the spirit of embodying mindfulness, we encourage you not only to be diligent in adequately preparing to use SoF for the first time, but also to go easy on yourself if you are not very successful the first few times you use the curriculum. Consider what you would tell a friend or colleague who is bold enough to use a new curriculum or to try a new activity for the first time and isn't as wildly successful in their initial attempt as they had intended. We suspect you'd tell them that of course you were not wildly successful—it was your first time, so go easy on yourself! It is interesting that we can be so thoughtful, kind, and gentle with others in our lives but are so quick to be harsh and condemning on ourselves. With this in mind, please go easy on yourself. Be kind to yourself. Allow for mistakes; indeed, you should expect them and embrace them as feedback for self-improvement. Do your best, but above all, embody the qualities we are trying to engender in our students. You aren't perfect and neither will you be in your first, second, or hundredth time in using SoF, but with practice, effort, and kindness you will do just fine.

PART I

Soles of the Feet for Students: Classroom Curriculum

PART I

Soles of the Feet for Students: Classroom Curriculum

CHAPTER 2

Class 1: Introducing Soles of the Feet

Materials Needed

- Handout—Knowing Your Feet (Appendix 1A)
- Worksheet—Knowing Your Feet (Appendix 1B)
- Handout—Belly Breathing (Appendix 1C)
- Handout—My Soles of the Feet Routine (Appendix 1D)

Class Outline

1.1. **Class Introduction:** Explain the purpose of the curriculum.
1.2. **Defining Behavior Expectations:** Set positive rules and expectations for the class.
1.3. **Instructing Posture:** Introduce and practice basic mindful posture seated in chair.

1.4. **Instructing Mindful Breathing:** Introduce and practice mindful breathing.
1.5. **Learning About the Foot:** Explain the anatomy of the feet.
1.6. **Practicing Paying Attention to the Feet:** Introduce and practice mindful awareness of feet.
1.7. **Practicing the Full Soles of the Feet Routine:** Practice combining mindful breathing and paying attention to the feet.
1.8. **Class Closure:** Review key content of Class 1.
1.9. **Assign Between-Class Practice:** Explain importance of practice and assign practice.
1.10. **Practice the Full Soles of the Feet Routine:** End the class with practice.

1.1. Class Introduction

Explain to the students that they will be starting a new curriculum called *Soles of the Feet*. Tell them how often you will meet (something that should be decided *before* you meet for the first time; see chapter 1 for details) and that they will be learning a great new tool for staying calm. Emphasize that the skill they will learn will help them to control their own feelings and emotions, which is very important for being a successful student and is an important part of becoming an adult. Communicate clearly and directly that during this first session, the students will learn about mindful breathing and how to do the Soles of the Feet routine.

We are going to be meeting to learn a special technique for staying calm when upset called Soles of the Feet. We will be meeting twice a week, on Mondays and Wednesdays, for a full class period, which is about 40 minutes.

Soles of the Feet is a really easy way to stay calm even if you feel very upset. Learning how to stay calm is really important for school and can be a great way to keep from getting in trouble. Also, learning how to stay calm is part of growing up, and it's something you'll use for the rest of your life.

Today, we're going to learn how to breathe mindfully and how to do the Soles of the Feet exercise.

1.2. Defining Behavior Expectations

Explain to your students the rules and expectations for the class. Expectations should be positively stated; that is, they should be about what the students should be doing, *not* what they shouldn't be doing or what isn't allowed. The expectations may be the same as the students' normal classroom rules, or they may be different and special for the times you meet with them. Sample rules to consider are "Be Safe, Be Responsible, and Be Respectful." In reviewing and defining the rules, we suggest that you work collaboratively with students to elicit positive expectations (i.e., what the students *should* be doing) concerning safety, following instructions, completing assignments between sessions, and establishing and maintaining confidentiality. This will increase students' buy-in to the agreed upon expectations. The general idea is to provide explicit instructions on rules and expectations, but in such a way that it enhances the students' motivation to engage in the instructions that follow.

Since we will be meeting together, we should talk about the special rules we are going to follow. I know that your normal classroom rules are Be Safe, Be Responsible, and Be Respectful. Who can remind me what these rules mean again? The first rule is "Be Safe."

What should being safe look like? ... Keeping our hands and feet to ourselves sounds like a great rule, let's definitely use that!

The second rule is "Be Responsible." What should that look like? ... Being ready for our meetings and doing the practice assignments works for me!

The last rule is "Be Respectful." What should that look like? ... One person talking at a time sounds good to me.

I'd also like to add a rule. Can we agree that the things we discuss during class will be kept among ourselves and just within this classroom? I won't share anything that we talk about during class unless it involves your safety or the safety of someone else; if I'm concerned about anyone's safety, I do have to let other adults know in order to keep everyone safe. If we can all agree that we won't share information we talk about during class, it'll make everyone feel much more comfortable, so let's add this to our list of rules.

1.3. Instructing Posture

Instruct the students that sitting up straight can be helpful when paying attention. Instruct them in the basics of how to position their bodies when paying attention while sitting: feet flat on the floor, hands on their lap, sitting up straight (but not rigid). You can invite the students to close their eyes if they would like to. However, some students feel more comfortable with keeping their eyes open and picking a neutral point (such as the middle of their desk) to softly gaze at. Note that some students who have had, or are currently having, adverse childhood experiences may feel threatened by closing their eyes in the classroom. So be clear that it is the students' choice whether they want to keep their eyes open or closed—it will not affect what they are going to learn. We have found that some students need a few practice runs to get their posture just right, so take your time and provide corrective feedback as needed. Transition from this section immediately to the next section (1.4, "Instructing Mindful Breathing").

To begin, we are going to discuss how to arrange our bodies. Our minds and bodies are connected, and it's important that we position our bodies in a way that will help our mind practice. Sitting up straight can make you more alert and attentive, just like lying down on a cozy couch can make you sleepy.

So now, sitting up straight in your chair, position your body so that it is awake, and make sure you are still comfortable. Now, make sure your feet are flat on the floor and place your hands comfortably on your lap. Next, you can keep your eyes open or you can keep them closed, because that makes no difference to what we are going to do next. If you keep your eyes open, gently let your gaze rest on the middle of your desk so that you are not watching, or distracting, anyone else in the classroom...

1.4. Instructing Mindful Breathing

Once your students have demonstrated good posture and are sitting calmly, instruct them to try "belly breathing," that is, mindful breathing. Have students place one hand on their stomach to foster somatic awareness of their breath in the abdominal region, and ask them to imagine breathing into and out of their belly or lower abdomen. Encourage them to breathe *low and slow,* that is, low into their belly and slowly on the exhale. Have the students continue to notice breathing this way for one or two minutes, giving prompts approximately every ten to thirty seconds, depending on your visual assessment of their in-the-moment engagement with this practice. End the activity by having the students practice taking ten belly breaths by themselves.

...And now that we are sitting up straight with our eyes closed, let's put one hand on our bellies. We are going to breathe low and slow: breathing through our nose and imagining that each breath goes down low into our belly and then out again slowly through our nose. [Pause for 10-30 seconds.] *Feeling the way your belly moves with each breath.* [Pause for 10-30 seconds.] *Just breathing naturally, breathing low into our bellies, slowly.* [Pause for 20-30 seconds.] *Feeling your breath coming into and out of your belly.*

Now, take ten belly breaths by yourselves, remembering to breath low and slow into your belly ... and when you are done, you can open your eyes.

1.5. Learning About the Foot

Communicate to the students that before they can learn the Soles of the Feet routine, they need to know some foot vocabulary. To help the students identify the parts of their feet, begin with a brief vocabulary activity to make sure that the students both know and are fluent with the anatomical parts of the foot. Use the "Knowing Your Feet" handout and worksheet (Appendices 1A and 1B) both to teach these parts of the foot and to check for understanding by having students complete the activity, noting that some students may need help writing in the responses, depending on their academic reading and writing ability. You may also choose to display these worksheets on a smartboard or other such projector to do this activity as a group.

Next, engage the students with some simple movement activities. The purpose of these exercises is to help the students become aware of the different somatic sensations of their feet by using balance, attention, and physical pressure. Be sure to keep these activities light-hearted and above all, have fun!

Ball and heel. Have the students stand up then rock forward as far as they can onto their toes without having to take a step forward, and explain that they are now balancing on the *ball of* their foot. Next, have the students rock all the way back as far as they can, lifting their toes, to identify their *heel.*

Toes and sole. Have the students stand with their feet flat on the floor. The entire bottom of their foot, which is what they are resting on and is where they can sense the pressure of their body weight, is called the *sole* or the *bottom of the foot.* Ask the students to wiggle their toes to identify their *toes.*

Ankle, arch, and top of foot. Either standing and balancing on one foot or sitting in a chair with one leg crossed on your lap, point to and press on the *ankle* with your finger, then proceed to the *arch* and *top of the foot.* Ask the students to point and press on their own body parts as they in turn label these parts of their feet.

Before we talk more about Soles of the Feet, let's take a minute to learn more about the parts of our feet. Here's a list of the different parts of the foot ... [Review the labels of the parts of the foot, using the "Knowing Your Feet" handout, Appendix 1A.]

Now, let's identify these parts of the feet on ourselves. First, stand up and lean forward as far as you can without falling and without going up on your tip toes ... that's the ball of your foot. Now lean back as far as you can, but don't fall over! That's your heel. Now stand normally with your feet flat on the ground. The flat bottom part where all your weight is pressing is the sole of the feet. Now, sit in your chair ... can you point to your toes? Ankle? Arch? Top of the foot? Very good!

Let's do one last quick activity, but first, put away the handout I just gave you. Here's a worksheet that is the same as the handout but with blank spaces and a vocabulary box. [Indicate blank spaces and vocabulary box on the "Knowing Your Feet" worksheet, Appendix 1B.] *See if you can fill out all the different parts of the foot using the vocab box. If you have any questions or need help, just raise your hand and I'll come to you ... Excellent work everyone, you've learned that really fast and you really know your feet!*

1.6. Practicing Paying Attention to the Feet

This next activity encourages students to start to identify different somatic sensations of their feet. Use prompt questions to structure detailed somatic attention to their feet. In asking questions, instruct the students that they should not answer your questions verbally, rather they should simply concentrate on the physical sensations of their feet by *following* your instructions. It is important not to require a verbal response from your students, because such a response moves their attention away from the somatic attention of their feet to looking and verbally responding to you, and it may be distracting to other students in the class. Instead, let your questions serve as guides for the students' exploration. End this section by checking in with the students to make sure that they were able to experience the somatic experiences of each part of the foot.

Next, we are going to practice focusing attention on the different physical feelings in our feet. To begin, let's sit in our chairs with our feet flat on the floor, backs straight, and hands on our lap, just as we practiced earlier.

Now, see if you can wiggle your toes.

> Can you feel the tip of your shoe?
>
> Can you feel your toes touching?
>
> Can you wiggle just one toe and not others?

Next, feel the very bottom of your feet, the soles of your feet.

> Can you feel your socks?
>
> Does it feel warm, cold, or neither?
>
> Can you feel the bottom of your shoe?

Now, focus on the arch.

> Can you feel the shoe pushing on the arch?
>
> Can you feel where it's most curved?
>
> Can you feel the sock against the arch of your shoe?

Next, let's focus on the ball of your feet.

Can you feel the shoe pressing against the ball?

If you lean your foot forward, picking up your heel slightly, do you feel more pressure?

Now, see if you can notice the top of your feet and your ankles.

Can you feel your shoes pressing on the top of your feet?

What do your socks feel like on the top of your feet?

See if you can notice where your socks touch your ankle, what does that feel like?

Last, focus on the heel against the back of your shoe.

Can you feel the shoe pressing against the heel?

Do you feel where your heel is pushing on the ground? Feeling the floor through your shoes?

If you push your foot back, picking up your toes slightly, does this change anything on your heel?

Nice work! I could tell you were all really concentrating hard! Was there any part of your foot that you could feel really strongly? Was there any part of the foot that you couldn't feel? What *does "no feeling" feel like, can you describe this more to me? Does anyone have any questions?*

1.7. Practicing a Full Soles of the Feet Activity

Walk the students through a combined activity by first engaging in the mindful breathing exercise then switching to paying attention to their feet (i.e., the elements of the full Soles of the Feet routine). Debrief by asking open-ended questions about the students' experience, taking special care to make sure that the students were all able to move their attention to the somatic experience of their feet.

A few important things to keep in mind as you are walking students through the Soles of the Feet activity for the first time:
- Use a slow-paced, low tone of voice to help model and embody a calm, intentional, and mindful manner of being.
- The statement *"quickly shift the focus of your attention to your feet"* should be given as a *direct and*

forceful command. The idea is that the students *quickly* move their attention to their feet to disengage their attention promptly.
- You should consider waiting about five or ten seconds initially between delivering separate Soles of the Feet commands (indicated with [PAUSE.] below), and then stretching this time longer based on the average student's attention span and developmental level.

Now that we've practiced belly breathing and paying attention to our feet, we'll combine the two. This is called the Soles of the Feet routine.

To begin, sitting up straight, placing your feet flat on the floor, allowing your eyes to close if this feels comfortable. [Check to make sure the students have assumed the correct posture.]

Placing one hand on your belly, and beginning to pay attention to your breath coming into and out of your belly. [Do this for approximately one to two minutes, reminding them every 10–30 seconds to pay attention to their breathing, as needed.]

Noticing your breathing.

Noticing your belly moving with your breath.

Breathing low and slow into your belly.

Now, **quickly shift the focus of your attention to your feet.** *[PAUSE.]*

All of your attention is on your feet. [PAUSE.]

Wiggling and noticing your toes. [PAUSE.]

Putting attention on the balls of your feet. [PAUSE.]

Focusing on the arches of your feet. [PAUSE.]

Going to the heels of your feet. [PAUSE.]

Putting your attention on the soles of your feet. [PAUSE.]

Feeling the entire foot. [PAUSE.]

Continuing to stay in your feet just by wiggling your toes and noticing your feet. [PAUSE.]

Now, slowly opening your eyes. [PAUSE.]

Nice work! You just used Soles of the Feet for the first time. Way to go! What was this like for you all? What did you notice when you moved your attention to your feet? What are you noticing about your feet right now? [Debrief with students accordingly, encouraging any report of their direct experience with noticing their feet.]

> ### STOP and CHECK for understanding
>
> Before continuing to Class 2, be sure that the students have attained the following goal: (1) Able to use Soles of the Feet routine by following verbal instructions.

1.8. Class Closure

Review the key concepts of the class.

We just finished the first class of Soles of the Feet, in which we will be learning an easy way to keep ourselves calm when we are upset. Today we learned about how to breathe with our bellies and pay attention to our feet. By first doing belly breathing and then shifting attention to our feet, we used Soles of the Feet for the first time ever!

1.9. Assign Between-Class Practice

Remind the students that to get good at anything, *practice is very important!* Provide an example of how practice yields expertise in any field (such as in sports, video games, or music). Assign the practice of the entire Soles of the Feet routine *at least once* per day at school (although more often is preferable), and have students indicate a specific time that they can practice by having a few students verbally share this with the class. Spend a few minutes troubleshooting barriers to practice or remembering to practice. Give the students the "Belly Breathing" handout (Appendix 1C) and the "My Soles of the Feet" handout (Appendix 1D) as reminders for how to do this activity. If the students would like, also distribute a special sticker or post-it note that you describe as "the Soles of the Feet reminder sticker," which they can affix to their desks or someplace else (such as their smartphones) to remind them to practice, noting that some students may not want this extra attention. (These stickers can easily be created using 8.5"x11" label sheets, which can be inexpensively purchased at any office supply store. As an example, a sticker template document with a picture of a foot, formatted for two-inch circular labels, can be downloaded from the New Harbinger website: http://www.newharbinger.com/44741.) Encourage students to practice with the handout for now. Mention that the Soles of the Feet routine is a covert behavior (i.e., no one will know they are doing it) in order to address any apprehension the students may feel about doing the practice around other people.

Practice is really important to improve our skills, and it's very important that you all practice between sessions to get better at Soles of the Feet so that you can stay calm even if you feel upset in school. It's just like being on a sports team: you practice to get better so you can win the game, and if you don't practice, you won't improve.

This week, practice doing the full Soles of the Feet routine during school at least once per day (although the more you practice, the better you'll get!). Here are a few handouts that detail the instructions for today. Eventually, you'll have the full Soles of the Feet routine memorized, but for now, practice using these handouts so that you do all of the steps.

Here's a special Soles of the Feet sticker to remind yourself to practice. Whenever you see this reminder sticker, remember that practicing Soles of the Feet is the best way to get better at it. Some students like to put these on their school desks or phones, but it's up to you where you want to put it.

When do you think would be a good time to practice Soles of the Feet in school? Let's get a few examples to share with the class, your idea might help other students! ... That's a great time to practice, thank you so much for sharing, I bet other students could practice at that same time too. Okay, and what do you think might cause you all to forget to practice? Let's hear a few examples, and maybe we can come up with some solutions as a class. [Troubleshoot their responses.] Remember, a really great thing about the Soles of the Feet practice is that no one knows when you are practicing, it's like your own secret practice!

1.10. Practice the Full Soles of the Feet Routine

End the class with a practice of the full Soles of the Feet routine. It is best if you yourself have all of the steps memorized to model the process of being able to recite the full Soles of the Feet routine without the aid of the printed sheet ("My Soles of the Feet Routine," Appendix 1D). Just be sure that you are using the exact language on the sheet in order to provide consistency to your students.

To begin, sitting up straight, placing your feet flat on the floor, allowing your eyes to close if this feels comfortable ... [Continue reciting the full Soles of the Feet routine (see "My Soles of the Feet Routine," Appendix 1D) as you practice with the students.]

CHAPTER 3

Class 2: Practicing with a Pleasant Feeling

Materials Needed

- Handout—My Soles of the Feet Routine (Appendix 1D)
- Worksheet—Eliciting Emotions Support Sheet (Appendix 1E)

Session Outline

2.1. **Practice Soles of the Feet:** Begin the class with practice.
2.2. **Review of Previous Class:** Review major content from Class 1.
2.3. **Review of Assigned Between-Class Practice:** Discuss how their practice went and troubleshoot barriers to practice.

2.4.	**Class Introduction:** Explain the activities and content to be covered during Class 2.
2.5.	**Identifying the Feeling of Happiness:** Provide basic psychoeducation on the emotion happiness.
2.6.	**Identifying a Happy Event:** Gather information to create an *in vivo* pleasant emotional experience.
2.7.	**Applying Soles of the Feet to a Happy Situation:** Practice making the pleasant emotion disappear or diminish by using the Soles of the Feet routine.
2.8.	**Post-Practice Discussion:** Debrief the practice.
2.9.	**Class Closure:** Review key content of Class 2.
2.10.	**Assign Between-Class Practice:** Reiterate importance of practice and assign practice.
2.11.	**Practice Soles of the Feet:** End the class with practice.

2.1. Practice Soles of the Feet

Classes 2 through 5 will always begin, and end, with a full Soles of the Feet practice to establish a routine and offer an additional opportunity to practice with feedback from the teacher. Debrief by asking open-ended questions about the students' experience, taking special care to make sure the students were able to move their attention to the somatic experience of their feet. Make sure to ask about what the students are noticing about their feet *right now* to continue to engender mindful attention to the present moment. Be mindful that you as the instructor are consistently using the same language for the Soles of the Feet practice and are referring to the students' "My Soles of the Feet Routine" handout (Appendix 1D) accordingly.

Before we start with new content today, let's start with a practice of the full Soles of the Feet routine. To begin, sitting up straight, placing your feet flat on the floor, allowing your eyes to close if this feels comfortable ... [Continue reciting the full Soles of the Feet routine (see "My Soles of the Feet Routine," Appendix 1D) as you practice with the students.]

Nice work! You just used Soles of the Feet again, way to go! What was this like for you? What did you notice when you moved your attention to your feet? What do you notice about your feet right now? What questions do you have about this practice we just did?

2.2. Review of Previous Class

To activate prior knowledge, remind the students the purpose of learning Soles of the Feet. Review why it is important to learn how to stay calm when we are upset, and that Soles of the Feet can help.

Ask if they can explain the important pieces of "Belly Breathing" (mindful breathing) to check for understanding and to troubleshoot any misconceptions if necessary. Ask the students to identify the feet vocabulary words from Class 1, referring back to the "Knowing

Your Feet" materials (which you can redistribute if they don't have it with them) and section 1.5 as needed. Refer to handouts from the previous session if necessary (Appendices 1A–1D).

During our last class, we learned about our new special activity, Soles of the Feet, which is a great way to remain calm when we become upset. Being able to stay calm when you're upset can help you do well in school and keep from getting in trouble, and it is also an important part of growing up. Last time we talked about the steps to Soles of the Feet—sitting up straight, taking belly breaths, and then focusing on parts of our feet. We also discussed the importance of practice, so that you all can become more skilled at using Soles of the Feet.

Can anyone remind me what the steps are to belly breathing? ... Great, you got it! And who can tell me about the different parts of the feet? ... What part is this? ... Great memory, you all know belly breathing and parts of the foot! Very impressive!

> ### STOP and CHECK for understanding
>
> Before continuing with Class 2, be sure that the students have achieved the following goals: (1) Fluency with mindful breathing, and (2) Memorization of vocabulary describing anatomy of the foot.

2.3. Review of Assigned Between-Class Practice

Review the idea that to get good at anything, practice is very important. Check to see if the students practiced the full Soles of the Feet routine and if they used the handout (Appendix 1D) to facilitate their practice.

If most of the students did not practice, spend time troubleshooting barriers to practice so that they have a concrete plan for practice before next class (see chapter 14 for more details on common barriers and solutions to establishing practice).

How was your practice of the full Soles of the Feet routine since last time we met? Can someone share what they noticed? Did you use the handouts? How did you use them? When and where did you practice at school? For those of you who did practice, what reminded you to practice? Wow, I'm impressed that some of you were able to practice every day, that's great! And for those of you who forgot to practice, what strategies do you think might help you remember next time? Great problem solving, I can't wait to hear how it goes.

2.4. Class Introduction

Explain to the students that during this class, they will be exploring what happens when they use Soles of the Feet while experiencing a pleasant emotion. We usually recommend focusing on *happiness,* but any other positive feeling can be equally as effective (see chapter 14 for a full discussion of modifications using other emotions). They will do this by talking about a recent memory, having you repeat back to the student the details of their memory, and then imagining this happy memory in order to elicit the pleasant feeling during the session (this is an example of *in vivo* practice). While experiencing the pleasant emotion, they will then apply the Soles of the Feet technique to make the emotional sensation disappear or diminish. The premise here is that the students are cultivating a greater nonjudgmental awareness of their emotional experience, and then they are given the opportunity to redirect their attention to the neutral somatic experience of breath and feet after they experience the emotion. Through repeated practice of bringing up awareness of an experience and then shifting attention to their feet, the students develop coping strategies that they may use to self-regulate their emotions and behavior. (See the Introduction for a more detailed discussion of the theory and mechanisms of Soles of the Feet and mindfulness-based programs.)

Today we're going to see what happens when we use Soles of the Feet while we are experiencing a pleasant feeling: happiness. I'm going to ask you all to recall some details about a time when you felt really, really happy, then

I will ask you to try to remember all of these details as you reimagine the happy memory, and then we're going to practice Soles of the Feet to see what happens.

2.5. Identifying the Feeling of Happiness

Facilitate a psychoeducational discussion about the pleasant emotion "happy." Explain that the feeling of happiness is a pleasant, comfortable emotion that feels good. Note that this is not the same thing as equating the feeling of happiness as *being* good. Labeling the feeling of happy as being a good feeling is judgmental and is thus incongruent with a mindful theoretical perspective. Focus on having the students describe the physiological experience of happiness, that is, what their bodies feel and look like when they are happy, as this is the most easily identifiable experience of emotions, because emotions may be an abstract concept for many students. Be sure that the students identify the subjective feeling of happiness (such as feeling warm or comfortable), the outward behavioral expression of happiness (such as smiling or laughing), and the internal physical experience of happiness (such as lightness, warmth, muscles relaxed).

Let's talk about the emotion "happy." Happiness is a pleasant, comfortable feeling, and it feels nice to be happy. How do you know when you are feeling happy? What does it feel like for you? How would I know if you were feeling happy? How would you know if someone else was feeling happy? I know when kids are feeling happy because they are smiling or laughing. If you were feeling happy, what would you look like and how would I know? Some kids say that they feel relaxed and warm when they are happy. What does your body feel like when you are happy? There are no right or wrong answers to this, because everyone experiences emotions like happiness in their own way, I'm just interested in what it feels like for you all.

2.6. Identifying a Happy Event

To elicit a strong pleasant emotional feeling, students will need to identify and recollect the details of a recent event in which they felt very happy. This can be tricky the first time you attempt to do this in a group, and we recommend you practice doing this with an individual first before you attempt it with a whole group. Chapter 14 provides more details on how to facilitate this group *in vivo* event, and we encourage you to read this prior to working with a group of students.

Events that happened more recently tend to work better for recalling details. The more detailed the memory and description the student can provide, the more likely it will elicit a strong emotional response. When facilitating this exercise, try to avoid vague recollections (such as memories from early childhood). Use the "Eliciting Emotions Support Sheet" (Appendix 1E) to guide your questioning. We've found it works best to have a few students share their memories and then to work quickly one-on-one with these students in front of the class in order to flesh out their memory and provide some examples to the class. If certain general phrases recur with these students, it may be worth taking a few short notes to repeat these phrases back to students. Guide the class by having them recall generalities of their event (What? Where? When? With whom?) and moving into specific multisensory details, such as What things did you hear? What were you wearing? Were there any smells you remember? We recommend that you use direct quotes from the students whenever possible, as this is likely to resonate the most strongly with their memory and experience; but you should also bear in mind that if a specific experience doesn't apply to the class, it might be distracting for the majority of students. Make sure to mention that sharing experiences during class is optional, that students should not discuss these in-class conversations outside of class, and that if they do choose to share an example, it should not be about another student or teacher whom someone else in the class knows. Again, we recommend that you practice this process of using details thoroughly beforehand to elicit an emotional experience.

Now I want you to recall a time recently when you remember feeling really happy. What was happening? Who was there? Now, I'm going to ask if any of you would like to share some of your memories—this is optional and it's totally fine if you don't want to do this. Also, let's remember that we agreed to not share what happens during class outside of class. I'd also ask that you not share an example that involves another student or teacher. Can someone share an example? ... That sounds like a great memory, but it seems like it was from many years ago, do you have a more recent memory that you can identify? Start to think about what you remember making you feel the most happy? What exactly made you feel so happy? Think about what you remember seeing? ... Would someone be willing to share some of their details with the class? [Continue gathering information from a few students using the "Eliciting Emotions Support Sheet" (Appendix 1E) to illustrate this process with the whole classroom.]

2.7. Applying Soles of the Feet to a Happy Situation

Explain that the purpose of the exercise is to apply Soles of the Feet when feeling a strong emotion, in this case the pleasant emotion happiness, and to see what happens. Do not tell the students beforehand that their emotions will disappear or diminish—this is a critical *insight* that the students must come to by themselves, and if you set this expectation beforehand, they might feel pressured to report this experience despite it not occurring. Have the students assume a relaxed posture and take ten belly breaths, and then guide them through the happy scenario they were recalling by walking them through it, recalling their experience with general guidance (such as with prompts from the "Eliciting Emotions Support Sheet"). Most students find it easiest to recreate the memory with their eyes shut, but this is optional.

Be sure to encourage students to recall as much detail as possible. Refer to notes you have taken on the "Eliciting Emotions Support Sheet" (Appendix 1E) as necessary if there are shared experiences that could apply to multiple students, and use the students' verbatim language as much as possible. Once you have facilitated their recollection of their memories in detail and you notice behavioral cues from the students that they are feeling happy (such as grins or smiles on most their faces), have them practice the Soles of the Feet routine beginning with the instruction *"Now, quickly shift the focus of your attention to your feet."* It is important that this instruction be given as a *direct and forceful command* so as to practice *quickly and deliberately* shifting attentional awareness away from the happy memory to a neutral focal point (in this case, the students' feet). Much of the effectiveness of Soles of the Feet lies in the students' being able to volitionally "snap" their attention *away* from strong emotions, thoughts, and physical sensations, and *to* their feet.

In this class, we are learning how to use Soles of the Feet to stay calm, even if we are feeling a strong emotion. Now we are going to practice Soles of the Feet while we're feeling happy.

To begin, sitting up straight, placing feet flat on the floor, allowing your eyes to close ... Placing one hand on your belly, and beginning to pay attention to your breath coming into and out of your belly ... Remembering the happy memory that you were just recalling ... Thinking back to this recent happy event in detail ... Remembering who was there, what people were saying ... You might imagine going back to this event and looking around—what do you see? Are there any sounds around you? Recalling what you might have been wearing, the time of day, what the temperature was like ... Thinking back to the exact moment when you remember feeling the most happiness, and how you knew you were feeling happy, perhaps smiling or feeling a warmth in your body ... Just staying here for a moment and remembering and feeling this pleasant happy memory ... Now, quickly shift the focus of your attention to your feet. [PAUSE.] *All of your attention is on your feet ...* [Continue verbal instruction of the full Soles of the Feet routine.]

2.8. Post-Practice Discussion

Discuss how the experience of shifting attention to the feet changed their happy feeling. We suggest that you model the attitudinal qualities of mindfulness in this discussion, namely a nonjudgmental curiosity about their experience simply as it is. Typically, students find that once they shift their attention from the happy memories to their feet, the happy feeling *disappears* almost immediately or *diminishes* substantially. If students do not experience this, which is not uncommon, you should take the time to "troubleshoot" their experience, which may include repeating steps 2.6 and 2.7 using a second or third different memory of a happy situation to practice (see chapter 14 for more details on troubleshooting this activity). Usually if students practice the Soles of the Feet routine a few times with and without the memory component, they will be able to experience the disappearance of pleasant happy feelings. Be sure to let these students know that it is okay if this does not happen the first time (thereby modeling and engendering the mindful qualities of nonjudgmental acceptance) and that they simply require more practice. Again, be sure that you do not set the expectation that the feeling of happiness will disappear or diminish: it is very important that students come to this insight on their own.

Once the students notice that through using Soles of the Feet, their emotional experience either disappears or is substantially diminished, praise this insight and the fact that the students were able to alter their emotional experience on their own. The importance of this insight cannot be overstated. Students' coming to the realization that when they experience a powerful emotion they now have the ability to return to a calm baseline (or said differently, to self-regulate their emotions) is the central mechanism of Soles of the Feet and the foundation for all further classes. It is possible that in a large classroom, not all students will have a powerful experience of feeling happiness or of making that feeling disappear (just as not all students will grasp a concept you are instructing in a whole group context). If this occurs, be sure to acknowledge that this is okay and provide encouragement to keep practicing. If possible, consider spending additional time with these students, referring to chapter 14 for ideas on how to support this process as needed.

You were just imagining a happy situation, and I noticed that many of you were smiling. Were you all feeling happy? What did it feel like to remember the happy situation? Did you feel happy? Can someone share their experience with recalling their happy memory? Okay, now when I said to quickly shift your attention to your feet, what happened next? I could tell you were concentrating on noticing your feet, just as we practiced. And when attention was on your feet, did you go back to the happy memory? Let's hear some examples of your experiences ... Good, so you were able to pay attention just to your feet. Now, here's the question: What happened to the happy feeling when you were paying attention to your feet? ... That's right, simply by paying attention to your feet you were able to eliminate the happy feeling, you've got it! This is really important and something we're going to talk more about: When you practice Soles of the Feet and shift your attention to your feet, the strong feelings can become much less powerful or even completely disappear! For those of you who didn't have this exact experience, don't worry, the more you practice, the easier it'll become.

> ## STOP and CHECK for understanding
>
> It is very important that most students are able to experience success in using Soles of the Feet to make a strong emotional response disappear or diminish. Before

> continuing to Class 3, be sure that the students have attained the following goals: (1) Able to identify the feeling of happiness and (2) Experience of making the feeling of happiness disappear or diminish.

2.9. Class Closure

Review the class and major content covered. Mention again that the objective of learning Soles of the Feet is to keep us calm during intense emotions, such as when upset.

Today we practiced the Soles of the Feet exercise with a happy feeling. When you all shifted your attention away from the strong feeling, in this case a feeling of being happy, and went to your feet, the strong feeling disappeared.

Normally we do not want a happy feeling to disappear. But sometimes, we may have different strong feelings that we may want to have disappear because they don't feel good and can lead to us getting in trouble in school. Soles of the Feet can be helpful for eliminating other strong feelings, like anger, so that you can stay calm even if you feel upset. Soles of the Feet is a great tool that will help you in school and for the rest of your life, and we'll continue to practice it more, using other strong emotions so that you become very skilled at keeping calm when you choose to.

2.10. Assign Between-Class Practice

Remind the students of the critical importance of practice and ask the students to practice Soles of the Feet at least daily before the next class. Give students another copy of the "My Soles of the Feet Routine" handout (Appendix 1D) and more reminder stickers if they need them, and err on the side of the students having more copies if you are unsure. This will help facilitate their practice.

Work with the students to identify a specific time and location when they will practice Soles of the Feet during school, and remind them that it is a covert activity. Collaboratively troubleshoot any potential barriers to practice that were identified at the onset of the session. (See chapter 14 for more details on how to facilitate more practice between classes.)

Remember, in order to become good at anything, practice is very important, and to become skilled at Soles of the Feet, it's also important that you practice! Your challenge is to practice Soles of the Feet at least once per day until we meet as a group again. If you practice more than once per day, that would be even better. You can use this handout to remind yourself of the steps in Soles of the Feet, and you can use this reminder sticker to remind yourself to practice.

Who can share with me when they found a good time during the school day to practice? ... Great! And for those of you who didn't practice last time, can you share with me what you're going to do differently so that you will remember to practice? Remember, no one knows when you're practicing, it's a secret practice! What do you think will keep you from practicing every day? How can we make sure you remember to practice? Let's make a plan together...

2.11. Practice Soles of the Feet

End the class with a practice of Soles of the Feet by having the students verbally recite the steps of the routine, similar to a choral reading exercise. Students should use the "My Soles of the Feet Routine" handout (Appendix 1D) to accomplish this. If the students are unable to read the steps, point to each step on the handout as you read it aloud, either by holding up the sheet for them to see or by referring to the smartboard or projector if you are using these technologies, and have them repeat each step back to you, step by step, as a group (choral repetition or echo-reading). Having the students verbally say the steps of the Soles of the Feet routine out loud will support their internalization of the routine.

Let's practice Soles of the Feet one more time before we end today, but this time, I want you to lead the practice as a group. Just read aloud from the handout to guide yourself through the practice, and we'll do this all together as a class...

CHAPTER 4

Class 3: Practicing with an Unpleasant Feeling

Materials Needed

- Handout—My Soles of the Feet Routine (Appendix 1D)
- Worksheet—Eliciting Emotions Support Sheet (Appendix 1E)

Session Outline

3.1. **Practice Soles of the Feet:** Begin the class with practice.
3.2. **Review of Previous Class:** Review major content from Class 2.
3.3. **Review of Assigned Between-Class Practice:** Discuss how their practice went and troubleshoot barriers to practice.

3.4.	**Class Introduction:** Explain the activities and content to be covered during Class 3.
3.5.	**Identifying the Feeling and Consequences of Anger:** Provide basic psychoeducation on the emotion anger and the differentiation between anger (feeling) and aggression (action).
3.6.	**Identifying an Angry Event:** Gather information to recreate an *in vivo* unpleasant emotional experience.
3.7.	**Applying Soles of the Feet to an Angry Situation:** Practice making the unpleasant emotion disappear or diminish by using the Soles of the Feet routine.
3.8.	**Post-Practice Discussion:** Debrief the practice.
3.9.	**Class Closure:** Review key content of Class 3.
3.10.	**Assign Between-Class Practice:** Reiterate importance of practice and assign practice.

3.11. **Practice Soles of the Feet:**
End the class with practice.

3.1. Practice Soles of the Feet

Soles of the Feet can be done sitting or standing, and from this class onward, alternate between sitting and standing with practice, depending on the needs and preferences of students in your group. Begin this class by explaining that Soles of the Feet can also be done standing, do a standing practice, and then debrief by asking open-ended questions about the students' experience, taking special care to make sure the students were able to move their attention to the somatic experience of their feet while standing. As always, encourage students to notice their feet *right now* to continue to engender mindful attention to the present moment. Be mindful that you as the instructor are consistently using the same language for the Soles of the Feet practice and are referring to the students' "My Soles of the Feet Routine" handout (Appendix 1D) accordingly.

So far, we've only practiced Soles of the Feet while sitting, but this activity can be done while standing too and it works just as effectively. Today, let's start by practicing the full Soles of the Feet routine while standing.

To begin, stand up behind your desks, standing up straight, making sure your feet are flat on the floor, and allowing your eyes to close if this feels comfortable ... [Continue reciting the full Soles of the Feet routine (see "My Soles of the Feet Routine," Appendix 1D) as you practice with the students.]

Nice work! You just used Soles of the Feet again, but this time while standing! What was this like for you? What did you notice when you moved your attention to your feet? What do you notice about your feet right now? What questions do you have about this practice we just did? Did anyone notice a difference between standing practice as compared to sitting practice?

3.2. Review of Previous Class

To activate prior knowledge, review the purpose of learning Soles of the Feet. Review why it is important to learn how to stay calm when we are upset, and that Soles of the Feet can help. Review that during the previous class, students learned how to use Soles of the Feet to make a strong pleasant feeling (in that case, being happy) disappear or diminish. Refer to handouts from last session if necessary (Appendices 1A–1D).

During our last class, we continued to learn about Soles of the Feet, which is a great way to remain calm when we become upset. Being able to stay calm when upset can help you do well in school and keep from getting in trouble, and it is also an important part of growing up.

Last time, we recalled a very pleasant emotional memory, a happy memory, and then experimented with using Soles of the Feet while remembering this happy feeling. Does anyone remember what happened after we used Soles of the Feet while feeling happy? ... That's right, the happy feeling disappeared or felt less intense because our attention was on our feet and not on the memory that was causing us to feel happy! Great remembering everyone! Does anyone have any questions about material we covered during the last class?

3.3. Review of Assigned Between-Class Practice

Review the idea that to get good at anything, practice is very important. Check to see if the students practiced the full Soles of the Feet Routine since the last class. If students did not practice, consider spending time troubleshooting barriers to practice so that they have a concrete plan for practice before the next class. (See chapter 14 for more details on common barriers and solutions to establishing practice.)

Check for students' progress in the curriculum by having them lead themselves through a Soles of the Feet routine without your verbal guidance. Students may still be reliant on reading from their sheets at this point in the curriculum; however, it would be best if students were able to walk themselves through the curriculum without this prop. Ask students to verbally recite the steps with a low-volume voice. If students are not able to do the Soles of the Feet routine without your direct assistance, spend time troubleshooting the sources of the difficulty (see chapter 14 for additional details).

How was your practice of the full Soles of the Feet routine since last time we met, can someone share what they noticed? Did you use the handouts? How did you use them? When and where did you practice at school? For those of you who did practice, what reminded you to practice? Wow, I'm so impressed that some of you were able to practice every day, that's great! And for those of you who forgot to practice, what strategies do you think might help you remember next time? Great problem solving, I can't wait to hear how it goes.

Let's practice Soles of the Feet one more time, but this time, I want you all to lead your own practice. If you already have all of the steps memorized, then this is fantastic! If you haven't quite memorized all the steps, take out the sheet that has the steps written on it. (I have more copies if you need them, just raise your hand and I'll come by.) What I'd like you to do is walk yourself through the routine by whispering the steps to yourself, like this. [Demonstrate to class by whispering the full Soles of the Feet routine to yourself.] *Does anyone have any questions? Okay, let's do another practice then!* [Begin reciting steps of the Soles of Feet routine to yourself, monitoring the class for students who are struggling and need additional support.]

STOP and CHECK for understanding

Before continuing with Class 3, be sure that the students have attained the following goal: (1) Ability to verbally recite the full Soles of the

Feet routine with or without reading off a sheet.

3.4. Class Introduction

Explain to the students that during this class, they will be exploring what happens when they use Soles of the Feet while experiencing an unpleasant emotion. For this purpose, we usually recommend *anger,* but any other negative feeling can be equally as effective (see chapter 14 for a full discussion of modifications using other emotions). They will do this in the exact same way as during Class 2, except instead of recalling a happy memory, they will recall an angry memory. The premise here is that the students are cultivating a greater nonjudgmental awareness of their unpleasant emotional experience, and then they are given the opportunity to redirect their attention to the neutral somatic experience of breath and feet after they experience the unpleasant emotion. Through repeated practice of bringing up awareness of the experience and then shifting attention to their feet, the students develop a coping strategy that they can use to self-regulate their emotions that typically lead to disruptive behavior. (See the Introduction for a more detailed discussion of the theory and mechanisms of Soles of the Feet and mindfulness-based programs.)

Today we're going to do something similar, but different, than last class. We're going see what happens when we use Soles of the Feet while we are experiencing an unpleasant feeling—in this case, a feeling of anger. Just like last class, I'm going to ask you all to recall some details about a time when you felt a powerful emotion, but this time instead of happiness, we'll use anger for the target emotion. I will ask for you to try to remember all of these details as you reimagine the angry memory, and then we're going to practice Soles of the Feet to see what happens.

3.5. Identifying the Feeling and Consequences of Anger

Facilitate a psychoeducational discussion about the unpleasant emotion "angry" and how the feeling of anger is different from aggressive *actions* one might do while feeling angry. Describe how the feeling of anger is an unpleasant, uncomfortable emotion that feels bad. Note that this is not the same thing as equating the feeling of anger as *being* bad. *No feeling or emotion is bad, and anger is a normal experience of all humans.* Labeling the feeling of anger as being a bad feeling is judgmental and is thus incongruent with a mindfulness theoretical perspective. Focus on having the students describe the physiological experience of anger, that is, what their bodies feel and look like when they are angry, as this is the most easily identifiable experience of emotions, which may be an abstract concept for many students. Be sure that the students identify the subjective feelings of anger (e.g., being hot or uncomfortable), the outward behavioral expression of anger (e.g., scowling, yelling, breathing fast, clenching fists or jaw), and the internal physical experience of anger (e.g., heaviness, muscles tensed).

Next, explain that anger can lead to actions that may get them into trouble or cause other people to get hurt, which are called aggression. Differentiate the feeling (anger) from the behavior (aggression). Refer to a specific example if you know one from school or share an example from your own life if this feels more appropriate. Explain that Soles of the Feet can be used to prevent anger from becoming aggression, which is a great strategy to have as a student for many reasons (such as for keeping friends and not getting in trouble).

Let's talk about the emotion "anger." Anger is an unpleasant and uncomfortable feeling. You know you are feeling angry when you are scowling or clenching your fists. Sometimes your body tells you that you're angry by tensing up and getting tight. How do you know when you are feeling angry?

What does your body feel like when you are angry? Can someone show me what it looks like when you feel angry? Feeling angry is not a bad thing, and feeling angry is not a good thing. Feeling angry is just a feeling that everyone has and it's totally normal. What is important, though, is what we choose to do when we feel angry.

Sometimes when we become angry, anger causes us to act in ways that we don't want to. We can do or say things that we don't mean and that cause other people to get hurt, which is called aggression. Acting aggressively when we feel angry can get us in trouble, like if you were to shove another student during recess and got a detention, or when you yell something mean to other kids and they don't want to be your friend anymore. But anger is not the same thing as aggression—anger is a feeling that we experience, aggression is what we do or act like when we feel angry. Soles of the Feet is a way to stay calm when we become angry so that we can keep ourselves from acting with aggression and instead act in a way that won't cause any problems for ourselves and other people. So it is a very useful skill to have.

3.6. Identifying an Angry Event

To elicit a strong unpleasant emotional feeling, students will need to identify and recollect the details of a recent event in which they felt very angry, following the same steps outlined in Class 2. Have students describe a recent event in which they felt very angry. Be sure to support students' recollecting as much detail as possible, referring to the "Eliciting Emotions Support Sheet" (Appendix 1E) as needed. Events that happened more recently tend to work better for recalling details. The more detailed the memory and description the student can provide, the more likely it will elicit a strong emotional response. Make sure to again mention that sharing experiences during class is optional, that students should not discuss conversations that happen during class outside of class, and that if they do choose to share an example, it should not be about another student or teacher whom someone else in the class knows. Again, we recommend that you practice this process of using details thoroughly beforehand to elicit an emotional experience.

Now, I want you to recall a time recently when you remember feeling really angry. What was happening? Who was there? I'm going to ask for people to share their examples, but let me remind you that this is optional, that we aren't going to discuss what happens during Soles of the Feet class outside of class, and that these examples should not be about someone else who other classmates may know, such as another student or a teacher. Can someone share an example? ... That sounds like a great memory, but it seems like it was from many years ago, do you have a more recent memory that you can identify? Start to think about what you remember making you feel really angry. What exactly made you feel so angry? Think about what you remember seeing.... Would someone be willing to share some of their details with the class? [Continue gathering information from a few students using the "Eliciting Emotions Support Sheet" (Appendix 1E) to illustrate this process with the whole classroom.]

3.7. Applying Soles of the Feet to an Angry Situation

Explain that the purpose of the exercise is to apply Soles of the Feet when feeling a strong emotion, in this case the emotion anger, and to see what happens. Do not tell the students beforehand that their emotions will disappear or diminish—this is a critical *insight* that the students must come to by themselves, and if you set this expectation beforehand, they might feel pressured to report this experience despite it not occurring. Have the students assume a relaxed posture and take ten belly breaths, then walk them through the angry scenario they were recalling using their own words or prompts from the "Eliciting Emotions Support Sheet." Most students find it easiest to recreate the memory with their eyes shut, but this is optional.

Once you've walked students through the memory in detail and you notice behavioral cues from the students that they are feeling angry (such as grimacing or clenching fists), instruct them to practice Soles of the Feet by beginning with the instruction: *"Now, quickly shift the focus of your attention to your feet."* It is important that this instruction be given as a *direct and forceful command* so as to practice *quickly* and *deliberately* shifting attentional awareness away from the angry memory to a neutral focal point (in this case, the students' feet). Much of the effectiveness of Soles of the Feet lies in the students' being able to volitionally "snap" their attention *away* from strong emotions, thoughts, and physical sensations, and *to* their feet.

In this class, we are learning how to use Soles of the Feet to stay calm, even if we are feeling a strong emotion. Now we are going to practice Soles of the Feet while we're feeling angry.

To begin, sitting up straight, placing feet flat on the floor, allowing your eyes to close ... Now placing one hand on your belly, and beginning to pay attention to your breath coming into and out of your belly ... Now remembering the angry memory that you were just recalling ... thinking back to this recent angry event in detail ... remembering who was there, what people were saying ... You might imagine going back to this event and looking around—what do you see? Are there any sounds around you? Recalling what you might have been wearing, the time of day, what the temperature was like ... Thinking back to the exact moment when you remember feeling angry, and how you know you were feeling really angry, perhaps clenching your teeth or making fists, or feeling hot and tense in your body ... Just staying here for a moment and remembering and feeling this unpleasant and super angry moment ... Now, **quickly shift the focus of your attention to your feet.** [PAUSE.] *All of your attention is on your feet ...* [Continue verbal instruction of the full Soles of the Feet routine.]

3.8. Post-Practice Discussion

Just as in Session 2, discuss with the students how the experience of shifting attention to the feet changed their angry feeling. Again, it is important that you model the attitudinal qualities of mindfulness in this discussion, namely a nonjudgmental curiosity about their experience simply as it is. Typically, students find that once they shift their attention from the angry memories to their feet, the angry feeling disappears almost immediately or diminishes substantially. If students do not experience this, which is not uncommon, you should take the time to troubleshoot their experience, which may include repeating steps 3.6 and 3.7 using a second or third different memory of an angry situation to practice. (See chapter 14 for more details on troubleshooting this activity.) Usually, if students practice the Soles of the Feet routine a few times with and without the memory component, they will be able to experience the disappearance of unpleasant angry feelings. Be sure to let these students know that it is okay if this does not happen the first time (thereby modeling and engendering the mindful qualities of nonjudgmental acceptance) and that they simply require more practice. Again, be sure that you do not set the expectation that the feeling of anger will disappear or diminish—it is very important that students come to this insight on their own.

Once the students notice that through using Soles of the Feet, their emotional experience either disappears or is diminished, praise this insight and the fact that the students were able to alter their emotional experience on their own. The importance of this insight cannot be overstated. In fact, students' gaining the ability to self-regulate their emotional experience by using the Soles of the Feet routine is the single most important aspect of the entire curriculum. It is possible that in a large classroom, not all students will have a powerful experience of feeling angry or of making that feeling disappear (just as not all students will grasp a concept you are instructing in a whole group context). If this occurs, be sure to acknowledge that this is okay and provide encouragement to keep practicing. If possible, consider spending additional time with these students, referring to chapter 14 for ideas on how to support this process as needed.

You were just imagining an angry situation, and I noticed that many of you were grimacing and clenching your fists. Were you all feeling angry? What did it feel like to remember being angry? Pleasant, unpleasant, or neutral? How do you know? Can someone share their experience with recalling their angry memory? ... Okay, now when I said to quickly shift your attention to your feet, what happened next? I could tell you were concentrating on noticing your feet, just as we practiced. And when attention was on your feet, did you go back to the angry memory? Let's hear some examples of people's experiences ... Great! So, you were able to pay attention just to your feet. Now, here's the question: What happened to the angry feeling when you were paying attention to your feet? That's right, simply by paying attention to your feet, you were able to eliminate the angry feeling—you've got it! This is really important and is actually the most important thing in Soles of the Feet—by shifting your attention to your feet when you experience strong feelings, like anger, the strong feelings can become much less powerful or even completely disappear! If you can do this, then you can prevent yourself from acting aggressively, which is the whole point of learning Soles of the Feet. For those of you who didn't have this exact experience, don't worry, the more you practice, the easier it'll become.

STOP and CHECK for understanding

It is *very* important that most students are able to experience success in using Soles of the Feet to make a strong emotional response disappear or diminish. Before continuing to Class 4, be sure that the students have attained the following goals: (1) Ability to identify the feeling of anger, and (2)

> Experience of making the feeling of anger disappear or diminish.

3.9. Class Closure

Review the class and the major content covered. Mention again that the objective of learning Soles of the Feet is to keep us calm during intense emotions, such as when we are angry or upset.

Today, we practiced the Soles of the Feet exercise with an angry feeling. When you all shifted your attention away from the strong feeling, like being angry, and went to your feet, the strong feeling disappeared, or at least it became weaker.

Feeling angry is not a bad thing, but sometimes when we feel angry, we act aggressively and hurt other people or get ourselves into trouble, which is not okay. You can use Soles of the Feet when you feel strong feelings like anger that you may want to have disappear because they don't feel good or because they can lead to getting in trouble in school. Soles of the Feet can be helpful for eliminating other strong feelings besides anger, like worry and frustration, so that you can stay calm even if you feel upset. Soles of the Feet is a great tool that will help you in school and for the rest of your life, and we'll continue to practice it more using other strong emotions so that you become very skilled at keeping calm when you choose to.

3.10. Assign Between-Class Practice

Remind the students of the critical importance of practice and ask them to practice Soles of the Feet at least daily, sitting or standing, before the next class and ideally when they feel angry, even if just a little bit angry. Give students another copy of the "My Soles of the Feet Routine" handout (Appendix 1D) and more reminder stickers if they need them. Err on the side of the students' having more copies if you are unsure, as this will help facilitate their practice.

Work with the students to identify a specific time and location when they will practice Soles of the Feet during school, and remind them that it is a covert activity. Collaboratively troubleshoot any potential barriers to practice that were identified at the onset of the session. (See chapter 14 for more details on how to facilitate more practice between classes.)

Remember, in order to become good at anything, practice is very, very important, and to become skilled at Soles of the Feet, it's also important that you practice! Your challenge is to practice Soles of the Feet at least once per day until we meet as a group again, and if you practice more than once per day, that would be even better. The best practice you can do, and your challenge before next class, is to use Soles of the Feet when you feel angry, even if you feel just a little bit angry. Remember, you can do Soles of the feet sitting or standing. You can use this handout to remind yourself of the steps in Soles of the Feet, and you can use this reminder sticker to remind yourself to practice.

Who can share with me when they found a good time during the school day to practice? ... Great! And for those of you who didn't practice last time, can you share with me what you're going to do differently so that you will remember to practice? Remember, no one knows when you're practicing, it's a secret practice! What do you think will keep you from practicing every day? How can we make sure you remember to practice? Let's make a plan together...

3.11. Practice Soles of the Feet

End the class with a practice of Soles of the Feet. Allow students the option to engage with the practice sitting or standing, by reading from their sheets or by reciting from memory, and by saying the steps to themselves in a quiet voice just as you did when beginning the class. If the students are unable to read the steps, point to each step on the handout as you read it aloud, either by holding up the sheet for them to see or by referring to the smartboard or projector if you are using these technologies, and have them repeat each step back to you, step by step, as a group (choral repetition or echo-reading). Having the students verbally say the steps of the Soles of the Feet routine out loud will support their internalization of the routine.

Let's practice Soles of the Feet one more time before we end today. You can do this practice sitting or standing, it's up to you. You can also do this practice by following along on the printed sheet, but it is best if you can recite all the steps just from memory, so give this a try if you feel ready to. We're going to lead ourselves through the practice again by whispering the steps to ourselves step-by-step. Does anyone have any questions? Okay, let's begin...

CHAPTER 5

Class 4: Practicing with the Triggers to an Unpleasant Feeling

Materials Needed

- Worksheet—Eliciting Emotions Support Sheet (Appendix 1E)
- Worksheet—Identifying Triggers Worksheet (Appendix 1F)

Session Outline

4.1. **Practice Soles of the Feet:** Begin the class with practice.
4.2. **Review of Previous Class:** Review major content from Class 3.
4.3. **Review of Assigned Between-Class Practice:** Discuss how their practice went

and troubleshoot barriers to practice.
4.4. **Class Introduction:** Explain the activities and content to be covered during Class 4.
4.5. **Identifying the Triggers of Anger:** Define and identify triggers for unpleasant emotion.
4.6. **Applying Soles of the Feet to the Triggers of Anger:** Practice making the unpleasant emotion disappear or diminish by using the Soles of the Feet routine.
4.7. **Post-Practice Discussion:** Debrief the practice.
4.8. **Class Closure:** Review key content of Class 4.
4.9. **Assign Between-Class Practice:** Reiterate importance of practice and assign practice.
4.10. **Practice Soles of the Feet:** End the session with practice.

4.1. Practice Soles of the Feet

Begin the class with a practice of Soles of the Feet, allowing students to choose either sitting or standing practice. Troubleshoot their use of the program as necessary and distribute additional copies of the "My Soles of the Feet Routine" handout (Appendix 1D) if students need them.

Debrief by asking open-ended questions about the students' experience, taking special care to make sure the students were able to move their attention to the somatic experience of their feet. Make sure to ask about what the students are noticing about their feet *right now* to continue to engender mindful attention to the present moment. Be mindful that you are consistently using the same language for the Soles of the Feet practice and are referring to the "My Soles of the Feet Routine" handout (Appendix 1D) accordingly.

Let's start class with a Soles of the Feet practice. You can choose to do this either sitting or standing.

To begin, sitting up straight, placing your feet flat on the floor, allowing your eyes to close if this feels comfortable ... [Continue reciting the full Soles of the Feet routine (see "My Soles of the

Feet Routine," Appendix 1D) as you practice with the students.]

Nice work! You all just used Soles of the Feet again, way to go! Would anybody like to share what this was like for you? What are you all noticing when you move your attention to your feet? What are you noticing about your feet right now? Does anyone need an extra copy of the "My Soles of the Feet Routine" to help you remember the steps? Does anybody have any questions about this practice we just completed?

4.2. Review of Previous Class

To activate prior knowledge, review that the purpose of learning Soles of the Feet is to learn how to stay calm when one becomes upset. Review the previous class's experience of using Soles of the Feet to make the strong negative emotion anger disappear or diminish.

We are continuing to learn about how to use Soles of the Feet, which is a great way to keep us calm even if we are upset. Being able to stay calm when you are upset can help you all do well in school and keep from getting in trouble, and it is also an important part of growing up.

During the last class, we practiced Soles of the Feet while you were imagining an unpleasant experience and experiencing the unpleasant emotion of anger. We practiced using Soles of the Feet while feeling angry, and you were able to experience making the angry feeling disappear or feel much less powerful.

4.3. Review of Assigned Between-Class Practice

Review that to get good at anything, practice is very important. Check to see if the students practiced Soles of the Feet since the last class, and whether they used Soles of the Feet while feeling angry (or even slightly angry or annoyed), and nonjudgmentally inquire how this practice went.

It is very important that the students practice Soles of the Feet between classes so that this new skill will generalize to other contexts. Make sure to praise students who have practiced and inquire how they remembered to practice so as to model for other students in the class. Also, give extra praise for students who were able to successfully apply Soles of the Feet when feeling angry: this is very important for demonstrating the utility to other students and will serve as powerful and influential testament to the benefits Soles of the Feet. If the students did not practice, be sure to take the time to troubleshoot why this occurred (see chapter 14 for more details).

Remember, in order to develop the skill of Soles of the Feet, you have to keep practicing! Your assignment from last class was to practice Soles of the Feet at least once per day, and to use Soles of the Feet when you were feeling angry, even if you felt only a little angry.

How did your practice go? When did you use Soles of the Feet, and what did you notice? ... Wow, that's great that you remembered to practice, excellent! How did you remember to practice it?

Did anyone use Soles of the Feet while feeling angry? ... That's great! So, you felt annoyed, or a little angry, and then used Soles of the Feet and felt calm again, great work! I'm so glad you shared this, thank you! This is the whole point of learning Soles of the Feet—it's a great way to stay calm even when you are feeling upset or angry.

> ### STOP and CHECK for understanding
>
> Before continuing with Class 4, be sure that the students have attained the following goal: (1) Ability to use the Soles of the Feet routine between classes.

4.4. Class Introduction

Communicate the purpose and objectives of the lesson clearly. Teach students the concept of a "trigger" or antecedent, that is, the internal event (such as thoughts and feelings) or external event that *causes* a targeted behavior (such as aggression). Use analogies to support the teaching of this idea if it is helpful. Explain that during this class, students are going to first identify the triggers to their angry feelings, then imagine an angry situation that includes these triggers similar to the activity from Class 3, and finally practice using the Soles of the Feet routine on these triggers to see what happens.

Today we are going to talk a little bit about "triggers." Do you know what a trigger is? That's right, a trigger is something that comes before an event and often causes the event to happen. Think about a videogame where, if you push a button on the controller, the character on the screen will perform an action, like jumping. The buttons on a video game controller are triggers for the character jumping; first you push a button on the controller, which then causes the character to jump. Today we're going to discuss triggers for our angry feelings.

Triggers for anger can come from inside of us, such as with a thought or a feeling. Sometimes students tell themselves "I don't want to do this!," and this thought triggers angry feelings. Other times, students feel an unpleasant emotion first, such as being worried about a big test, and then this worried feeling triggers their anger.

Triggers for anger can come from outside of us too. If someone mocks me, or if I lose while playing a sport, these events can trigger feelings of anger. First, someone calls me a mean name, then this triggers anger. First, I lose a basketball game, then this triggers anger.

Today, we'll see what happens when we use Soles of the Feet with triggers to our angry feelings. I'm going to ask you to remember a time recently when you felt really, really angry, and to remember what the trigger was to the feeling of anger. Then we'll practice Soles of the Feet to see what happens.

4.5. Identifying the Triggers of Anger

Facilitate a discussion about what the students' triggers for anger are. Define an anger trigger as any situation or event that results in feeling angry, including internal events (such as clenching one's fists, or having a thought that "this isn't fair!") and external events (such as a teacher giving you a warning for misbehavior or a peer calling you a name). Work with the students as a group to identify triggers from the examples discussed during Class 3.

Next, have students identify triggers to their angry feelings. You may ask that the students use the anger example that they identified from the Class 3, or you can support students in identifying some other recent occurrence of anger, using the "Eliciting Emotions Support Sheet" (Appendix 1E). Make sure that everyone in the class has an event in mind where they felt angry and that they are able to identify some of their own triggers.

Depending on the size of the class, you may not have time to check individually with each student to hear their specific example. If this is the case, you can ask if any student is having trouble with this. If that is the case, you can try to work with them quickly to identify their anger event and trigger to the feeling of anger, or you can work with the student outside of whole class instructional time to support this student's individual needs. (See chapter 14 for more details on troubleshooting this situation.) The overarching objective here is to help students identify what the triggers to their anger are, homing in specifically on their thoughts, feelings, and physical sensations that trigger their anger.

Most of the time when we experience an unpleasant emotion, like anger, something happens in our lives that triggers our anger. Let's think back to some of the situations from last class that we talked about ... [Describe to the class one or two examples of the angry emotional memories that students shared during class.]

So, in these examples, can anyone think of what may have triggered the feeling of anger? What are some of the internal triggers, that is, thoughts, feelings, or physical sensations, that might have triggered anger? ... What are some of the external triggers, that is, things that happened or things people said that might have triggered anger? ... [Spend time identifying internal and external triggers to anger, using the examples being discussed.]

Now, let's identify triggers to our own anger. Can you all recall the memory that you used during last class when you felt really angry? Good. Now, thinking back to your angry memory, what were some of the internal and external triggers for your anger? Were there any specific thoughts? Feelings? Physical sensations? Things that happened or things that people said? Raise your hand if you need help identifying your triggers to anger ... [Spend time supporting students in identifying their own internal and external triggers to their angry memory.]

4.6. Applying Soles of the Feet to the Triggers of Anger

Clearly explain the purpose of the exercise: to imagine their anger triggers and then use Soles of the Feet *right before* they get angry. Have students assume a relaxed posture, and then guide them through an *in vivo* memory of the angry scenario they just identified containing their triggers. Try to have students recall as much detail as possible, including multiple senses, in order to elicit a strong memory.

Focus on the moments right *before* the student became angry, when they first noticed their trigger, specifically the thoughts, feelings, and physical sensations that occurred right *before* they became angry. Then, have them practice the Soles of the Feet routine. It is important that this instruction be given as a *direct and forceful command* so as to practice *quickly and deliberately* shifting attentional awareness away from the angry memory (and more specifically, the triggers to their anger) to a neutral focal point (in this case, to the student's feet). Refer to the "Eliciting Emotions Support Sheet" (Appendix 1E) if you need support in asking generic questions about the overview and details of the memory.

In this class, we are learning how to use Soles of the Feet to stay calm, even if something is triggering a strong emotion. Now we are going to practice Soles of the Feet during a trigger that occurred right before we became angry.

To begin, sitting up straight, placing feet flat on the floor, allowing your eyes to close if this feels comfortable ... Placing one hand on your belly, and beginning to pay attention to your breath coming into and out of your belly ... Remembering the angry memory that you have identified ... recalling what was happening ... where you were ... who was with you ... Remembering any sights you saw at the time, what time of day it was, what clothes you were wearing ... As best you can, remember what sounds were happening at the time ... if people were talking, what they said ... if there were any smells, tastes, or tactile sensations, recalling these too ... thinking about this angry memory, remembering what it was you were thinking about at the time and remembering what it felt like to be angry...

And now, remembering those triggers to the angry feeling ... thoughts that you may have had right before you became angry ... physical sensations that occurred right before you felt angry ... things that happened, or things that people said, that triggered the feelings of anger. See if you can replay in your memory those exact triggers that happened right before the moment you felt angry. Now, **quickly shift the focus of your attention to your feet.** *[PAUSE.] All of your attention is on your feet ...* [Continue verbal instruction of the full Soles of the Feet routine.]

4.7. Post-Practice Discussion

Discuss how the experience of shifting attention to the feet while the students were recalling the triggers to anger actually interrupted the feeling of anger, either preventing the angry feeling from happening, or causing the anger to disappear, or reducing its intensity. This interruption helped them to remain calm. Typically, students find that when they shift their attention from the trigger to their feet, they do not become angry in the first place, or the anger that does arise is much less intense. If students do not experience this, which is not uncommon, you should take the time to troubleshoot their experience just as you did during the previous classes, which may include repeating steps 4.5 and 4.6 (see chapter 14 for more details on troubleshooting this activity).

We were just imagining an angry situation, and then I said to shift your attention to your feet as you were recalling the triggers to your anger. What did it feel like to remember the angry situation? Did you feel angry? And then, were you able to identify and remember those triggers to your anger?

What happened to your angry feeling after you shifted your attention? ... That's right—when you practice Soles of the Feet and shift your attention to your feet during the first indication that you are becoming angry, the trigger, then the angry feeling disappears or does not even occur in the first place!

When we become angry, sometimes we let our anger control our behavior.

When this happens, we may say things we don't mean, and do things that get us in trouble. Soles of the Feet is a way to stay calm so that we can act in a way that won't cause any problems for ourselves and other people. Using Soles of the Feet when we notice the triggers to our anger is a great way to keep us from becoming angry in the first place, thus helping to keep us out of trouble at school.

STOP and CHECK for understanding

It is *very* important that students are able to experience success in using Soles of the Feet on triggers to a strong negative emotional response of anger. Before continuing to Class 5, be sure that the students have attained the following goals: (1) Ability to identify triggers to feeling of anger, and (2) Experience of applying Soles of the Feet routine to triggers of anger, thus preventing the feeling of anger from arising, or making it disappear or diminish.

4.8. Class Closure

Review the lesson for the day with the students. Be sure to mention that the objective of learning Soles of the Feet is to keep calm during intense unpleasant emotions such as anger, and that the benefit of staying calm instead of being angry is so the students do not get into trouble from their anger. It's important that you clarify that anger is not a "bad" thing, but rather that by using coping strategies like Soles of the Feet before they become angry, students have the ability to remain calm even if they are angry or upset. Be sure to mention that next class will be the last time you meet with the students for this training.

Today we practiced the Soles of the Feet exercise with triggers that made us angry. When we shift our attention away from strong feelings, like anger, and turn our attention to our feet, often the strong feeling disappears. Remember, anger is just a feeling and it isn't good or bad; however, sometimes when we become angry, we act in a way that gets us in trouble, like becoming aggressive. Soles of the Feet is an important skill for you to have because you can keep yourself calm when you want to, even if you are feeling a strong feeling like anger. Next time we meet will be our last class of Soles of the Feet curriculum.

4.9. Assign Between-Class Practice

Remind the students the critical importance of practice and ask them to practice Soles of the Feet at least daily before the next session, preferably when they notice the triggers to their anger. Remind them that if they do not experience an intense period of anger, they should still practice Soles of the Feet daily, either on feelings of slight anger, or simply as practice. They may do the practice either sitting or standing. Give the students another copy of the "My Soles of the Feet Routine" handout (Appendix 1D) and more stickers if they need them. Err on the side of the students' having more copies if you are unsure, as this will help facilitate their practice. Work with students to troubleshoot any potential barriers to practice if necessary (see chapter 14 for more details on this).

Remember, in order to become good at anything, practice is very, very important, and to become skilled at Soles of the Feet, it's also important that you practice! Practice Soles of the Feet every day whenever you notice a trigger to angry feelings. It's best if you practice Soles of the Feet on triggers before you are feeling angry, as it will help you remain calm and not act aggressively or in a way that can get you into trouble. If you don't notice any triggers or intense feelings of anger, you can still practice Soles of the Feet on small feelings of anger, such as being annoyed, or simply practice it all by itself. Remember, no one knows when you're practicing, and you can do the practice sitting or standing.

You can use the handout sheet to remind yourself of the steps in Soles of the Feet, and you can use these reminder stickers to remind yourself to practice. Does anyone have any ideas for when they think is a good time during the school day to practice Soles of the Feet? What things do you all think will keep you from practicing every day, either on a trigger of anger or otherwise? How can we make sure you remember to practice?

4.10. Practice Soles of the Feet

End class with a practice of Soles of the Feet by having the students verbally recite the steps of the routine. Students may use the "My Soles of the Feet Routine" handout (Appendix 1D) to help them to accomplish this, but it's best at this point in the training if students are able to do the Soles of the Feet routine without any additional support if possible.

Let's practice Soles of the Feet one more time before we end today. You can follow along with the practice using the Soles of the Feet handout, but it's best if you can do this without using any handout at all, because if you have Soles of the Feet memorized, then you can use it any time you want. This time, I want you to lead the practice.

To begin, sitting up straight, placing your feet flat on the floor, allowing your eyes to close if this feels comfortable ... [Continue reciting the full Soles of the Feet routine (see "My Soles of the Feet routine," Appendix 1D) as you practice with the students.]

CHAPTER 6

Class 5: Planning to Use Soles of the Feet in Daily Life

Materials Needed

- Worksheet—"Using Soles of the Feet in Daily Life" worksheet (Appendix 1G)

Session Outline

5.1. **Practice Soles of the Feet:** Begin the class with practice.
5.2. **Review of Previous Class:** Review major content from Class 4.
5.3. **Review of Assigned Between-Class Practice:** Discuss how their practice went and troubleshoot barriers to practice.

5.4.	**Class Introduction:**	Explain the activities and content to be covered during Class 5.
5.5.	**Curriculum Review:**	Review the major content from the entire curriculum.
5.6.	**Discussing the Importance of Practice:**	Discuss the importance of practice.
5.7.	**Making a Plan for Future Practice and Application:**	Work together to create a plan for future Soles of the Feet practice and utilization.
5.8.	**Check for Mastery:**	Work with the class to make sure that all students are fluent with major elements of the curriculum.
5.9.	**Curriculum Closure:**	Facilitate final discussion with the class to terminate the curriculum and the relationship (if needed).
5.10.	**Practice Soles of the Feet:**	End the session with practice.

5.1. Practice Soles of the Feet

Begin class with a practice of Soles of the Feet, allowing students to choose either sitting or standing practice. Troubleshoot their use of the intervention as necessary and distribute additional copies of the "My Soles of the Feet Routine" handout (Appendix 1D) if students need them.

Debrief by asking open-ended questions about the students' experience, taking special care to make sure the students were able to move their attention to the somatic experience of their feet. Make sure to ask about what the students are noticing about their feet *right now* so as to continue to engender mindful attention to the present moment. Be mindful that you are consistently using the same language for the Soles of the Feet practice and are referring to the "My Soles of the Feet Routine" handout (Appendix 1D) accordingly.

Let's start class with a Soles of the Feet practice. You can choose to do this either sitting or standing.

To begin, sitting up straight, placing your feet flat on the floor, allowing your eyes to close if this feels comfortable ... [Continue reciting the full Soles of the Feet routine (see "My Soles of the Feet Routine," Appendix 1D) as you practice with the students.]

Nice work! You all just used Soles of the Feet again, way to go! Would anybody like to share what this was like for you? What are you all noticing when you move your attention to your feet? What are you noticing about your feet right now? Does anyone need an extra copy of the "My Soles of the Feet Routine" to help you remember the steps? Does anybody have any questions about this practice we just completed?

5.2. Review of Previous Class

To activate prior knowledge, review the purpose of learning Soles of the Feet. Review what a trigger is, and why it's important to use Soles of the Feet on triggers.

We have been practicing Soles of the Feet to learn how to stay calm even if we are feeling upset. Last time, we discussed triggers, which are things that happen before an unpleasant emotion, and which often cause the unpleasant emotion to arise. Triggers can be many things, such as words people say, places we are, things we think about, or sensations we notice in our bodies. In the last class, we practiced using Soles of the Feet when we experienced triggers to anger, and this either prevented the anger from happening or made it much less intense. It's important to remember that when we recognize that something is triggering our unpleasant feelings, like anger, we practice using Soles of the Feet so that we can stay calm and not act in ways that cause problems.

5.3. Review of Assigned Between-Class Practice

Review the idea that to get good at anything, practice is very important.

Check to see if the students practiced Soles of the Feet during a trigger to their strong unpleasant emotion, anger, or practiced when they noticed mild unpleasant feelings, and nonjudgmentally inquire how this practice went. If students did not practice, spend time troubleshooting with them if needed (see chapter 14 for details).

Check for understanding that the students are able to correctly use the Soles of the Feet routine with minimal, or preferably no, assistance from you or the printed materials. Ask the students to guide themselves through the practice by having them quietly whisper the steps of Soles of the Feet as they go through the entire routine, without using a visual prompt, if possible. Troubleshoot this exercise accordingly (see chapter 14 for details).

Remember, in order to develop the skill of Soles of the Feet, you have to keep practicing! Your practice assignment from last class was to practice Soles of the Feet at least once per day and to use Soles of the Feet when you noticed the triggers to feeling anger, even if you felt only a little angry. How was your practice since the last time we met? When did you use it and what did you notice?...

Let's practice Soles of the Feet one more time, but this time, I want you all to lead yourselves through the entire practice. If you can do this without using the handout, great! If you still need to reference the handout, then that is okay too. To lead yourselves through the routine, use a very quiet whisper voice to repeat all the steps. Let's begin...

STOP and CHECK for understanding

Before continuing with Class 5, be sure that the students have attained the following goal: (1) Fluency with using the Soles of the Feet routine outside of the session with minimal or no external supports.

5.4. Class Introduction

Communicate the purpose and objectives of the lesson clearly. Remind students that this is the final class. Discuss with the students the importance of integrating Soles of the Feet into their everyday life.

Today is our last class of the Soles of the Feet curriculum. You've learned how to identify triggers to your unpleasant feelings and are all now very good at using Soles of the Feet to keep yourself calm. Today we're going to spend some time reviewing all the classes and the content that we've covered. We'll also spend some time discussing the importance of practice and how to make a plan for using Soles of the Feet during "real life" situations when you notice triggers to unpleasant feelings like anger.

5.5. Curriculum Review

Review the major content from the earlier classes. If it's helpful, you may distribute previously printed materials for students so that they have a full copy of all materials you have used in the class.

Let's take a moment to review the content we've covered. During the first class, you learned why Soles of the Feet is important, how to belly breathe (low and slow!), how to pay attention to the different parts of the foot, and how to combine belly breathing with paying attention to your feet, which is what we call the Soles of the Feet routine.

During the second class, we practiced using Soles of the Feet while you were imagining a pleasant memory and were feeling a pleasant emotion, "happiness," and you noticed that the pleasant feeling went away or became much less intense after using Soles of the Feet because your attention wasn't on the happy memory.

During the third class, you practiced using Soles of the Feet with an unpleasant memory and with an unpleasant feeling of anger. After practice, you noticed that the angry feeling went away or became much less intense after using Soles of the Feet because your attention wasn't on the anger, it was on your feet!

During the fourth class, we identified the triggers to your anger, and you practiced using Soles of the Feet on the triggers of anger in order to prevent *the large unpleasant feelings of anger from arising in the first place. We noticed that using Soles of the Feet on the triggers to big unpleasant feelings can either reduce how strong the feelings become or prevent them from occurring in the first place, which is a great way to stay calm so you don't do things that get you in trouble.*

5.6. Discussing the Importance of Practice

Facilitate a discussion about how important practice is for becoming an expert at Soles of the Feet. You should use an example from some other field (such as sports, music, or art skill development) to help communicate the idea that it is only through practice that skill is developed, and that skill is needed to use any ability when the time comes.

When you practice Soles of the Feet repeatedly on your own, you can become so skilled at it that you start using it almost without thinking. Think about when you learned how to ride a bike: with enough practice, it became super easy, and you now don't have to think about how to ride a bike, you just do it. Think about basketball players when they shoot those tough shots at the end of very close games—how did they get so good at making those baskets when the game is on the line? That's right, from practicing over and over again. It's the same thing with Soles of the Feet. What you need to do now is practice Soles of the Feet so that you become an expert at it and can use it without thinking too much when it's really important, like when you are so angry you're about to do something that could get you in trouble. Being able to remain calm no matter what happens is a really important skill to have as students, and as adults!

There will be situations in the future that will make you angry, and sometimes we become so angry we do things that get us in trouble. When this happens, if you can notice the triggers that are starting to make you angry, and you are an expert at Soles of the Feet, you can use Soles of the Feet to have the power to stay calm during *situations where you used to become angry and got in trouble during school.*

5.7. Making a Plan for Future Practice and Application

Clearly explain to the students that the purpose of the next section is to make a list of times and situations that students can practice using Soles of the Feet. Distribute the "Using Soles of the Feet in Daily Life" worksheet (Appendix 1G to the students). Lead the class through the independent work activity of identifying both triggers and settings where they can use the Soles of the Feet routine. Make sure that all the students have a copy of any and all Soles of the Feet materials that you've used in Classes 1 through 4 so that they can reference this activity in the future.

So now that we've practiced using Soles of the Feet on our triggers, you're ready to use it in your everyday life. The last step is for us to create a plan for times when you think you'll need to use it. Here's a worksheet to help you identify triggers and situations when it would be useful to practice Soles of the Feet.

Let's think about all the different triggers that cause strong unpleasant feelings like anger. We'll first discuss this as a group, and then I'll give you a chance to fill out your own triggers for yourself on the sheet. What kind of thoughts do you have that trigger anger? Does anyone have an example they'd like to share? ... [Continue leading students through the "Triggers" section of "Using Soles of the Feet in Daily Life" worksheet (Appendix 1G), pausing to allow students time to write in their responses.]

Now, let's think about all the different situations that could happen when you think that it might be a good time to practice Soles of the Feet. You can think of situations for yourself that you know you'll want to practice. You can also think of situations that might happen when it would be a good idea to practice. Does anyone have an example of a situation at school when they think it'd be a good time to practice Soles of the Feet that they would like to share? ... [Continue leading students through the "Situations" section of "Using Soles of the Feet in Daily Life" worksheet (Appendix 1G), pausing to allow students time to write in their responses.]

In case you forget some of the material we've covered during our sessions, I have extra copies of all the handouts that we've used so that you can use to remind yourself in the future. Does anyone need any extra copies?

5.8. Check for Mastery

Now that students have practiced Soles of the Feet extensively, they should be able to identify the triggers to their strong unpleasant feelings and use Soles of the Feet to make those feeling disappear or diminish. Using the "Using Soles of the Feet in Daily Life" worksheet (Appendix 1G) they just completed, lead students through a self-guided Soles of the Feet practice. Debrief with students after the practice what they would expect the outcome of their Soles of the Feet practice to be and how that may differ from the typical outcome without practice. Try to provide as little prompting as necessary in order to check for their own mastery of the procedure.

Let's do another practice with Soles of the Feet, but this time I want you to lead yourself through all the steps. Look at the "Using Soles of the Feet in Daily Life" worksheet you just completed. Pick one of the situations you wrote down and remind yourselves what your triggers are as well. I'll help lead you through creating the memory for your situation, and then I'll say "Quickly shift the focus of your attention to your feet" as a cue for you to practice. I won't say anything after that, and it'll be your job to lead yourself through the rest of the practice. If you need help remembering the steps, you can use the other handout, but do try hard to lead yourself simply from your own memory.

Imagine your situation when you think you'll need Soles of the Feet. Think about where you'll be, who will be with you, and what things people *might be doing or saying. Try to imagine what you'll see in this situation, and any sounds you'll hear ...* [Continue leading them through an *in vivo* recollection of their situation.] *Now, think about the triggers of your anger. What thoughts, sensations, or things others are doing or saying are causing you to feel angry? ... Now, quickly shift the focus of your attention to your feet ...* [Pause to allow students time to self-direct themselves through the full Soles of the Feet routine.]

How did that go for everyone? What things did you notice from this practice? Thinking about your situation, when you use Soles of the Feet, what do you think will happen next? How is this different than the normal outcome? [Continue to facilitate class discussion about their experience and the expected outcomes of using Soles of the Feet when they notice a trigger to their unpleasant feelings.]

> STOP and CHECK for understanding

> Before completing Class 5 and the Soles of the Feet curriculum, be sure that the students have attained the following final goals: (1) Fluency with using Soles of the Feet during proximal antecedents of anger and while feeling angry and (2) Ability to identify settings/events/times when they can use Soles of the Feet.

5.9. Curriculum Closure

Thank the students for their participation in learning Soles of the Feet. Encourage them to use the skill in their daily lives at school and at home.

You've done a great job learning Soles of the Feet. I'm confident that you will be able to use this new skill whenever you need to stay calm while experiencing strong emotions. You know how to do Soles of the Feet, you know when and where to do it, and you all now have the ability to stay calm when you have unpleasant emotions, which will keep you from getting in trouble at school and will also help you as you get older and become an adult!

5.10. Practice Soles of the Feet

End class with a final practice of Soles of the Feet, allowing students to choose either sitting or standing practice.

Let's practice Soles of the Feet one more time before we end the class. You can practice along with me, either sitting or standing, either whispering the steps to yourself or practicing in silence. To begin, sitting up straight, placing your feet flat on the floor, allowing your eyes to close if this feels comfortable ... [Continue reciting the full Soles of the Feet routine (see "My Soles of the Feet Routine," Appendix 1D) as you practice with the students.]

CHAPTER 7

Follow-up Booster Session

Note: *Some teachers find that after completing the full Soles of the Feet curriculum (i.e., Classes 1 through 5), students may need a brief refresher on the materials. This chapter details a booster session that can be used to review all of the materials covered during the Soles of the Feet classes. Although it can be covered during a single class period, we suggest that teachers assess students' understanding and fluency with the materials, and adjust their rate of instruction to match the students' understanding. Some teachers may find that a single booster class is sufficient to review all the previous materials, but other teachers may find that their students require multiple booster classes to review critical elements of the curriculum. Some teachers find it useful to* *redistribute all the materials from previous sessions as well.*

Materials (as needed)

- Handout—Knowing Your Feet (Appendix 1A)
- Worksheet—Knowing Your Feet (Appendix 1B)
- Handout—Belly Breathing (Appendix 1C)
- Handout—My Soles of the Feet Routine (Appendix 1D)
- Worksheet—Eliciting Emotions Support Sheet (Appendix 1E)
- Worksheet—Identifying Triggers Worksheet (Appendix 1F)
- Worksheet—Using Soles of the Feet in Daily Life (Appendix 1G)

Session Outline

B.1. **Practice and Review the Soles of the Feet Routine:** Begin class with practice and check that students are able to self-guide through practice.

B.2. **Review Purpose of Soles of the Feet and Booster Class:**

Review purpose of learning Soles of the Feet.

B.3. **Review Soles of the Feet Between-Class Practice:** Check that students are able to practice outside of class.

B.4. **Review Content from Classes 2 and 3:** Review major content from Classes 2 and 3.

B.5. **Review and Revisit Content from Class 4:** Review major content from Class 4.

B.6. **Applying Soles of the Feet to the Triggers of Anger:** Practice making the unpleasant emotion disappear or diminish by using the Soles of the Feet routine.

B.7. **Post-Practice Discussion:** Debrief the practice using Soles of the Feet with anger trigger.

B.8. **Making a Plan for Future Practice and Application:** Work together to create a plan for future Soles of the Feet practice and utilization.

B.9. **Booster Class Closure and Practice:** Remind students of the utility of Soles of the Feet and end the class with practice.

B.1. Practice and Review the Soles of the Feet Routine

Begin class with a full Soles of the Feet practice to revisit the routine and offer an additional opportunity to practice with feedback. To review previous content, debrief by asking open-ended questions about the students' experience, taking special care to make sure the students were able to move their attention to the somatic experience of their feet *with minimal or no external supports.*

Note that to be able to use the Soles of the Feet routine, students must have the ability to self-guide through practice, which may require you to make probing multiple checks to assess their understanding. Make sure to ask about what the students are noticing about their feet *right now* in order to continue to engender their mindful attention to the present moment. Be mindful that you as the instructor are consistently using the same language for the Soles of the Feet practice that you established during the previous classes. Do not proceed with the booster class unless students are able to self-deliver the full Soles of the Feet routine with minimal support.

Let's start today with a practice of the full Soles of the Feet routine. I want you all to lead your own practice. If you remember all of the steps, great! If you can't quite remember all of the steps, just raise your hand and I'll come by with a handout.

What I'd like you to do is walk yourself through the routine by whispering the steps to yourself, like this. [Demonstrate to class by whispering the full Soles of the Feet routine to yourself.] *Does anyone have any questions? Okay, let's practice!* [Begin reciting steps of Soles of Feet routine to yourself, monitoring class for students who are struggling and need additional support.] *You just used Soles of the Feet, way to go! How was this practice? Did anyone have trouble remembering the steps of Soles of the*

Feet? What questions do people have about Soles of the Feet? ... [Distribute and review Appendices 1A–1D as needed. Probe students to check for understanding before moving forward.]
What was this practice like for you? What did you notice when you moved your attention to your feet? What do you notice about your feet right now? What questions do you have about this practice we just did?

STOP and CHECK for understanding

Before continuing with the booster class, be sure that the students have attained the following goals: (1) Ability to use Soles of the Feet routine by following verbal instructions, (2) Fluency with mindful breathing, (3) Memorization of vocabulary describing anatomy of the foot, (4) Ability to verbally recite the full Soles of the Feet routine with or without reading from their sheets, and (5) Fluency with using the Soles of the Feet routine outside of the session with minimal or no external supports.

B.2. Review Purpose of Soles of the Feet and Booster Class

To activate prior knowledge, review the purpose of learning Soles of the Feet. Review that it is important to learn how to stay calm when we are upset, and that Soles of the Feet can help.

A few months ago, we learned about a special activity, Soles of the Feet, which is a great way to remain calm when we become upset. Being able to stay calm when you're upset can help you do well in school and keep you from getting in trouble, and it is also an important part of growing up. We learned all about the steps to Soles of the Feet—sitting up straight, taking belly breaths, and then focusing on parts of our feet. We also discussed the importance of practice so that you all can become more skilled at using Soles of the Feet.

Today we are going to review Soles of the Feet to remind ourselves about the practice and how it can be useful for ourselves in school.

B.3. Review Soles of the Feet Between-Class Practice

Review that to get good at anything, practice is very important. Check to see if the students have practiced the full Soles of the Feet routine at any point since the curriculum was completed.

If most of the students did not practice, spend time troubleshooting barriers to practice so that they have a concrete plan for practice before the next class. (See chapter 14 for more details on common barriers and solutions to establishing practice.)

Remember, in order to develop the skill of Soles of the Feet, you have to keep practicing! Since we completed the Soles of the Feet curriculum, has anyone used the practice? When? Did you use the handouts? How did you use them? When and where did you practice at school? For those of you who did practice, what reminded you to practice? Wow, I'm impressed that some of you were able to practice to stay calm when you were upset, that's great!

> ### STOP and CHECK for understanding
>
> Before continuing with the booster class, be sure that the students have attained the following goal: (1) Ability to use Soles of the Feet routine between lessons.

B.4. Review Content from Classes 2 and 3

To activate prior knowledge, review the major content from Classes 2 and 3. Review that students learned how to use Soles of the Feet to make a strong pleasant feeling (happiness) and a strong unpleasant feeling (anger) disappear or diminish. Check for understanding by having students describe what happiness and anger are. Check that students remember being able to make these strong feelings disappear or diminish.

If students do not remember any of the specific content from these sessions, it may be worth revisiting this material. Refer back to the previous chapters to revisit session content as needed. Do not proceed with the booster class unless students are able to recognize, via their direct experience, that Soles of the Feet can be used to make a strong feeling disappear or become less intense.

In our previous classes, we discussed a few very powerful emotions: happiness and anger. Can anyone describe what "happiness" is? ... Yes, that's right—happiness is a pleasant, comfortable feeling. We can usually tell when we, or other people, are feeling happy because they are smiling or laughing (although this is different for everybody).

Can someone now describe what "anger" is? ... You got it—anger is an unpleasant and uncomfortable feeling. We can usually tell when we, or other people, are feeling angry because of how their face or body looks, such as scowling and clenching fists (although this is different for everybody).

Sometimes when we become angry, anger causes us to act in ways that we don't want to. We may do or say things we don't mean, and which cause other people to get hurt, which is called aggression. Acting aggressively when we feel angry can get us in trouble. But anger is not the same thing as aggression—anger is a feeling that we experience, aggression is what we do or act like when we feel angry.

Now, does anyone remember what happened when we remembered a really happy event and practiced Soles of the Feet? ... That's right, we experienced having the happy feeling by remembering that happy event, and then after we practiced Soles of the Feet, the feeling of happiness pretty much went away. And what about the angry memory followed by Soles of the Feet practice, does anyone remember that? ... Good remembering! When we imagined the angry memory, we felt angry, and when we practiced Soles of the Feet while feeling angry, the anger disappeared.

> ### STOP and CHECK for understanding
>
> Before continuing with the booster class, be sure that the students have attained the following goals: (1) Ability to identify the feeling of happiness, (2) Experience of making the feeling of happiness disappear or diminish, (3) Ability to identify the feeling of anger, and (4) Experience making the feeling of anger disappear or diminish.

B.5. Review and Revisit Content from Class 4

Facilitate a discussion about what the students' triggers are for anger. Next, have students identify their specific triggers to their angry feelings. Support students in identifying a recent occurrence of anger using the "Eliciting Emotions Support Sheet" (Appendix 1E). Make sure that everyone in the class has an event in mind where they felt angry, and that they are able to identify some of their own triggers.

Recall that usually when we experience an unpleasant emotion, like anger, something happens in our lives before the angry feeling. Does anyone remember what the word for that is? That's right, we call it a trigger. We're going to take a minute to remember what our own personal triggers for anger are, for example ... [Describe to the class one or two examples of the angry emotional memories that students shared during class.]

So, in these examples, can anyone think of what may have triggered the feeling of anger? What are some of the internal triggers, that is, thoughts, feelings, or physical sensations, that might have triggered anger? ... What are some of the external triggers, that is, things that happened or things people said that might have triggered anger? ... [Spend time identifying internal and external triggers to anger using the examples being discussed.]

Now, let's identify triggers to our own anger. Think about a time recently when you felt really, really angry. Now, thinking back to your angry memory, what were some of the internal and external triggers for your anger? Were there any specific thoughts? Feelings? Physical sensations? Things that happened or things that people said? Raise your hand if you need help identifying an angry memory or the triggers to your anger ... [Spend time supporting students in identifying their own internal and external triggers to their angry memory.]

> ### STOP and CHECK for understanding
> Before continuing with the booster class, be sure that the students have attained the following goal: (1) Ability to identify triggers to feeling of anger.

B.6. Applying Soles of the Feet to the Triggers of Anger

Clearly explain the purpose of the exercise: to imagine their anger triggers and then use Soles of the Feet *right before* they get angry. Have students assume a relaxed posture, and then guide them through an *in vivo* memory of the angry scenario they just identified containing their triggers. Try to have students recall as much detail as possible, including multiple senses, in order to elicit a strong memory.

Focus on the moments right *before* the students became angry, when they first noticed their trigger, specifically the thoughts, feelings, and physical sensations that occurred right *before* they became angry. Then, have them practice the Soles of the Feet routine. It is important that this instruction be given as a *direct and forceful command* so as to practice *quickly and deliberately* shifting attentional awareness away from the angry memory (and more specifically, the triggers to their anger) to a neutral focal point (in this case, the students' feet). Refer to the "Eliciting Emotions Support Sheet" (Appendix 1E) if you need support asking generic questions about the overview and details of the memory.

Remember that we use Soles of the Feet to stay calm, even if something is triggering a strong emotion. Now we are going to practice Soles of the Feet during a trigger that occurred right before we became angry.

To begin, sitting up straight, placing feet flat on the floor, allowing your eyes to close if this feels comfortable ... Placing one hand on your belly, and beginning to pay attention to your breath coming into and out of your belly ... Remembering the angry memory that you have just identified ... recalling what was happening ... where you were ... who was with you ... Remembering any sights you saw at the time, what time of day it was, what clothes you were wearing ... As best you can, remember what sounds were happening at the time ... if people were talking, what they said ... if there were any smells, tastes, or tactile sensations, recalling these too ... Thinking about this angry memory, remembering what it was you were thinking about at the time and remembering what it felt like to be angry...

And now, remembering those triggers to the angry feeling. Thoughts that you may have had right before you became angry. Physical sensations that occurred right before you felt angry.

Things that happened, or things that people said, that triggered the feelings of anger. See if you can replay in your memory those exact triggers that happened right before the moment you felt angry. Now, quickly shift the focus of your attention to your feet. [PAUSE.] *All of your attention is on your feet ...* [Continue verbal instruction of the full Soles of the Feet routine.]

B.7. Post-Practice Discussion

Discuss how the experience of shifting attention to the feet while the students were recalling the triggers to anger actually interrupted the feeling of anger, either preventing the angry feeling from happening in the first place, or eliminating the anger, or reducing its intensity. This interruption helped them to remain calm. You should take the time to troubleshoot their experience just as you did during the previous classes, which may include repeating steps B.5 and B.6 (see chapter 14 for more details on troubleshooting this activity).

We were just imagining an angry situation, and then I said to shift your attention to your feet as you were recalling the triggers to your anger. What did it feel like to remember the angry situation? Did you feel angry? And then, were you able to identify and remember those triggers to your anger?

What happened to your angry feeling after you shifted your attention? ... That's right: when you practice Soles of the Feet and shift your attention to your feet during the first indication that you are becoming angry, the trigger, then the angry feeling disappears or does not even occur in the first place!

When we become angry, sometimes we let our anger control our behavior. When this happens, we may say things we don't mean, and do things that get us in trouble. Soles of the Feet is a way to stay calm so that we can act in a way that won't cause any problems for ourselves and other people. Using Soles of the Feet when we notice the triggers to our anger is a great way to keep us from becoming angry in the first place, and this can keep us out of trouble at school.

> **STOP and CHECK for understanding**
>
> Before continuing with the booster class, be sure that the students have attained the following goals: (1) Experience applying Soles of the Feet routine to triggers of anger, thus preventing the feeling of anger from arising, or causing it to disappear or diminish, (2) Fluency with using Soles of the Feet during proximal antecedents of anger and while feeling angry.

B.8. Making a Plan for Future Practice and Application

Clearly explain to the students that the purpose of this portion of the booster class is to make a list of times and situations that students can practice using Soles of the Feet. Distribute the "Using Soles of the Feet in Daily Life" worksheet (Appendix 1G) to the students. Lead the class through the independent work activity of identifying both triggers and settings where they can use the Soles of the Feet routine.

So we just practiced using Soles of the Feet on our triggers. Remember—you are able to use Soles of the Feet in your everyday life. Let's create a plan for times when you think you'll need to use it. Here's a worksheet to help you identify triggers and situations when it would be useful to practice Soles of the Feet.

Let's think about all the different triggers that cause strong unpleasant feelings like anger. We'll first discuss this as a group, and then I'll give you a chance to fill out your own triggers for yourself on the sheet. What kind of thoughts do you have that trigger anger? Does anyone have an example they'd like to share? ... [Continue leading students through the "Triggers" section of "Using Soles of the Feet in Daily Life" worksheet (Appendix 1G), pausing to allow students time to write in their responses.]

Now, let's think about all the different situations that could happen when you think that it might be a good time to practice Soles of the Feet. You can think of situations for yourself when you know you'll want to practice. You can also think of situations that might happen when it'd be a good idea to practice. Does anyone have an example of a situation at school when they think it'd be a good time to practice Soles of the Feet that they would like to share? ... [Continue leading students through the "Situations" section of "Using Soles of the Feet in Daily Life" worksheet (Appendix 1G), pausing to allow students time to write in their responses.]

In case you forget some of the material we've covered during our classes, I have extra copies of all the handouts that we've used so that you can use them to remind yourself in the future. Does anyone need any extra copies?

STOP and CHECK for understanding

Before completing the booster class, be sure that the students have attained the following final goal: (1)

> Ability to identify settings/events/times when they can use Soles of the Feet.

B.9. Booster Class Closure and Practice

Encourage students to use the skill in their daily lives at school and at home. End this booster class with a final Soles of the Feet practice.

You've done a great job remembering all of the parts of Soles of the Feet. I'm confident that you will be able to use this new skill whenever you need to stay calm while experiencing strong emotions. You know how to do Soles of the Feet, you know when and where to do it, and you all now have the ability to stay calm when you have unpleasant emotions, which will keep you from getting in trouble at school and will also help you as you get older and become an adult!

Let's practice Soles of the Feet one more time before we end the class. You can practice along with me, either sitting or standing, either whispering the steps to yourself or practicing in silence. To begin, sitting up straight, placing your feet flat on the floor, allowing your eyes to close if this feels comfortable ... [Continue reciting the full Soles of the Feet routine (see "My Soles of the Feet Routine," Appendix 1D) as you practice with the students.]

PART II

Soles of the Feet for Students: Individual Program

PART II

Soles of the Feet for Students; Individual Program

CHAPTER 8

Session 1: Introducing Soles of the Feet

Materials Needed

- Handout—Knowing Your Feet (Appendix 1A)
- Worksheet—Knowing Your Feet (Appendix 1B)
- Handout—Belly Breathing (Appendix 1C)
- Handout—My Soles of the Feet Routine (Appendix 1D)

Session Outline

1.1. **Session Introduction:** Explain the purpose of the curriculum.
1.2. **Defining Behavior Expectations:** Set positive rules and expectations for the sessions.

1.3.	**Instructing Posture:** Introduce and practice basic mindful posture seated in chair.
1.4.	**Instructing Mindful Breathing:** Introduce and practice mindful breathing.
1.5.	**Learning About the Foot:** Explain the anatomy of the feet.
1.6.	**Practicing Paying Attention to the Feet:** Introduce and practice mindful awareness of feet.
1.7.	**Practicing the Full Soles of the Feet Routine:** Practice combining mindful breathing and paying attention to the feet.
1.8.	**Session Closure:** Review key content of Session 1.
1.9.	**Assign Between-Session Practice:** Explain importance of practice and assign practice.
1.10.	**Practice the Full Soles of the Feet Routine:** End the session with practice.

1.1. Session Introduction

Explain to the student that they will be starting a new curriculum, *Soles of the Feet.* Tell the student how often you will meet (something that is decided *before* you meet for the first time; see chapter 1 for details), and that they will be learning a great new tool for staying calm. Emphasize that the skill they will learn will help them to control their own feelings and emotions, which is very important for being a successful student and is an important part of becoming an adult. Communicate clearly and directly that during this first session, the student will learn about mindful breathing and how to do the Soles of the Feet routine.

We are going to be meeting to learn a special technique for staying calm when upset, called Soles of the Feet. We will be meeting every other day for about thirty minutes.

Soles of the Feet is a really easy way to stay calm even if you feel very upset. Learning how to stay calm is really important for school and can be a great way to keep from getting in trouble. Learning how to stay calm is also part of growing up, and is something you'll use for the rest of your life.

Today, we're going to learn how to breathe mindfully and how to do the Soles of the Feet exercise.

1.2. Defining Behavior Expectations

Explain to your student the rules and expectations for the session. Expectations should be positively stated; that is, they should be about what the student should be doing, *not* what they shouldn't be doing or what isn't allowed. The expectations may be the same as the student's normal classroom rules, or they may be different and special for the time you meet with them. Sample rules to consider are "Be Safe, Be Responsible, and Be Respectful." In reviewing and defining the rules, we suggest that you work collaboratively with the student to elicit positive expectations (i.e., what the student *should* be doing) concerning safety, following instructions, completing assignments between sessions, and establishing and maintaining confidentiality. This will increase the student's buy-in to the agreed expectations. The general idea is to provide explicit instructions on rules and expectations, but in such a way that it enhances the student's motivation to engage in the instructions that follow.

Since we will be meeting together, we should talk about the special rules we are going to follow. I see that your classroom rules are Be Safe, Be Responsible, and Be Respectful. Can you tell me about these rules? The first rule is "Be Safe." What do you think being safe should look like? ... Keeping our chairs flat on the ground and our feet off of the desk sounds like a good rule, let's use that!

The second rule is "Be Responsible." What should that look like? ... Being ready for our meetings and doing the practice assignments works for me!

The last rule is "Be Respectful." What should that look like? ... Only one of us should be talking at a time. I like that, we'll be able to hear each other much better this way!

I'd also like to add that I want you to know that the things we discuss during these sessions will be kept between you and me, unless it involves your safety or the safety of someone else. If I'm concerned about safety, I do have to let other adults know to keep everyone safe.

1.3. Instructing Posture

Instruct the student that sitting up straight can be helpful when paying attention. Instruct the student in the basics of how to position their body when paying attention while sitting: feet flat on the floor, hands on the lap, sitting up straight (but not rigid). You can invite the student to close their eyes if they would like to, but remember that some students feel more comfortable with keeping their eyes open and picking a neutral point (such as the middle of their desk) to softly gaze at. Note that a student who has had, or is currently having, adverse childhood experiences may feel threatened by closing their eyes. So be clear that it is the student's choice whether they want to keep their eyes open or closed, because it will not affect what they are going to learn. We have found that some students need a few practice runs to get the posture just right, so take your time and provide corrective feedback as needed. Transition from this section immediately into the next section.

To begin, we are going to discuss how to arrange our bodies. Our minds and bodies are connected, and it's important that we position our bodies in a way that will help our mind practice. Sitting up straight can make you more alert and attentive, just like lying down on a cozy couch can make you sleepy.

So now, sitting up straight in your chair ... position your body so that it is awake, and make sure you are still comfortable. Now, make sure your feet are flat on the floor, and place your hands comfortably on your lap. Next, you can keep your eyes open or you can keep them closed because it makes no difference to what we are going to do next. If you keep your eyes open, gently let your gaze rest on the middle of your desk...

1.4. Instructing Mindful Breathing

Once the student has demonstrated good posture and is sitting calmly, instruct them to try "belly breathing," that is, mindful breathing. Have the student place one hand on their stomach to foster somatic awareness of the breath in the abdominal region, and ask them to imagine breathing into and out of their belly or lower abdomen. Encourage the student to breathe *low and slow,* that is, low into the belly and slowly on the exhale. Have the student continue to notice breathing this way for one or two minutes, giving prompts approximately every ten to thirty seconds depending on your visual assessment of the student's in-the-moment engagement with this practice. End the activity by having the student practice taking ten belly breaths by themselves.

...And now that we are sitting up straight with our eyes closed, let's put

one hand on our belly. We are going to breathe low and slow: breathing through our nose and imagining that each breath goes down low into our belly and then out again slowly through our nose. [Pause for 10–30 seconds.] *Feeling the way your belly moves with each breath.* [Pause for 10–30 seconds.] *Just breathing naturally, breathing low into your belly, slowly.* [Pause for 20–30 seconds.] *Feeling your breath coming into and out of your belly.*

Now, take ten belly breaths by yourself, remembering to breathe low and slow into your belly ... and when you are done, you can open your eyes and return to our session together.

1.5. Learning About the Foot

Communicate to the student that before they can learn the Soles of the Feet routine, they need to know some foot vocabulary. To help the student identify the parts of their feet, begin with a brief vocabulary activity to make sure that the student both knows and is fluent with the anatomical parts of the foot. Use the "Knowing Your Feet" handout and worksheet (Appendices 1A and 1B) both to teach these parts of the foot and to check for understanding by having the student complete the activity, noting that the student may need help writing in the responses depending on their academic reading and writing ability.

Next, engage the student with some simple movement activities. The purpose of these exercises is to help the student become aware of the different somatic sensations of their feet by using balance, attention, and physical pressure. Be sure to keep these activities light-hearted and, above all, have fun!

Ball and heel. Have the student stand up and rock forward as far as they can onto their toes without having to take a step forward, and explain that they are now balancing on the **ball** of their foot. Next, have the student rock all the way back as far as they can, lifting their toes to identify their **heel**.

Toes and sole. Have the student stand with their feet flat on the floor. The entire bottom of their foot, which is what they are resting on and where they can sense the pressure of their body weight, is called the **sole** or the **bottom of the foot.** Ask the student to wiggle their toes to identify their **toes.**

Ankle, arch, and top of foot. Either standing and balancing on one foot or sitting in a chair with one leg crossed on your lap, point to and press on the **ankle** with your finger, then proceed to the **arch** and the **top of the foot.** Ask the student to point to and press on their own body parts as they in turn label these parts of their feet.

Before we talk more about Soles of the Feet, let's take a minute to learn more about the parts of our feet. Here's a list of the different parts of the foot ... [Review the labels of the parts of the foot using the "Knowing Your Feet" handout, Appendix 1A.]

Now, let's identify these parts of the feet on ourselves. First, stand up and lean forward as far as you can without falling and without going up on your tip toes ... that's the ball of your foot. Now lean back as far as you can, but don't fall over! That's your heel. Now stand normally with your feet flat on the ground. The flat bottom part where all your weight is pressing is the sole of the foot. Now, sit in your chair ... can you point to your toes? Ankle? Arch? Top of the foot? Very good!

Let's do one last quick activity, but first put away the handout I just gave you. Here's a worksheet that is the same as the handout but with blank spaces and a vocabulary box. [Indicate blank spaces and vocabulary box on the "Knowing Your Feet" worksheet, Appendix 1B.] *See if you can fill out all the different parts of the foot using the vocab box. Excellent work, you learned that really fast and you really know your feet!*

1.6. Practicing Paying Attention to the Feet

This next activity encourages the student to start to identify different somatic sensations of their feet. Use prompt questions to structure detailed somatic attention of their feet. In asking questions, instruct the student that they should not answer your questions verbally, rather they should simply concentrate on the physical sensations of their feet by *following* your instructions. It is important not to require a verbal response from your student, because that moves their attention away from the somatic attention of their feet to looking at and verbally responding to you. Instead, let your questions serve as guides for the student's exploration. End this section by checking in with the student to make sure that they were able to experience the somatic experiences of each part of the foot.

Next we are going to practice focusing attention on the different physical feelings on our feet. To begin, let's sit in our chairs with our feet flat on the floor, backs straight, and hands on our lap, just as we practiced earlier.

Now, see if you can wiggle your toes.

> *Can you feel the tip of your shoe?*
> *Can you feel your toes touching?*
> *Can you wiggle just one toe and not others?*

Next, feel the very bottom of your feet, the soles of your feet.

Can you feel your socks?

Does it feel warm, cold, or neither?

Can you feel the bottom of your shoe?

Now, focus on the arch.

Can you feel the shoe pushing on the arch?

Can you feel where it's most curved?

Can you feel the sock against the arch of your shoe?

Next, let's focus on the ball of your foot.

Can you feel the shoe pressing against the ball?

If you lean your foot forward, picking up your heel slightly, do you feel more pressure?

Now, see if you can notice the top of your feet and your ankles.

Can you feel your shoes pressing on the top of your feet?

What do your socks feel like on the top of your feet?

See if you can notice where your socks touch your ankle—what does that feel like?

Last, focus on the heel against the back of your shoe.

Can you feel the shoe pressing against the heel?

Do you feel where your heel is pushing on the ground? Feeling the floor through your shoes?

If you push your foot back, picking up your toes slightly, does this change anything on your heel?

Nice work! I could tell you were really concentrating hard! Was there any part of your foot that you could feel really strongly? Was there any part of the foot that you couldn't feel? What does "no feeling" feel like, can you describe this more to me? What questions do you have?

1.7. Practicing the Full Soles of the Feet Routine

Walk the student through a combined activity by first engaging in the mindful breathing exercise, then switching to paying attention to their feet (i.e., the two basic elements of the full Soles of the Feet routine). Debrief by asking open-ended questions about the student's experience, taking special care to make sure the student was able to move their attention to the somatic experience of their feet.

A few important things to keep in mind as you are walking the student through the Soles of the Feet activity for the first time:

- Use a slow-paced, low tone of voice to help model and embody a calm, intentional, and mindful manner of being.
- The statement *"quickly shift the focus of your attention to your feet"* should be given as a *direct and forceful command.* The idea is that the student *quickly* moves their attention to their feet to disengage their attention promptly.
- You should consider waiting about five or ten seconds initially between delivering separate Soles of the Feet commands (indicated with [PAUSE.] below), and then stretching this time based on the student's

attention span and developmental level.

Now that we've practiced belly breathing and paying attention to our feet, we'll combine the two. This is called the Soles of the Feet routine.

To begin, sitting up straight, placing your feet flat on the floor, allowing your eyes to close if this feels comfortable. [Check to make sure the student has assumed the correct posture.]

Placing one hand on your belly, and beginning to pay attention to your breath coming into and out of your belly. [Do this for approximately one to two minutes, prompting every 10-30 seconds (as needed) to remind student to pay attention to their breathing.]

Noticing your breathing.

Noticing your belly moving with your breath.

Breathing low and slow into your belly.

Now, quickly shift the focus of your attention to your feet. [PAUSE.]

All of your attention is on your feet.

Wiggling and noticing your toes. [PAUSE.]

Putting attention on the ball of your feet. [PAUSE.]

Focusing on the arches of your feet. [PAUSE.]

Going to the heel of your feet. [PAUSE.]

Putting your attention on the soles of your feet. [PAUSE.]

Feeling the entire foot. [PAUSE.]

Continuing to stay in your feet just by wiggling your toes and noticing your feet. [PAUSE.]

Now, slowly opening your eyes. [PAUSE.]

Nice work! You just used Soles of the Feet for the first time. Way to go! What was this like for you? What did you notice when you moved your attention to your feet? What do you notice about your feet right now? [Debrief with the student, encouraging any report of their direct experience with noticing their feet.]

STOP and CHECK for understanding

Before continuing to Session 2, be sure that the student has attained the

> following goal: (1) Ability to use Soles of the Feet routine by following verbal instructions.

1.8. Session Closure

Review the key concepts of the session.

We just finished the first class of Soles of the Feet. We will be learning an easy way to keep ourselves calm when we are upset. Today we learned about how to breathe with our belly and pay attention to our feet. By first doing belly breathing and then shifting attention to our feet, we used Soles of the Feet for the first time ever!

1.9. Assign Between-Session Practice

Remind the student that to get good at anything, *practice is very important!* Provide an example of how practice yields expertise in any field (such as in sports, video games, or music). Assign the practice of the entire Soles of the Feet routine *at least once* (although more is preferable) per day at school, and have the student indicate a specific time that they can practice. Spend a few minutes troubleshooting barriers to practice or to remembering to practice. Give the student the "Belly Breathing" handout (Appendix 1C) and the "My Soles of the Feet" handout (Appendix 1D) as reminders for how to do this activity. If the student would like, also distribute a special sticker or post-it note that you label as the "Soles of the Feet reminder sticker," which they can affix to their desk or someplace else (such as their smartphone) to remind them to practice, noting that the student may not want this extra attention. These stickers can easily be created using 8.5"x11" label sheets, which can be inexpensively purchased at any office supply store. (As an example, a sticker template document with a picture of a foot, formatted for two-inch circular labels, can be downloaded from the New Harbinger website: http://www.newharbinger.com/44741.) Encourage the student to practice with the handout for now. Mention that the Soles of the Feet routine is a covert behavior (i.e., no one will know they are doing it) in order to address any apprehension the student may feel about doing the practice around other people.

Practice is really important to improve our skills, and it's very important that you practice between sessions to get better at Soles of the Feet so that you can stay calm even if you feel upset in school. It's just like being on a sports team: you practice getting better so you can win the game, and if you don't practice, you won't improve.

This week, practice doing the full Soles of the Feet routine during school at least once per day (although the more you practice, the better you'll get!). Here are a few handouts that detail the instructions for today. Eventually, you'll have the full Soles of the Feet routine memorized, but for now, practice using these handouts so that you do all of the steps.

Here's a special Soles of the Feet sticker to remind yourself to practice; whenever you see this reminder sticker remember that practicing Soles of the

Feet is the best way to get better at it. Some students like to put these on their school desks or phones, but it's up to you where you want to put it.

When do you think would be a good time to practice Soles of the Feet in school? Okay, and what do you think might cause you to forget to practice or not practice? [Troubleshoot their response.] *A really great thing about the Soles of the Feet practice is that no one knows when you are practicing—it's like your own secret practice session!*

1.10. Practice the Full Soles of the Feet Routine

End the session with a practice of the full Soles of the Feet routine. It is best if you have all of the steps memorized to model the process of being able to recite the full Soles of the Feet routine without the aid of the printed sheet ("My Soles of the Feet Routine," Appendix 1D). Just be sure that you are using the exact language on the sheet in order to provide consistency to your student.

To begin, sitting up straight, placing your feet flat on the floor, allowing your eyes to close if this feels comfortable ... [Continue reciting the full Soles of the Feet routine (see "My Soles of the Feet Routine," Appendix 1D) as you practice with the student.]

CHAPTER 9

Session 2: Practicing with a Pleasant Feeling

Materials Needed

- Handout—My Soles of the Feet Routine (Appendix 1D)
- Worksheet—Eliciting Emotions Support Sheet (Appendix 1E)

Session Outline

2.1. **Practice Soles of the Feet:** Begin the session with practice.
2.2. **Review of Previous Session:** Review major content from Session 1.
2.3. **Review of Assigned Between-Session Practice:** Discuss how their practice went and troubleshoot barriers to practice.

2.4.	**Session Introduction:** Explain the activities and content to be covered during Session 2.
2.5.	**Identifying the Feeling of Happiness:** Provide basic psychoeducation on the emotion happiness.
2.6.	**Identifying a Happy Event:** Gather information to create an *in vivo* pleasant emotional experience.
2.7.	**Applying Soles of the Feet to a Happy Situation:** Practice making the pleasant emotion disappear or diminish by using the Soles of the Feet routine.
2.8.	**Post-Practice Discussion:** Debrief the practice.
2.9.	**Session Closure:** Review key content of Session 2.
2.10.	**Assign Between-Session Practice:** Reiterate importance of practice and assign practice.
2.11.	**Practice Soles of the Feet:** End the session with practice.

2.1. Practice Soles of the Feet

Sessions 2 through 5 will always begin and end with a full Soles of the Feet practice to establish a routine and offer an additional opportunity to practice with feedback from you. Debrief by asking open-ended questions about the student's experience, taking special care to make sure the student was able to move their attention to the somatic experience of their feet. Make sure to ask about what the student is noticing about their feet *right now* to continue to engender mindful attention to the present moment. Be mindful that you are consistently using the same language for the Soles of the Feet practice and are referring to the student's "My Soles of the Feet Routine" handout (Appendix 1D) accordingly.

Before we start with new content today, let's start with a practice of the full Soles of the Feet routine.

To begin, sitting up straight, placing your feet flat on the floor, allowing your eyes to close if this feels comfortable

... [Continue reciting the full Soles of the Feet routine (see "My Soles of the Feet Routine," Appendix 1D) as you practice with the student.]

Nice work! You just used Soles of the Feet again, way to go! What was this like for you? What did you notice when you moved your attention to your feet? What do you notice about your feet right now? What questions do you have about this practice we just did?

2.2. Review of Previous Session

To activate prior knowledge, review the purpose of learning Soles of the Feet. Review why it is important to learn how to stay calm when we are upset, and that *Soles of the Feet* can help.

Ask if the student can explain the important pieces of "Belly Breathing" (mindful breathing) to check for understanding and to troubleshoot any misconceptions if necessary. Ask the student to identify the feet vocabulary words from Session 1, referring back to the "Knowing Your Feet" materials (which you can redistribute if they don't have it with them) and section 1.5 as needed. Refer to handouts from last session if necessary (Appendices 1A–1D).

During our last meeting, we learned about our new special activity, Soles of the Feet, which is a great way to remain calm when we become upset. Being able to stay calm when you're upset can help you do well in school and keep from getting in trouble, and it is also an important part of growing up. Last time we talked about the steps for Soles of the Feet—sitting up straight, taking belly breaths, and then focusing on parts of our feet. We also discussed the importance of practice so that you can become more skilled at using Soles of the Feet.

Remind me what the steps are to belly breathing? Great, you got it! Remind me about the different parts of the feet ... What part is this? ... Great memory, you know all about belly breathing and parts of the foot!

> ### STOP and CHECK for understanding
>
> Before continuing with Session 2, be sure that the student has attained the following goals: (1) Fluency with mindful breathing, and (2) Memorization of vocabulary describing the anatomy of the foot.

2.3. Review of Assigned Between-Session Practice

Review that to get good at anything, practice is very important. Check to see if the student practiced the full Soles of the Feet routine, and if they used the handout to facilitate their practice (Appendix 1D).

If the student did not practice, spend time troubleshooting barriers to practice so that you have a concrete plan for practice before the next session. (See chapter 14 for more details on common barriers and solutions to establishing practice.)

How was your practice of the full Soles of the Feet routine since the last time we met? Did you use the handouts? How did you use them? When and where did you practice at school? Wow, I'm impressed that you were able to practice every day, excellent!

2.4. Session Introduction

Explain to the student that during this session, they will be exploring what happens when they use Soles of the Feet while experiencing a pleasant emotion. For this purpose, we usually recommend using *happiness,* although any other positive feeling can be equally as effective (see chapter 14 for a more full discussion of modifications using other emotions). They will do this by talking about a recent memory, then you will repeat back to the student the details of their memory, and then they will reimagine this happy memory in order to elicit the pleasant feeling during the session (*in vivo* practice). While experiencing the pleasant emotion, they will then apply the Soles of the Feet technique to make the emotional sensation disappear or diminish. The premise here is that the student is cultivating a greater nonjudgmental awareness of their emotional experience, and then they are given the opportunity to redirect their attention to the neutral somatic experience of breath and feet after they experience the emotion. Through repeated practice of bringing awareness of experience and then shifting attention to their feet, the student develops a coping strategy that they may use self-regulate their emotions and behavior. (See Introduction for a more detailed discussion of the theory and mechanisms of Soles of the Feet and mindfulness-based programs.)

Today we're going to see what happens when we use Soles of the Feet while we are experiencing a pleasant feeling: happiness. I'm going to ask you some details about a time when you felt really, really happy, then I will repeat these details back to you as you reimagine the happy memory, and then we're going to practice Soles of the Feet to see what happens.

2.5. Identifying the Feeling of Happiness

Facilitate a psychoeducational discussion about the pleasant emotion "happy." Explain that the feeling of happiness is a pleasant, comfortable emotion that feels good. Note that this is not the same thing as equating the feeling of happiness with being a "good" feeling. Labeling the feeling of happy as being a good feeling is judgmental and is thus incongruent with a mindful theoretical perspective. Focus on having the student describe the physiological experience of happiness, that is, what their body feels and looks like when they are happy, as this is the most easily identifiable experience of emotions, which can be an abstract concept for many students. Be sure that the student identifies the subjective feeling of happiness (e.g., warm and comfortable), the outward behavioral expression of happiness (e.g., smiling or laughing), and the internal physical experience of happiness (e.g., lightness, warmth, muscles relaxed).

Let's talk about the emotion "happy." Happiness is a pleasant, comfortable feeling, and it feels nice to be happy. How do you know when you are feeling happy? What does it feel like for you? I know when kids are feeling happy, because they are smiling or laughing. If you were feeling happy, what would you look like and how would I know? Some kids say that they feel relaxed and warm when they are happy. What does your body feel like when you are happy?

2.6. Identifying a Happy Event

To elicit a strong pleasant emotional feeling, have the student describe a recent event in which they felt very happy. Events that happened more recently tend to work better for recalling details. The more detailed the memory and description the student can provide, the more likely it will elicit a strong emotional response. When facilitating this exercise, try to avoid vague recollections (such as memories from early childhood). Use the "Eliciting

Emotions Support Sheet" (Appendix 1E) to guide your questioning and to take short notes if necessary, beginning with generalities about the event (What? Where? When? With whom?) and moving into specific multisensory details (What things did you hear? What were you wearing? Were there any smells you remember?). We recommend that you use direct quotes from the student whenever possible, as this is likely to resonate strongly with their memory and experience. We also recommend that you practice beforehand this process of gathering notes and using these details to elicit an emotional experience.

Now, tell me about a time recently when you were feeling really happy. What was happening? Who was there? What do you remember making you feel happy? Tell me about what you remember seeing ... [Continue taking notes and gathering information using the "Eliciting Emotions Support Sheet" (Appendix 1E).]

2.7. Applying Soles of the Feet to a Happy Situation

Explain that the purpose of the exercise is to apply Soles of the Feet when feeling a strong emotion, in this case the pleasant emotion happiness, and to see what happens. Do not tell the student beforehand that they will make the emotion disappear or diminish—this is a critical *insight* that the student must come to by themselves; if you set this expectation beforehand they might feel pressured to report this experience despite its not occurring. Have the student assume a relaxed posture and take ten belly breaths, then guide them through the happy scenario they have just described to you. Most students find it easiest to recreate the memory with their eyes shut, but this is always an optional element to the activity.

Be sure to include as much detail as possible to create a continuous vivid narrative that will elicit the memory for the student. Refer to notes you have taken on the "Eliciting Emotions Support

Sheet" (Appendix 1E), as necessary, and use the student's verbatim description whenever you can. Once you've described the scenario to them in detail and you notice behavioral cues from the student that they are feeling happy (such as a grin or smile on their face), have them practice the Soles of the Feet routine, beginning with the instruction: "*Now, quickly shift the focus of your attention to your feet.*" It is important that this instruction be given as a *direct and forceful command* so as to practice *quickly and deliberately* shifting attentional awareness away from the happy memory to a neutral focal point (in this case, the student's feet). Much of the effectiveness of Soles of the Feet lies in the student being able to volitionally "snap" their attention *away* from strong emotions, thoughts, and physical sensations, and *to* their feet.

In this session, we are learning how to use Soles of the Feet to stay calm, even if we are feeling a strong emotion. Now we are going to practice Soles of the Feet while we're feeling happy.

To begin, sitting up straight, placing feet flat on the floor, allowing your eyes to close.

Placing one hand on your belly, and beginning to pay attention to your breath coming into and out of your belly...

Remembering the happy memory that you were just sharing ... You were at the carnival with your mom and brother ... You remember the smell of popcorn in the air, and all the laughter from people on rides ... Your mom bought you cotton candy, which you shared with you brother, and he said "This tastes awesome!" ... You played a game and knocked over three bottles to win a stuffed animal and felt so excited and happy that you were laughing and laughing ... Now, quickly shift the focus of your attention to your feet. [PAUSE.] *All of your attention is on your feet ...* [Continue verbal instruction of the full Soles of the Feet routine.]

2.8. Post-Practice Discussion

Discuss how the experience of shifting attention to the feet changed their happy feeling. We suggest that you model the attitudinal qualities of mindfulness in this discussion, namely a nonjudgmental curiosity about their experience simply as it is. Typically, students find that once they shift their attention from the happy memories to their feet, the happy feeling disappears almost immediately or is diminished substantially. If the student does not experience this, which is not uncommon, you should take the time to "troubleshoot" their experience, which may include repeating steps 2.6 and 2.7 using a second or third different memory of a happy situation to practice (see chapter 14 for more details on troubleshooting this activity). Usually if the student practices the Soles of the Feet routine a few times with and without the memory component, they will be able to experience the disappearance of pleasant happy feelings. Be sure to let the student know that it is okay if this does not happen the first time (thereby modeling and engendering the mindful qualities of nonjudgmental acceptance) and that they simply require more practice. Again, be sure that you do not set the expectation that they will make the feeling of happiness disappear or diminish: it is very important that the student comes to this insight on their own.

Once the student notices that through using Soles of the Feet, their emotional experience either disappears or diminishes, praise both this insight and the fact that the student was able to alter their emotional experience on their own. The importance of this insight cannot be overstated. The student coming to the realization that when they experience a powerful emotion, they now have the ability to return to a calm state (or said differently, to self-regulate their emotions) is the central mechanism to Soles of the Feet and the foundation for all further sessions.

You were just imagining a happy situation, and I noticed you were smiling. Were you feeling happy? What did it feel like to remember the happy situation? Did you feel happy? Okay, and then when I said to quickly shift your attention to your feet, what happened next? I see, so you were noticing your feet, just as we practiced. And when your attention was on your feet, did you go back to the happy memory? Good, so you were able to pay attention just to your feet. Now, here's the question: What happened to the happy feeling when you were paying attention to your feet? That's right, simply by paying attention to your feet, you were able to eliminate the happy feeling. You got it! This is really important and something we're going to talk more about: When you practice Soles of the Feet and shift your attention to your feet, the strong feelings can become much less powerful or even completely disappear!

STOP and CHECK for understanding

It is very important that the student is able to experience success

> in using Soles of the Feet to make a strong emotional response disappear or diminish. Before continuing to Session 3, be sure that the student has attained the following goals: (1) Ability to identify the feeling of happiness, and (2) Experience of making the feeling of happiness disappear or diminish.

2.9. Session Closure

Review the session and major content covered. Mention again that the objective of learning Soles of the Feet is to keep us calm during intense emotions, such as when we are upset.

Today we practiced the Soles of the Feet program with a happy feeling. When you shifted your attention away from the strong feeling, like being happy, and went to your feet, the strong feeling disappeared.

Normally we do not want a happy feeling to disappear. But sometimes you may have different strong feelings that you may want to have disappear because they don't feel good and can lead to you getting in trouble in school. Soles of the Feet can be helpful for eliminating other strong feelings, like anger, so that you can stay calm even if you feel upset. Soles of the Feet is a great tool that will help you in school and for the rest of your life, and we'll continue to practice it more using other strong emotions so that you become very skilled at keeping calm when you choose to.

2.10. Assign Between-Session Practice

Remind the student the critical importance of practice and ask the student to practice Soles of the Feet at least daily before the next session. Give the student another copy of the "My Soles of the Feet Routine" handout (Appendix 1D) and more reminder tickers if they need them, and err on the side of the student having more copies if you are unsure, as this will help facilitate their practice.

Work with the student to identify a specific time and location when they will practice Soles of the Feet during school, and remind the student that it is a covert activity. Collaboratively troubleshoot any potential barriers to practice that were identified at the onset of the session (see chapter 14 for more details on how to facilitate more practice between sessions).

Remember, in order to become good at anything, practice is very, very important, and to become skilled at Soles of the Feet, it's also important that you practice! Your challenge is to practice Soles of the Feet at least once per day until we meet again, and if you practice more than once per day, that would be even better. You can use this handout to remind yourself of the steps in Soles of the Feet, and you can use this reminder sticker to remind yourself to practice.

When is a good time during the school day that you think you'll want to practice Soles of the Feet? Remember, no one knows when you're practicing—it's a secret practice! What do you think will keep you from practicing every day? How can we make sure you remember to practice? Let's make a plan together...

2.11. Practice Soles of the Feet

End the session with a practice of Soles of the Feet by having the student verbally recite the steps of the routine. The student should use the "My Soles of the Feet Routine" handout (Appendix 1D) to help them accomplish this. If the student is unable to read the steps, point to each step on the handout as you read it aloud, and have them repeat each step back to you, step by step. Having the student verbally say the steps of the Soles of the Feet routine out loud will support their internalization of the routine.

Let's practice Soles of the Feet one more time before we end today, but this time, I want you to lead the practice. Just read aloud from the handout to guide yourself through the practice ... [Continue with the student reciting the full Soles of the Feet routine (see "My Soles of the Feet Routine," Appendix 1D) as you practice with the student.]

CHAPTER 10

Session 3: Practicing with an Unpleasant Feeling

Materials Needed

- Handout—My Soles of the Feet Routine (Appendix 1D)
- Worksheet—Eliciting Emotions Support Sheet (Appendix 1E)

Session Outline

3.1. **Practice Soles of the Feet:** Begin the session with practice.
3.2. **Review of Previous Session:** Review major content from Session 2.
3.3. **Review of Assigned Between-Session Practice:** Discuss how the student's practice went and troubleshoot barriers to practice.

3.4.	**Session Introduction:** Explain the activities and content to be covered during Session 3.
3.5.	**Identifying the Feeling and Consequences of Anger:** Provide basic psychoeducation on the emotion anger and the differentiation between anger (feeling) and aggression (action).
3.6.	**Identifying an Angry Event:** Gather information to create an *in vivo* unpleasant emotional experience.
3.7.	**Applying Soles of the Feet to an Angry Situation:** Practice making the unpleasant emotion disappear or diminish by using the Soles of the Feet routine.
3.8.	**Post-Practice Discussion:** Debrief the practice.
3.9.	**Session Closure:** Review key contents of Session 3.
3.10.	**Assign Between-Session Practice:** Reiterate importance of practice and assign practice.

3.11. **Practice Soles of the Feet:**
End the session with practice.

3.1. Practice Soles of the Feet

Soles of the Feet can be done sitting or standing. From this session onward, alternate between sitting and standing, with practice depending on the needs and preference of your student. Begin this session by explaining that Soles of the Feet can also be done standing, do a standing practice, and then debrief by asking open-ended questions about the student's experience, taking special care to make sure that the student is able to move their attention to the somatic experience of their feet while standing. As always, encourage the student to notice their feet *right now* to continue to engender mindful attention to the present moment. Be mindful that you are consistently using the same language for the Soles of the Feet practice and are referring to the student's "My Soles of the Feet Routine" handout (Appendix 1D) accordingly.

So far, we've only practiced Soles of the Feet while sitting, but this activity can also be done while standing, and it works just as effectively. Today, let's start by practicing the full Soles of the Feet routine while standing.

To begin, stand up behind your desk, standing up straight, making sure your feet are flat on the floor, and allowing your eyes to close if this feels comfortable ... [Continue reciting the full Soles of the Feet routine (see "My Soles of the Feet Routine," Appendix 1D) as you practice with the student.]

Nice work! You just used Soles of the Feet again, but this time while standing! What was this like for you? What did you notice when you moved your attention to your feet? What do you notice about your feet right now? What questions do you have about this practice we just did? Did you notice a difference between standing practice as compared to sitting practice?

3.2. Review of Previous Session

To activate prior knowledge, review the purpose of learning Soles of the Feet. Review why it is important to learn how to stay calm when one becomes upset, and that Soles of the Feet can help. Review that during the previous session, the student learned how to use Soles of the Feet to make a strong pleasant feeling (happy) disappear or diminish. Refer to handouts from last session if necessary (Appendices 1A–1D).

During our last session, we continued to learn about Soles of the Feet, which is a great way to remain calm when we become upset. Being able to stay calm when you're upset can help you do well in school and keep you from getting in trouble, and it is also an important part of growing up.

Last time, we used a very pleasant emotional memory, a happy feeling, and then experimented with using Soles of the Feet while remembering this happy feeling. Do you remember what happened after we used Soles of the Feet while feeling happy? That's right, you found that the happy feeling disappeared because your attention was on your feet and not on the memory that was causing you to feel happy! Great remembering! Do you have any questions about material we covered during last session?

3.3. Review of Assigned Between-Session Practice

Review that to get good at anything, practice is very important. Check to see if the student practiced the full Soles of the Feet routine since the last session. If the student did not practice, spend time troubleshooting barriers to practice so that they have a concrete plan for practice before the next session. (See chapter 14 for more details on common barriers and solutions to establishing practice.)

Check your student's progress in the curriculum by having them lead themselves through a Soles of the Feet routine practice without your verbal guidance. The student may still be reliant on reading from their sheets at this point in the curriculum, but it would be best if the student were able to walk through the curriculum without this prop. Ask your student to verbally recite the steps with a low-volume voice. If your student is not able to use the Soles of the Feet routine without your direct assistance, spend time troubleshooting the sources of the difficulty (see chapter 14 for additional details).

How was your practice of the full Soles of the Feet routine since the last time we met? Did you use the handouts? How did you use them? When and where did you practice at school? What reminded you to practice? Wow, I'm so impressed that you were able to practice every day, that's great!

Let's practice Soles of the Feet one more time, but this time, I want you to lead yourself through the practice. If you already have all of the steps memorized, then this is fantastic! If you haven't quite memorized all the steps, take out the sheet that has the steps written on it (I have more copies if you need one). What I'd like you to do is walk yourself through the routine by whispering the steps to yourself, like this: [Demonstrate to the student by whispering the full Soles of the Feet routine to yourself.] *Do you have any questions? Okay, let's do another practice then!* [Begin reciting the steps of the Soles of the Feet routine to yourself, monitoring if your student needs additional support.]

> ### STOP and CHECK for understanding
>
> Before continuing with Session 3, be sure that your student has attained the following goal: (1) Ability to verbally recite the full Soles of the Feet routine with or without reading off a sheet.

3.4. Session Introduction

Explain to your student that during this session, they will be exploring what happens when they use Soles of the Feet while experiencing an unpleasant emotion. For this purpose we usually recommend *anger,* although any other negative feeling can be equally as effective. (See chapter 14 for a fuller discussion of modifications using other emotions.) They will do this in the exact same way as during Session 2, except instead of recalling a happy memory, they will recall an angry memory. The premise here is that students are cultivating a greater nonjudgmental awareness of their unpleasant emotional experience, and then they are given the opportunity to redirect their attention to the neutral somatic experience of breath and feet after they experience the unpleasant emotion. Through repeated practice of bringing up awareness of the experience and then shifting attention to their feet, students develop a coping strategy that they can use to self-regulate their emotions that typically lead to disruptive behavior. (See the Introduction for a more detailed discussion of the theory and mechanisms of Soles of the Feet and mindfulness-based programs.)

Today we're going to do something similar, but a little different than last session. We're going see what happens when we use Soles of the Feet while we are experiencing an unpleasant feeling: anger. Just like last session, I'm going to ask you to recall some details about a time when you felt a really, really strong emotion, but this time instead of happiness, we'll discuss anger. Then I will ask you to try to remember all of the details as you reimagine the angry memory, and then we're going to practice Soles of the Feet to see what happens.

3.5. Identifying the Feeling and Consequences of Anger

Facilitate a psychoeducational discussion about the unpleasant emotion "anger" and how the feeling of anger is different from actions one does while feeling angry (aggression). Explain that the feeling of anger is an unpleasant, uncomfortable emotion that feels bad. Note that this is not the same thing as equating the feeling of anger with *being* bad. *No feeling or emotion is bad, and anger is a normal experience of all humans.* Labeling the feeling of anger as being a bad feeling is judgmental and is thus incongruent with a mindfulness theoretical perspective. Focus on having your student describe the physiological experience of anger, that is, what their body feels and looks like when they are angry, as this is the most easily identifiable experience of emotions, which can be an abstract concept for many students. Be sure that your student can identify the subjective feeling of anger (e.g., feeling hot and uncomfortable), the outward behavioral expression of anger (e.g., scowling, yelling, breathing fast, and clenching fists or jaw), and the internal physical experience of anger (e.g., heaviness, muscles tensed).

Next, explain that anger can lead to actions (aggression) that can cause other people to get hurt or get them in trouble. Differentiate the feeling (anger) from the behavior (aggression). Refer to a specific example if you know one from school or share an example from your own life if this feels more appropriate. Explain that Soles of the Feet can be used to prevent anger from becoming aggression, which is a great strategy to have as a student for many reasons (such as keeping friends and not getting in trouble).

Let's talk about the emotion "anger." Anger is an unpleasant and uncomfortable feeling. You know you are feeling angry when you are scowling or clenching your fists. Sometimes your body tells you that you're angry by tensing up and getting tight. How do you know when you are feeling angry? What does your body feel like when you are angry? Can you show me what it looks like when you feel angry? Feeling angry is not a bad thing, and feeling angry is not a good thing. Feeling angry is just a feeling that everyone has and it's totally normal. What is important, though, is what we choose to do when we feel angry.

Sometimes when we become angry, anger causes us to act in ways that we don't want to. We can do or say things that we don't mean, and that may cause other people to get hurt, which is called aggression. Acting aggressively when we feel angry can get us in trouble, like if you were to shove another student during recess and got a detention, or when you yell something *mean to another kid and they don't want to be your friend anymore. But anger is not the same thing as aggression—anger is a feeling that we experience, aggression is what we do or act like when we feel angry. Soles of the Feet is a way to stay calm when we become angry so that we can keep ourselves from being aggressive and act in a way that won't cause any problems for ourselves and other people. It is a very useful skill to have.*

3.6. Identifying an Angry Event

To elicit a strong unpleasant emotional feeling, your student will need to identify and recollect the details of a recent event in which they felt very angry, following the same steps outlined in Session 2. Have the student describe a recent event in which they felt very angry. Be sure to support the student to recollect as much detail as possible, referring to the "Eliciting Emotions Support Sheet" (Appendix 1E) as needed. Events that happened more recently tend to work better for recalling details. The more detailed the memory and description the student can provide, the more likely it will elicit a strong emotional response.

Use the "Eliciting Emotions Support Sheet" (Appendix 1E) to guide your questioning and to take short notes if necessary, begin with generalities about the event (What? Where? When? With whom?) and move into specific multisensory details (What things did you hear? What were you wearing? Were there any smells you remember?). We recommend that you use direct quotes from the student whenever possible, as this is likely to resonate the most strongly with their memory and experience. Again, we strongly encourage that you practice beforehand this process of using details to elicit an emotional experience.

Now, I want you to recall a time recently when you felt really angry. What was happening? Who was there? That sounds like a great memory, but it seems like it was from many years ago, do you have a more recent memory that you can identify? ... Start to think about what you remember making you feel angry. What exactly made you feel so angry? Think about what you remember seeing ... [Continue gathering information from the student using the "Eliciting Emotions Support Sheet" (Appendix 1E) to gather details and direct quotes from your student.]

3.7. Applying Soles of the Feet to an Angry Situation

Explain that the purpose of the exercise is to apply Soles of the Feet when feeling a strong emotion, in this case the unpleasant emotion "anger," and to see what happens. Do not tell the student beforehand that they will make their emotion disappear or diminish—this is a critical *insight* that the student must come to by themselves, and if you set this expectation beforehand, then they might feel pressured to report this experience despite its not occurring. Have your student assume a relaxed posture and take ten belly breaths, and then guide them through the angry scenario they were recalling by walking them through recalling their experience with general guidance (such as prompts from the "Eliciting Emotions Support Sheet," Appendix 1E). The student may find it easier to recreate the memory with their eyes shut, but this is always an optional element to the activity.

Once you've walked the student through the memory in detail and you notice behavioral cues that they are feeling angry (such as grimacing or clenching fists), instruct them to practice Soles of the Feet by beginning with the instruction: *"Now, quickly shift the focus of your attention to your feet."* It is important that this instruction be given as a *direct and forceful command* so as to practice *quickly and deliberately* shifting attentional awareness away from the angry memory to a neutral focal point (in this case, the student's feet). Much of the effectiveness of Soles of the Feet lies in the student's being able to volitionally "snap" their attention *away* from strong emotions, thoughts, and physical sensations, and *to* their feet.

In this session we are learning how to use Soles of the Feet to stay calm, even if we are feeling a strong emotion.

Now we are going to practice Soles of the Feet while we're feeling angry.

To begin, sitting up straight, placing feet flat on the floor, allowing your eyes to close.

Placing one hand on your belly, and beginning to pay attention to your breath coming into and out of your belly...

Remembering the angry memory that you were just recalling ... Thinking back to this recent angry event in detail ... Remembering who was there, what people were saying ... You might imagine going back to this event and looking around—what do you see? You can recall all the details of the playground, the other students, the game of kickball happening. Then, you are about to kick the ball, and you completely miss it and Clarence shouts out "Good one!" and you become angry. You can remember getting hot, clenching your fists, and thinking to yourself "That jerk! I'm going to get him!" [PAUSE.] *Now, quickly shift the focus of your attention to your feet.* [PAUSE.] *All of your attention is on your feet ...* [Continue verbal instruction of the full Soles of the Feet routine.]

3.8. Post-Practice Discussion

Just as in Session 2, discuss with the student how their experience of shifting attention to the feet changed their angry feeling. Again, it is important that you model the attitudinal qualities of mindfulness in this discussion, namely a nonjudgmental curiosity about their experience simply as it is. Typically, students find that once they shift their attention from the angry memories to their feet, the angry feeling disappears almost immediately or diminishes substantially. If your student does not experience this, which is not uncommon, you should take the time to troubleshoot their experience, which may include repeating steps 3.6 and 3.7 using a second or third different memory of an angry situation to practice (see chapter 14 for more details on troubleshooting this activity). Usually, if a student practices the Soles of the Feet routine a few times with and without the memory component, they will be able to experience the disappearance of unpleasant angry feelings. Be sure to let your student know that it is okay if this does not happen the first time (modeling and engendering the mindful qualities of nonjudgmental acceptance) and that they simply require more practice. Again, be sure that you do not set the expectation that they will make the feeling of anger disappear or diminish, because it is very important that your student comes to this insight on their own.

Once your student notices that through using Soles of the Feet, their emotional experience disappears or diminishes, praise this insight and the fact that your student was able to alter their emotional experience on their own. The importance of this insight cannot be overstated, and, furthermore, the student's gaining the ability to self-regulate their emotional experience by using the Soles of the Feet routine is the single most important aspect of the entire curriculum. It is possible that your student will not have a powerful experience of feeling angry or of making that feeling disappear or diminish (just as not all students will grasp a concept when you are instructing in a whole group context). If this occurs, be sure to acknowledge that this is okay and provide encouragement to keep practicing, and refer to chapter 14 for ideas on how to support this student as needed.

You were just imagining an angry situation, and I noticed that you were grimacing and clenching your fists. Were you feeling angry? What did it feel like to remember the angry situation? Pleasant, unpleasant, or neutral? How do you know? Okay, now when I said to quickly shift your attention to your feet, what happened next? I could tell you were concentrating on being in your feet, just as we had practiced. And when your attention was on your feet, did you go back to the angry memory? Great! So, you were able to pay attention to just your feet. Now here's the question: what happened to the angry feeling when you were paying attention to your feet? That's right, simply by paying attention to your feet, you were able to eliminate the angry feeling. You've got it! This is really important and is actually the most important thing in Soles of the Feet—by shifting your attention to your feet when you experience strong feelings, like anger, the strong feelings can become much less powerful or even completely disappear! If you can do this, then you can prevent yourself from acting aggressively, which is the whole point of learning Soles of the Feet. The more you practice, the easier it'll become.

STOP and CHECK for understanding

It is very important that your student is able to experience success in using Soles of the Feet to make a strong emotional response disappear or diminish. Before continuing to Session 4, be sure that your student has attained the following goals: (1) Ability to identify the feeling of anger, and (2) Experience of making the feeling of anger disappear or diminish.

3.9. Session Closure

Review the session and major contents covered. Mention again that the objective of learning Soles of the Feet is to keep us calm during intense emotions, such as when we are upset.

Today, we practiced the Soles of the Feet program with an angry feeling. When you shifted your attention away from the strong feeling, like being angry, and went to the soles of your feet, the strong feeling disappeared or at least became weaker.

Feeling angry is not a bad thing, but sometimes when we feel angry, we act aggressively and hurt other people or get ourselves into trouble, which is not okay. You can use Soles of the Feet when you have strong feelings like anger that you may want to have disappear because they don't feel good or because they can lead to getting in trouble in school. Soles of the Feet can be helpful for eliminating other strong feelings, like anger, so that you can stay calm even if you feel upset. Soles of the Feet is a great tool that will help you in school and for the rest of your life, and we'll continue to practice it more using other strong emotions so that you become very skilled at keeping calm when you choose to.

3.10. Assign Between-Session Practice

Remind the student of the critical important of practice and ask the student to practice Soles of the Feet at least daily, sitting or standing, before the next session and ideally when they feel angry, even if just a little bit angry. Give your student another copy of the "My Soles of the Feet Routine" handout (Appendix 1D) and more reminder stickers if they need them. Err on the side of the student having more copies if you are unsure, because this will help facilitate their practice.

Work with the student to identify a specific time and location when they will practice Soles of the Feet during school, and remind the student that it is a covert activity. Collaboratively troubleshoot any potential barriers to practice (see chapter 14 for more details on how to facilitate more practice between sessions).

Remember, in order to become good at anything, practice is very, very important, and to become skilled at Soles of the Feet, it's also important that you practice! Your challenge is to practice Soles of the Feet at least once per day until we meet again, and if you practice more than once per day, that would be even better. The best practice you can do, and your special challenge before next session, is to use Soles of the Feet when you feel angry, even if you feel just a little bit angry. Remember, you can do Soles of the Feet sitting or standing. You can use this handout to remind yourself of the steps in Soles of the Feet, and you can use this reminder sticker to remind yourself to practice.

When do you think would be a good time during the school day to practice? Great! Remember, no one knows when you're practicing—it's a secret practice! What do you think will keep you from practicing every day? How do you think we can make sure you remember to practice do you think? Let's make a plan together...

3.11. Practice Soles of the Feet

End the session with a practice of Soles of the Feet. Allow the student the option to engage in the practice sitting or standing, by reading off the sheet or by reciting from memory, and by saying the steps to themselves in a quiet voice just as you did when beginning the session. If the student is unable to read the steps, point to each step on the handout as you read it aloud, and have them repeat each step back to you, step by step. Having the student verbally state the steps of the Soles of the Feet routine out loud will support their internalization of the routine.

Let's practice Soles of the Feet one more time before we end today. You can do this practice sitting or standing, it's up to you. You can also do this practice by following along on the printed sheet, but it is best if you can recite all the steps just from memory, so give this a try if you feel ready to. I want you to lead yourself through the practice again by whispering the steps to yourself step-by-step. Do you have any questions? Okay, let's begin...

To begin, sitting up straight, placing your feet flat on the floor, allowing your eyes to close if this feels comfortable ... [Have the student recite the full Soles of the Feet routine (see "My Soles of the Feet Routine," Appendix 1D) as you practice with the student.]

CHAPTER 11

Session 4: Practicing with the Triggers to an Unpleasant Feeling

Materials Needed

- Worksheet—Eliciting Emotions Support Sheet (Appendix 1E)
- Worksheet—Identifying Triggers Worksheet (Appendix 1F)

Session Outline

4.1. **Practice Soles of the Feet:** Begin the session with practice.
4.2. **Review of Previous Session:** Review major content from Session 3.
4.3. **Review of Assigned Between-Session Practice:** Discuss how their practice went

and troubleshoot barriers to practice.
4.4. **Session Introduction:** Explain the activities and content to be covered during Session 4.
4.5. **Identifying the Triggers of Anger:** Define and identify triggers for unpleasant emotion.
4.6. **Applying Soles of the Feet to the Triggers of Anger:** Practice making the unpleasant emotion disappear or diminish by using the Soles of the Feet routine.
4.7. **Post-Practice Discussion:** Debrief the practice.
4.8. **Session Closure:** Review key content of Session 4.
4.9. **Assign Between-Session Practice:** Reiterate importance of practice and assign practice.
4.10. **Practice Soles of the Feet:** End the session with practice.

4.1. Practice Soles of the Feet

Begin the session with a practice of Soles of the Feet, allowing your student to choose either sitting or standing practice. Troubleshoot their use of the intervention, as necessary, and distribute an additional copy of the "My Soles of the Feet Routine" handout (Appendix 1D) if the student needs one.

Debrief by asking open-ended questions about the student's experience, taking special care to make sure the student was able to move their attention to the somatic experience of their feet. Make sure to ask about what the student is noticing about their feet *right now* to continue to engender mindful attention to the present moment. Be mindful that you are consistently using the same language for the Soles of the Feet practice and are referring to the "My Soles of the Feet Routine" handout (Appendix 1D) accordingly.

Let's start our session with a Soles of the Feet practice. You can choose to do this either sitting or standing.

To begin, sitting up straight, placing your feet flat on the floor, allowing your eyes to close if this feels comfortable ... [Continue reciting the full Soles of the Feet routine (see "My Soles of the

Feet Routine," Appendix 1D) as you practice with the student.]

Nice work! You just used Soles of the Feet again, way to go! What was this like for you? What are you noticing when you move your attention to your feet? What are you noticing about your feet right now? Do you need an extra copy of the "My Soles of the Feet Routine" to help you remember the steps? Do you have any questions about this practice we just completed?

4.2. Review of Previous Session

To activate prior knowledge, review that the purpose of learning Soles of the Feet is to learn how to stay calm when one becomes upset, and that Soles of the Feet can help. Review the previous session's experience of using Soles of the Feet to make the strong negative emotion anger disappear or diminish.

We are continuing to learn about how to use Soles of the Feet, which is a great way to keep us calm even if we are upset. Being able to stay calm when you are upset can help you do well in school and keep from getting in trouble, and it is also an important part of growing up.

During the last session, we practiced Soles of the Feet while you were imagining an unpleasant experience and experiencing the unpleasant emotion of anger. We practiced using Soles of the Feet while feeling angry, and you were able to experience making the angry feeling disappear or feel much less powerful.

4.3. Review of Assigned Between-Session Practice

Review that to get good at anything, practice is very important. Check to see if the student practiced Soles of the Feet since the last session, and whether they used Soles of the Feet while feeling angry (or even slightly angry or annoyed), and nonjudgmentally inquire how this practice went.

It is very important that the student practices Soles of the Feet between sessions so that this new skill will generalize to other contexts. Make sure to praise your student for practicing and inquire how they remembered to practice. Also, give extra praise if the student successfully applied Soles of the Feet when feeling angry. If the student did not practice, be sure to take the time to troubleshoot why this occurred (see chapter 14 for more details).

Remember, in order to develop the skill of Soles of the Feet, you have to keep practicing! Your assignment from last session was to practice Soles of the Feet at least once per day, and to use Soles of the Feet when you were feeling angry, even if you felt only a little angry.

How did your practice go? When did you use Soles of the Feet, and what did you notice? ... Wow, that's great that you remembered to practice, excellent! How did you remember to practice it? Did you use Soles of the Feet while feeling angry? ... That's great! So, you felt annoyed, or a little angry, and then used Soles of the Feet and felt calm again, great work! I'm so glad you gave this a shot! This is the whole point of learning Soles of the

Feet—it's a great way to stay calm even when you are feeling upset or angry.

> **STOP and CHECK for understanding**
>
> Before continuing with Session 4, be sure that the student has attained the following goal: (1) Ability to use Soles of the Feet routine between sessions.

4.4. Session Introduction

Communicate the purpose and objectives of the lesson clearly. Teach your student the concept of a "trigger" or antecedent, that is, the internal event (e.g., thoughts and feelings) or external event that causes a targeted behavior (e.g., aggression). It may be helpful to use analogies to support the teaching of this idea. Explain that during this session the student is first going to identify the triggers to their angry feelings, then imagine an angry situation that includes these triggers similar to the activity from Session 3, and then practice using the Soles of the Feet routine on these triggers to see what happens.

Today we are going to talk a little bit about "triggers." Do you know what a trigger is? That's right, a trigger is something that comes before an event and often causes the event to happen. Think about a videogame where, if you push a button on the controller, the character on the screen will perform an action, such as jumping. The buttons on a video game controller are triggers for the character jumping; first you push a button on the controller, which then causes the character to jump. Today we're going to discuss triggers for our angry feelings.

Triggers for anger can come from inside of us, such as with a thought or a feeling. Sometimes students tell themselves, "I don't want to do this!," and this thought triggers angry feelings. Other times, students feel an unpleasant emotion first, such as being worried about a big test, and then this worried feeling triggers their anger.

Triggers for anger can also come from outside of us. If someone mocks me, or if I lose while playing a sport, *these events can trigger feelings of anger. If someone calls me a mean name, then that triggers anger. If I lose a basketball game, then that triggers anger.*

Today, we'll see what happens when we use Soles of the Feet with triggers to our angry feelings. I'm going to ask you to remember a time recently when you felt really, really angry, and to remember what the trigger was to that feeling of anger. Then we'll practice Soles of the Feet to see what happens.

4.5. Identifying the Triggers of Anger

Facilitate a discussion about what the student's triggers for anger are. Define an angry trigger as any situation or event that results in them feeling angry, including external events (e.g., a teacher giving you a warning for misbehavior or a peer calling you a name) or internal events (e.g., a thought like "This isn't fair!" or clenching fists, or beginning to breathe quickly and shallowly). Work with the student to identify triggers from the examples discussed during Session 3.

Next, have the student identify triggers to their angry feelings. You may ask that the student use the angry example that they identified from the Session 3, or you can support the student in identifying another new recent occurrence of anger using the "Eliciting Emotions Support Sheet" (Appendix 1E). Make sure that the student has an event in mind where they felt angry and that they are able to identify some of their own triggers. The overarching objective here is to help your student identify what are the triggers to their anger, homing in specifically on their thoughts, feelings, and physical sensations that trigger their anger.

Most of the time when we experience an unpleasant emotion like anger, something happens in our lives that triggers our anger. Let's think back to some of the situations from last session that we talked about ... [Recap the memory of an angry situation that the student shared with you during the previous session.]

So, in this example, can you think of what may have triggered the feeling of anger? What are some of the internal triggers, that is, thoughts, feelings, or physical sensations, that might have triggered anger? ... What are some of the external triggers, that is, things that happened or things people said, that might have triggered anger? ... [Spend time identifying internal and external triggers to anger, using the example being discussed.]

Now, let's identify all the triggers that we can from this memory. Can you recall the memory that you used during last session when you felt really angry? Good. Now, thinking back to your memory of being angry, what were some of the internal and external triggers for your anger? Were there any specific thoughts? Feelings? Physical sensations? Things that happened or things that people said? ... Ah, so it was when the student said "Nice kick!" in a really sarcastic voice that seemed to trigger your anger. And it seems that you thinking to yourself "That jerk!" actually made you feel even angrier. Nice job identifying those triggers, you have a great memory! [Spend time supporting the student in identifying their own internal and external triggers to their angry memory.]

4.6. Applying Soles of the Feet to the Triggers of Anger

Clearly explain the purpose of the exercise: to work out the triggers to their anger and then use Soles of the Feet *right before* they became angry. Have the student assume a relaxed posture, and then guide them through an *in vivo* memory of the angry scenario they just identified containing their triggers. Try to have the student recall as much detail as possible, including multiple senses, in order to elicit a strong memory.

Focus on the moments right *before* the student became angry, when they first noticed their trigger, specifically the thoughts, feelings, and physical sensations that occurred right *before* they became angry. Then, have the student practice the Soles of the Feet routine. It is important that this instruction be given as a *direct and forceful command* so as to practice *quickly and deliberately* shifting attentional awareness away from the angry memory (and more specifically, the triggers to their anger) to a neutral focal point (in this case, the student's feet). Refer to the "Eliciting Emotions Support Sheet" (Appendix 1E) if you need support in asking generic questions about the overview and details of the memory.

In this curriculum, we are learning how to use Soles of the Feet to stay calm, even if something is triggering a strong emotion. Now we are going to practice Soles of the Feet during a trigger that occurred right before you became angry.

To begin, sitting up straight, placing feet flat on the floor, allowing your eyes to close if this feels comfortable ... Placing one hand on your belly, and beginning to pay attention to your breath coming into and out of your belly ... Remembering the angry memory that you identified ... recalling what was happening ... where you were ... who was with you ... Remembering any sights you saw at the time, what time of day it was, what clothes you were wearing ... As best you can, remember what sounds were happening at the time ... if people were talking, what they said ... if there were any smells, tastes, or tactile sensations, recalling these too ... Thinking about this angry memory, remembering what it was like to play kickball on that day ... the clothes you were wearing, the sounds and sights of the playground.

And now remembering those triggers to the angry feeling. Thoughts that you may have had right before you became angry. Remembering what the student who said "Nice kick!" was wearing, and remembering exactly how you felt and how you thought to yourself "That jerk!" right after he made that mean comment ... Now quickly shift the focus of your attention to your feet. [PAUSE.] All of your attention is on your feet ... [Continue verbal instruction of the full Soles of the Feet routine.]

4.7. Post-Practice Discussion

Discuss how the experience of shifting attention to the feet while the student was recalling the triggers to anger actually interrupted the feeling of anger, either preventing the angry feeling from happening in the first place or causing the anger to disappear or diminish. This interruption helped the student to remain calm. Typically, students report that when they shift their attention from the trigger to their feet, they do not become angry in the first place, or the anger that does arise is much less intense. If your student did not experience this, which is not uncommon, you should take the time to troubleshoot their experience just as you did during the previous sessions, which may include repeating steps 4.5 and 4.6 (see chapter 14 for more details on troubleshooting this activity).

We were just imagining an angry situation, and then I said to shift your attention to your feet as you were recalling the triggers to your anger.

What did it feel like to remember the angry situation? Did you feel angry? And then, were you able to identify and remember those triggers to your anger?

What happened to your angry feeling after you shifted your attention? You got it, when you practice Soles of the Feet and shift your attention to your feet during the first indication that you are becoming angry, the trigger, then the angry feeling is less intense, or even does occur in the first place!

When we become angry, sometimes we let our anger control our behavior. When this happens, we may say things we don't mean and do things that get us in trouble. Soles of the Feet is a way to stay calm so that we can act in a way that won't cause any problems for ourselves and other people. Using Soles of the Feet when we notice the triggers to our anger is a great way to keep us from becoming angry in the first place, and thus can keep us out of trouble at school.

> STOP and CHECK for understanding

> It is very important that your student is able to experience success in using Soles of the Feet on triggers to a strong negative emotional response, anger. Before continuing to Session 5, be sure that the student has attained the following goals: (1) Ability to identify triggers to feelings of anger and (2) Experience in applying Soles of the Feet routine to triggers of anger, thus preventing the feeling of anger from arising, or causing it to disappear or diminish.

4.8. Session Closure

Review the lesson for the day with the student. Be sure to mention that the objective of learning Soles of the Feet is to keep calm during intense unpleasant emotions such as anger, and that the benefit of staying calm instead of becoming angry is that the student does not get in trouble from their anger. It's important that you clarify that anger is not a "bad" thing; rather, that by using coping strategies like Soles of the Feet before they become angry, students have the ability to remain calm even if they are angry or upset. Be sure to mention that the next session will be the last time you meet with the student about this program.

Today we practiced the Soles of the Feet program with triggers that made us angry. When we shift our attention away from strong feelings, like anger, and go to the soles of our feet, often the strong feeling disappears. Remember, anger is just a feeling and it isn't good or bad; but sometimes when we become very angry, we act in a way that gets us in trouble, like becoming aggressive. Soles of the Feet is an important skill for you to have because you can keep yourself calm when you want to, even if you have a strong feeling like anger. The next time we meet will be our last session of Soles of the Feet program.

4.9. Assign Between-Session Practice

Remind the student of the critical importance of practice, and ask the student to practice Soles of the Feet at least daily before the next session, preferably when they notice the triggers to their anger. Remind the student that if they do not experience an intense period of anger, they should still practice Soles of the Feet daily, either on feelings of slight anger or simply as practice. They can practice Soles of the Feet every day while sitting or standing. Give the student another copy of the "My Soles of the Feet Routine" handout (Appendix 1D) and more reminder stickers if the student needs them. Err on the side of the student having more copies if you are unsure, because this will help facilitate their practice. Work with your student to troubleshoot any potential barriers to practice if necessary (see chapter 14 for more details on this).

Remember, in order to become good at anything, practice is very, very important, and to become skilled at Soles of the Feet, it's also important that you practice! Practice Soles of the Feet every day, whenever you notice a trigger to angry feelings. It's best if you practice Soles of the Feet on triggers before you are feeling angry, as this will help you remain calm and not act aggressively or in a way that can get you in to trouble. If you don't notice any triggers or intense feelings of anger, you can still practice Soles of the Feet on small feelings of anger, such as being annoyed, or simply practice it all by itself. Remember, no one knows when you're practicing, and you can do the practice sitting or standing.

You can use the handout sheet to remind yourself of the steps in Soles of the Feet, and you can use these reminder stickers to remind yourself to practice. Do you have any ideas about when a good time will be during the school day to practice Soles of the Feet? What things do you think might keep you from practicing every day, either on a trigger of anger or otherwise? How can we make sure you remember to practice?

4.10. Practice Soles of the Feet

End the session with a practice of Soles of the Feet by having the student verbally recite the steps of the routine. The student may use the "My Soles of the Feet Routine" handout (Appendix 1D) to accomplish this; however, it is best at this point in the training if the student is able to use Soles of the Feet without any additional support, if at all possible.

Let's practice Soles of the Feet one more time before we end today, but this time I want you to lead your practice. You can follow along with the practice using the Soles of the Feet handout; however, it's best if you can do this without using any handout at all, because if you have Soles of the Feet memorized, then you can use it at any time you want!

To begin, sitting up straight, placing your feet flat on the floor, allowing your eyes to close if this feels comfortable ... [Have the student recite the full Soles of the Feet routine (see "My Soles of the Feet Routine," Appendix 1D) as you practice with the student.]

CHAPTER 12
Session 5: Planning to Use Soles of the Feet in Daily Life

Materials Needed

- Worksheet—"Using Soles of the Feet in Daily Life" worksheet (Appendix 1G)

Session Outline

5.1. **Practice Soles of the Feet:** Begin the session with practice.
5.2. **Review of Previous Session:** Review major content from Session 4.
5.3. **Review of Assigned Between-Session Practice:** Discuss how their practice went and troubleshoot barriers to practice.

5.4. **Session Introduction:** Explain the activities and content to be covered during Session 5.
5.5. **Curriculum Review:** Review the major content from the entire curriculum.
5.6. **Discussing the Importance of Practice:** Stress again the importance of practice.
5.7. **Making a Plan for Future Practice and Application:** Work together to create a plan for future Soles of the Feet practice and utilization.
5.8. **Check for Mastery:** Work with the student to make sure that they are fluent with major elements of the curriculum.
5.9. **Curriculum Closure:** Facilitate discussion to end the session, the curriculum, and (if applicable) the therapeutic relationship.
5.10. **Practice Soles of the Feet:** End the session with practice.

5.1. Practice Soles of the Feet

Begin the session with a practice of Soles of the Feet, allowing the student to choose either sitting or standing practice. Troubleshoot the student's use of the program, as necessary, and distribute an additional copy of the "My Soles of the Feet Routine" handout (Appendix 1D) if the student needs one.

Debrief by asking open-ended questions about the student's experience, taking special care to make sure that your student was able to move their attention to the somatic experience of their feet. Make sure to ask about what the student is noticing about their feet *right now* to continue to engender mindful attention to the present moment. Be mindful that you are consistently using the same language for the Soles of the Feet practice and are referring to the "My Soles of the Feet Routine" handout (Appendix 1D) accordingly.

Let's start this session with a Soles of the Feet practice. You can choose to do this either sitting or standing.

To begin, sitting up straight, placing your feet flat on the floor, allowing your eyes to close if this feels comfortable ... [Continue reciting the full Soles of the Feet routine (see "My Soles of the Feet Routine," Appendix 1D) as you practice with the student.]

Nice work! You just used Soles of the Feet again, way to go! What was this like for you? What are you noticing when you move your attention to your feet? What are you noticing about your feet right now? Do you need an extra copy of the "My Soles of the Feet Routine" to help you remember the steps? Do you have any questions about this practice we just completed?

5.2. Review of Previous Session

To activate prior knowledge, review the purpose of learning Soles of the Feet. Review what a trigger is, and why it's important to use Soles of the Feet on triggers.

We have been practicing Soles of the Feet to learn how to stay calm even if we are feeling upset. Last time, we discussed triggers, which are things that happen before an unpleasant emotion, and which often cause the unpleasant emotion to happen. Triggers can be many things, such as words people say, places we are, things we think about, or sensations we notice in our bodies. In the last session, we practiced using Soles of the Feet when we experienced triggers to anger, and this either prevented the anger from happening or made it much less intense. It's important to remember that when we recognize that something is triggering our unpleasant feelings, like anger, we then practice using Soles of the Feet so that we can stay calm and not act in ways that cause problems.

5.3. Review of Assigned Between-Session Practice

Review that to become good at anything, practice is very important. Check to see if the student practiced Soles of the Feet during a trigger to their strong unpleasant emotion, anger, or practiced when the student noticed mild unpleasant feelings. Nonjudgmentally inquire how this practice went. If the student did not practice, spend time troubleshooting with the student, if needed (see chapter 14 for details).

Check that the student was able to use the Soles of the Feet routine with fidelity with minimal, or preferably no, assistance from you or the printed materials. Ask the student to guide themself through the practice by having them quietly whisper the steps of Soles of the Feet as they go through the entire routine, without using a visual prompt, if possible. Troubleshoot this exercise accordingly (see chapter 14 for details).

Remember, in order to develop the skill of Soles of the Feet, you have to keep practicing! Your practice assignment from the last session was to practice Soles of the Feet at least once per day and to use Soles of the Feet when you noticed the triggers to feeling angry, even if you felt only a little angry. How was your practice since the last time we met? When did you use it and what did you notice?...

Now let's practice Soles of the Feet one more time, but this time, I want you to lead the entire practice. If you can do this without using the handout, great! If you still need to reference the handout, that is okay too. To lead yourself through the routine, use a very quiet whisper voice to repeat all the steps. Let's begin...

STOP and CHECK for understanding

Before continuing with Session 5 (which will complete the Soles of the Feet curriculum), be sure that the student has attained the following goal: (1) Fluency with using Soles of the Feet routine outside of the session with minimal or no external supports.

5.4. Session Introduction

Communicate the purpose and objectives of the session clearly. Remind your student that this is the final session. Explain to your student that today you are going to talk about the importance of integrating Soles of the Feet into their everyday life.

Today is our last session of the Soles of the Feet curriculum. You've learned how to identify triggers to your unpleasant feelings and are now very good at using Soles of the Feet to keep yourself calm. Today we're going to spend some time reviewing all the content that we've covered. We'll also spend some time discussing the importance of practice and how to make a plan for using Soles of the Feet during "real life" situations when you notice triggers to unpleasant feelings like anger.

5.5. Curriculum Review

Review the major contents from the earlier sessions. If it's helpful, you may distribute previously printed materials for the student so that they have a full set of all the materials you've used in the sessions.

Let's take a moment to review the content we've covered. During the first session, you learned why Soles of the

Feet is important, how to belly breathe (low and slow!), how to pay attention to the different parts of the foot, and how to combine belly breathing with paying attention to your feet, which is what we call the Soles of the Feet routine.

During the second session, we practiced using Soles of the Feet while you were imagining a pleasant memory and were feeling a pleasant emotion, happiness, and you noticed that the pleasant feeling went away or became much less intense after using Soles of the Feet because your attention wasn't on the happy memory.

During the third session, you practiced using Soles of the Feet with an unpleasant memory and with an unpleasant feeling of anger. You noticed that the angry feeling went away or became much less intense after using Soles of the Feet because your attention wasn't on the anger, it was on your feet!

During the fourth session, we identified the triggers to our anger and you practiced using Soles of the Feet on the triggers of anger in order to prevent the unpleasant feelings of anger from arising in the first place. We noticed that using Soles of the Feet on the triggers to unpleasant feelings can either reduce how strong the feelings become or prevent them from occurring at all, which is a great way to stay calm so you don't do things that get you in trouble.

5.6. Discussing the Importance of Practice

Facilitate a discussion about how important practice is for becoming an expert at Soles of the Feet. You should use a comparison (such as sports, music, or art skill development) to help communicate the idea that it is only through practice that skill is developed, and that skill is needed to use any ability when the time comes.

When you practice Soles of the Feet repeatedly on your own, you can become so skilled at it that you start to use it almost without thinking. Think about when you learned how to ride a bike. With enough practice, it became super easy, and you now don't have to think about how to ride a bike, you just do it. Think about basketball players when they shoot those tough shots at the end of very close games. How did they get so good at making those baskets when the game is on the line? That's right, from practicing over and over again. It's the same thing with Soles of the Feet. What you need to do now is practice Soles of the Feet so that you become an expert at it and can use it without thinking too much when it's really important, like when you are so angry you're about to do something that could get you in trouble. Being able to remain calm no matter what happens is a really important skill to have as students, and as adults!

There will be situations in the future that will make you angry, and sometimes we become so angry we do things that get us in trouble. When this happens, if you can notice the triggers that are starting to make you angry and you are an expert at Soles of the Feet, you can use Soles of the Feet to have the power to stay calm during situations where you used to become angry and got in trouble during school.

5.7. Making a Plan for Future Practice and Application

Clearly explain to the student that the purpose of the next section is to make a list of times and situations that the student can practice using Soles of the Feet. Distribute the "Using Soles of the Feet in Daily Life" worksheet (Appendix 1G) to the student. Lead the student through the independent work activity of identifying both triggers and settings where they can use the Soles of the Feet routine. Make sure that the student has a copy of all the Soles of the Feet materials that you've used in Sessions 1 through 4 so that they can reference this activity in the future.

Now that you have practiced using Soles of the Feet on your triggers to anger, you're ready to use it in your everyday life. The last step is for us to create a plan for times when you think you'll need to use it. Here's a worksheet to help us identify triggers and situations when it would be useful to practice Soles of the Feet.

Let's think about all the different triggers that cause strong unpleasant feelings like anger. I'll give you a chance to fill out your own triggers for yourself on the sheet. What kind of thoughts do you have that trigger anger? ... [Continue leading the student through the "Triggers" section of "Using Soles of the Feet in Daily Life" worksheet (Appendix 1G), pausing to allow the student time to write in their responses.]

Now, let's think about all the different situations that could happen when you think that it might be a good time to practice Soles of the Feet. Think of all situations that you know you'll want to practice. You can also think of situations that might happen when it'd be a good idea to practice. Do you have an example of a situation at school when you think it'd be a good time to practice Soles of the Feet? ... [Continue leading the student through the "Situations" section of the "Using Soles of the Feet in Daily Life" worksheet (Appendix 1G), pausing to allow the student time to write in their responses.]

In case you forget some of the material we've covered during our sessions, I have extra copies of all the handouts that we've used so that you can use them to remind yourself in the future. Do you need any extra copies?

5.8. Check for Mastery

Now that your student has practiced Soles of the Feet extensively, they should be able to identify the triggers to their strong unpleasant feelings and use Soles of the Feet to make those feelings disappear or diminish. Using the "Using Soles of the Feet in Daily Life" worksheet (Appendix 1G) they just completed, lead your student through a self-guided Soles of the Feet practice. Debrief with the student after the practice what they would expect the outcome of their Soles of the Feet practice to be and how that may differ from the typical outcome without practice. Try to provide as little prompting as necessary in order to verify that the student can use the full procedure without your explicit guidance. By doing so, you are checking that the student has mastered Soles of the Feet and is able to use the procedure independently in their daily life.

Let's do another practice with Soles of the Feet, but this time I want you to lead yourself through all the steps. Look at the "Using Soles of the Feet in Daily Life" worksheet you just completed. Pick one of the situations that you wrote down, and remind yourself what your triggers are as well. I'll help lead you through creating the memory for your situation, and then I'll say "quickly shift the focus of your attention to your feet" as a cue for you to practice. I won't say anything after that, and it'll be your job to lead yourself through the rest of the practice. If you need help remembering the steps, you can use the other handout, but do try lead yourself simply from your own memory.

Imagine a situation when you think you'll need Soles of the Feet. Think about where you'll be, who will be with you, and what things people might be doing or saying. Try to imagine what you'll see in this situation, and any sounds you'll hear ... [Continue leading the student through an *in vivo* recollection of their situation.] *Now, think about the triggers of your anger. What thoughts, sensations, or things other people are doing or saying are causing you to feel angry? ... Now, quickly shift the focus of your attention to your feet.* [Pause to allow the student time to self-direct through the full Soles of the Feet routine.]

How did that go for you? What things did you notice from this practice? Thinking about your situation, when you use Soles of the Feet what do you think will happen next? How is this different from the normal outcome? [Continue to facilitate session discussion about the student'sr experience and the expected outcomes of using Soles of the Feet when they notice a trigger to their unpleasant feelings.]

STOP and CHECK for understanding

Before completing Session 5 and the Soles of the Feet curriculum, be sure that the student has attained the following final goals: (1) Fluency with

> using Soles of the Feet during proximal antecedents of anger and while feeling angry, and (2) Ability to identify settings/events/times when they can use Soles of the Feet.

5.9. Curriculum Closure

Thank the student for participating in learning Soles of the Feet. Encourage the student to use the skill in daily life at school and at home.

You've done a great job learning Soles of the Feet. I'm confident that you will be able to use this new skill whenever you need to stay calm while experiencing strong emotions. You know how to do Soles of the Feet, you know when and where to do it, and you now have the ability to stay calm when you have unpleasant emotions, which will keep you from getting in trouble at school and will also help you as you get older and become an adult!

5.10. Practice Soles of the Feet

End the session with a final practice of Soles of the Feet, allowing your student to choose either sitting or standing practice.

Let's practice Soles of the Feet one more time before we end this last session. You can practice along with me, either sitting or standing, either whispering the steps to yourself or practicing in silence. To begin, sitting up straight, placing your feet flat on the floor, allowing your eyes to close if this feels comfortable ... [Continue reciting the full Soles of the Feet routine (see "My Soles of the Feet Routine," Appendix 1D) as you practice with the student.]

CHAPTER 13

Follow-up Booster Session

Note: *Some teachers find that after completing the full Soles of the Feet curriculum (i.e., Sessions 1 through 5), the student may need a brief refresher on the materials. This chapter details a booster session that can be used to review all of the materials covered during the Soles of the Feet sessions. Although it can be covered during a single session, we suggest that teachers assess their student's understanding and fluency with the materials, and adjust their rate of instruction to match the student's understanding. Some teachers may find that a single booster session is sufficient to review all the previous materials, while others may find that their student requires multiple booster sessions to review critical elements of the curriculum. Some teachers find it useful to redistribute all the materials from previous sessions as well.*

Materials (as needed)

- Handout—Knowing Your Feet (Appendix 1A)
- Worksheet—Knowing Your Feet (Appendix 1B)
- Handout—Belly Breathing (Appendix 1C)
- Handout—My Soles of the Feet Routine (Appendix 1D)
- Worksheet—Eliciting Emotions Support Sheet (Appendix 1E)
- Worksheet—Identifying Triggers Worksheet (Appendix 1F)
- Worksheet—Using Soles of the Feet in Daily Life (Appendix 1G)

Session Outline

B.1. **Practice and Review the Soles of the Feet Routine:** Begin the session with practice and check that the student is able to self-guide through practice.

B.2. **Review Purpose of Soles of the Feet and Booster Session:** Review the purpose of learning Soles of the Feet.

B.3. **Review Soles of the Feet Between-Session Practice:** Check that the student is able to practice outside of session.

B.4. **Review Content from Sessions 2 and 3:** Review major content from Sessions 2 and 3.

B.5. **Review and Revisit Content from Session 4:** Review major content from Session 4.

B.6. **Applying Soles of the Feet to the Triggers of Anger:** Practice making the unpleasant emotion disappear or diminish by using the Soles of the Feet routine.

B.7. **Post-Practice Discussion:** Debrief the practice using Soles of the Feet with anger trigger.

B.8. **Making a Plan for Future Practice and Application:** Work together to create a plan for future Soles of the Feet practice and utilization.

B.9. **Booster Session Closure and Practice:** Remind the student of the utility of Soles of the

Feet and end the class with practice.

B.1. Practice and Review the Soles of the Feet Routine

Begin the session with a full Soles of the Feet practice to revisit the routine and offer an additional opportunity to practice with feedback. To review previous content, debrief by asking open-ended questions about the student's experience, taking special care to make sure that the student is able to move their attention to the somatic experience of their feet *with minimal or no external supports.*

Note that to be able to use the Soles of the Feet routine, the student must have the ability to self-guide through practice, which may require probing multiple checks of their understanding. Make sure to ask about what the student is noticing about their feet *right now* to continue to engender mindful attention to the present moment. Be mindful that you as the instructor are consistently using the same language for the Soles of the Feet practice that you established during the previous classes. Do not proceed with the booster session unless your student is able to self-deliver the full Soles of the Feet routine with minimal support.

Let's start today with a practice of the full Soles of the Feet routine. I want you to lead your own practice. If you remember all of the steps, great! If you can't quite remember all of the steps, use this handout. What I'd like you to do is walk yourself through the routine by whispering the steps to yourself, like this. [Demonstrate to student by whispering the full Soles of the Feet routine to yourself.] *Do you have any questions? Okay, let's do the practice then!* [Begin reciting steps of Soles of Feet routine to yourself, monitoring your student if they need additional support.]

You just used Soles of the Feet, way to go! How was this practice? Did you have trouble remembering the steps to Soles of the Feet? What questions do you have about Soles of the Feet? ... [Distribute and review Appendices 1A–1D as needed. Probe student to check for understanding before moving forward.] *What was this practice like for you? What did you notice when you moved your attention to your feet? What do you notice about your feet right now? What questions do you have about this practice we just did?*

> ## STOP and CHECK for understanding
>
> Before continuing with the booster session, be sure that the student has attained the following goals: (1) Ability to use the Soles of the Feet routine by following verbal instructions, (2) Fluency with mindful breathing, (3) Memorization of vocabulary describing anatomy of the foot, (4) Ability to verbally recite the full Soles of the Feet routine with or without reading from their sheet, and (5) Fluency with using the Soles of the Feet routine outside of the sessions with minimal or no external supports.

B.2. Review Purpose of Soles of the Feet and Booster Session

To activate prior knowledge, review the purpose of learning Soles of the Feet. Review that it is important to learn how to stay calm when we are upset, and that Soles of the Feet can help.

A few months ago, we learned about a special activity, Soles of the Feet, which is a great way to remain calm when we become upset. Being able to stay calm when you are upset can help you do well in school and keep you from getting in trouble, and it is also an important part of growing up. We learned all about the steps to Soles of the Feet—sitting up straight, taking belly breaths, and then focusing on parts of our feet. We also discussed the importance of practice so that you can become more skilled at using Soles of the Feet.

Today we are going to review Soles of the Feet to remind ourselves about the practice and how it can be useful for ourselves in school.

B.3. Review Soles of the Feet Between-Session Practice

Review that to get good at anything, practice is very important. Check to see if the student has practiced the full Soles of the Feet routine at any point since the curriculum was completed.

If your student did not practice, spend time troubleshooting barriers to practice so that they have a concrete plan for practice before the next class. (See chapter 14 for more details on common barriers and solutions to establishing practice.)

Remember, in order to develop the skill of Soles of the Feet, you have to keep practicing! Since we completed the Soles of the Feet curriculum, have you used the practice? When? Did you use the handouts? How did you use them? When and where did you practice at school? What reminded you to practice? Wow, I'm impressed that you were able to practice to stay calm when you were upset, that's great!

> **STOP and CHECK for understanding**
>
> Before continuing with the booster session, be sure that the student has attained the following goal: (1) Ability to use Soles of the Feet routine between lessons.

B.4. Review Content from Sessions 2 and 3

To activate prior knowledge, review the major content from Sessions 2 and 3. Verify that your student learned how to use Soles of the Feet to make a strong pleasant feeling (happiness) and a strong unpleasant feeling (anger) disappear or become less intense. Check for understanding by having the student describe what happy and angry feelings are. Check that your student remembers being able to make those strong feelings disappear or diminish.

If your student does not remember any of the specific content from these sessions, it may be worth revisiting this material. Refer back to the previous chapters to revisit session content as needed. Do not proceed with the booster session unless the student is able to recognize, via their direct experience, that Soles of the Feet can be used to make a strong feeling disappear or diminish.

In our previous meetings, we discussed a few very powerful emotions: happiness and anger. Can you describe what a "happy" feeling is? What's it like for you? ... Yes that's right—happiness is a pleasant, comfortable feeling. We can usually tell when we, or other people, are feeling happy because they are smiling or laughing (although this is different for everybody).

Can you now tell me what "anger" is? What's anger like for you? ... You got it—anger is an unpleasant and uncomfortable feeling. We can usually tell when we, or other people, are feeling angry because of how their face or body looks, such as scowling and clenching fists (although this is different for everybody). Sometimes when we become angry, anger causes us to act in ways that we don't want to. We can do or say things that we don't mean, and that may cause other people to get hurt, which is called aggression. Acting aggressively when we feel angry can get us in trouble. But anger is not the same thing as aggression—anger is a feeling that we experience, aggression is what we do or act like when we feel angry.

Now, do you remember what happened when you remembered a really happy event and practiced Soles of the Feet? [Obtain example from student.] *That's right, you experienced having the happy feeling by remembering that happy event, and then after you practiced Soles of the Feet the feeling of happiness pretty much went away. And what about the angry memory followed by Soles of the Feet practice, do you remember that?* [Obtain example from student.] *Good remembering! When you imagined the angry memory, you felt angry, and when you practiced Soles of the Feet while feeling angry, the anger disappeared.*

> ### STOP and CHECK for understanding
>
> Before continuing with the booster session, be sure that the student has attained the following goals: (1) Ability to identify the feeling of happiness, (2) Experience of making the feeling of happiness disappear or diminish, (3) Ability to identify the feeling of anger, and (4) Experience of making the feeling of anger disappear or diminish.

B.5. Review and Revisit Content from Session 4

Facilitate a discussion about what the student's triggers are for anger. Next, have your student identify their specific triggers to their angry feelings. Support the student in identifying a recent occurrence of anger using the "Eliciting Emotions Support Sheet" (Appendix 1E). Make sure that your student is able to identify some of their own triggers.

Most of the time when we experience an unpleasant emotion, like anger, something happens in our lives that triggers our anger. Let's think about a particular situation ... [Discuss a memory of an angry situation that the student shared with you during the previous session.]

So, in this example, can you think of what may have triggered the feeling of anger? What are some of the internal triggers, such as thoughts, feelings, or physical sensations, that might have triggered anger? ... What are some of the external triggers, such as things that happened or things people said, that might have triggered anger? ... [Spend time identifying internal and external triggers to anger using the example being discussed.]

Now, let's identify all the triggers that we can from this memory. Can you recall a situation when you felt really, really angry? Good. Now, thinking back to your memory of being angry, what were some of the internal and external triggers for your anger? Were there any specific thoughts? Feelings? Physical sensations? Things that happened or things that people said? ... Ah, so it was when the student said "Nice kick!" in a really sarcastic voice that seemed to trigger your anger. And it seems that your thinking to yourself "That jerk!" actually made you feel even angrier. Nice job identifying those triggers, you have a great memory! [Spend time supporting the student in identifying their own internal and external triggers to their angry memory.]

STOP and CHECK for understanding

Before continuing with the booster session, be sure that the student has attained the following goal: (1) Ability to identify triggers to feeling of anger.

B.6. Applying Soles of the Feet to the Triggers of Anger

Clearly explain that the purpose of the exercise: to imagine the student's anger triggers and then use Soles of the Feet *right before* they get angry. Have the student assume a relaxed posture, and then guide them through an *in vivo* memory of the anger scenario they just identified containing their triggers. Try to have the student recall as much detail as possible, including multiple senses, in order to elicit a strong memory.

Focus on the moments right *before* the student became angry, when they first noticed their trigger, specifically the thoughts, feelings, and physical sensations that occurred right *before* they became angry. Then, have them practice the Soles of the Feet routine. It is important that this instruction be given as a *direct and forceful command* so as to practice *quickly and deliberately* shifting attentional awareness away from the angry memory (and more specifically, the triggers to their anger) to a neutral focal point (in this case, the student's feet). Refer to the "Eliciting Emotions Support Sheet" (Appendix 1E) if you need support asking generic questions about the overview and details of the memory.

In this curriculum, we learned how to use Soles of the Feet to stay calm, even if something is triggering a strong emotion. Now we are going to practice Soles of the Feet during a trigger that occurred right before we became angry.

To begin, sitting up straight, placing feet flat on the floor, allowing your eyes to close if this feels comfortable ... Placing one hand on your belly, and beginning to pay attention to your breath coming into and out of your belly ... Remembering the angry memory that you identified ... Recalling what was happening ... where you were ... who was with you ... Remembering any sights you saw at the time, what time of day it was, what clothes you were wearing ... As best you can, remembering what sounds were happening at the time ... If people were talking, what they said ... If there were any smells, tastes, or tactile sensations, recalling these too ... Thinking about this angry memory, remembering what it was like to play kickball on that day ... the clothes you were wearing, the sounds and sights of the playground.

And now remembering those triggers to the angry feeling. Thoughts that you may have had right before you became angry. Remembering what the student who said "Nice kick!" was wearing, and remembering exactly how you felt and how you thought to yourself, "That jerk!" right after he made that mean comment ... Now, quickly shift the focus of your attention to your feet. [PAUSE.] *All of your attention is on your feet ...* [Continue verbal instruction of the full Soles of the Feet routine.]

B.7. Post-Practice Discussion

Discuss how the experience of shifting attention to the feet while the student was recalling the triggers to anger actually interrupted the feeling of anger, either preventing the angry feeling from arising in the first place or making it disappear or diminish. This interruption helped them to remain calm. You should take the time to troubleshoot their experience just as you did during the previous classes, which may include repeating steps B.5

and B.6 (see chapter 14 for more details on troubleshooting this activity).

You were just imagining an angry situation, and then I said to shift your attention to your feet as you were recalling the triggers to your anger. What did it feel like to remember the angry situation? Did you feel angry? And then, were you able to identify and remember those triggers to your anger?

What happened to your angry feeling after you shifted your attention? You got it, when you practice Soles of the Feet and shift your attention to your feet during the trigger, the first indication that you are becoming angry, then the angry feeling disappears or does not occur in the first place!

When we become angry, sometimes we let our anger control our behavior. When this happens, we may say things we don't mean and do things that get us in trouble. Soles of the Feet is a way to stay calm go so that we can act in a way that won't cause any problems for ourselves and other people. Using Soles of the Feet when we notice the triggers to our anger is a great way to keep us from becoming angry in the first place, and thus it can keep us out of trouble at school.

> ### STOP and CHECK for understanding
>
> Before continuing with the booster session, be sure that the student has attained the following goals: (1) Experience applying the Soles of the Feet routine to triggers of anger, thus preventing the feeling of anger from arising or making it disappear or diminish, and (2) Fluency with using Soles of the Feet during proximal antecedents of anger and while feeling angry.

B.8. Making a Plan for Future Practice and Application

Clearly explain to the student that the purpose of this part of the session is to make a list of times and situations that the student can practice using Soles of the Feet. Give the student a copy of the "Using Soles of the Feet in

Daily Life" worksheet (Appendix 1G) and lead them through the independent work activity of identifying both triggers and settings where they can use the Soles of the Feet routine.

So, we just practiced using Soles of the Feet on our triggers. Remember—you are able to use Soles of the Feet in your everyday life. Let's create a plan for times when you think you'll need to use it. Here's a worksheet to help us identify triggers and situations when it would be useful to practice Soles of the Feet.

Let's think about all the different triggers that cause strong unpleasant feelings like anger. I'll give you a chance to fill out your own triggers for yourself on the sheet ... What kind of thoughts do you have that trigger anger? ... [Continue leading the student through the "Triggers" section of the "Using Soles of the Feet in Daily Life" worksheet (Appendix 1G), pausing to allow the student time to write in their responses.]

Now, let's think about all the different situations that could happen when you think that it might be a good time to practice Soles of the Feet. You can think of situations for yourself when you know you'll want to practice. You can also think of situations that might happen when it'd be a good idea to practice. What is a situation at school when you think it'd be a good time to practice Soles of the Feet? ... [Continue leading the student through the "Situations" section of the "Using Soles of the Feet in Daily Life" worksheet (Appendix 1G), pausing to allow the student time to write in their responses.]

In case you forget some of the material we've covered during our classes, I have extra copies of all the handouts that we've used so that you can use them to remind yourself in the future.

> ## STOP and CHECK for understanding
>
> Before completing the booster session, be sure that the student has attained the following final goal: (1) Ability to identify settings/events/times when they can use Soles of the Feet.

B.9. Booster Session Closure and Practice

Encourage the student to use the skill in their daily lives at school and at home. End this booster session with a final Soles of the Feet practice.

You've done a great job remembering all of the parts of Soles of the Feet. I'm confident that you will be able to use this new skill whenever you need to stay calm while experiencing strong emotions. You know how to do Soles of the Feet, you know when and where to do it, and you have the ability to stay calm when you have unpleasant emotions, which will keep you from getting in trouble at school and will also help you as you get older and become an adult!

Let's practice Soles of the Feet one more time before we end for today. You can practice along with me, either sitting or standing, either whispering the steps to yourself or practicing in silence. To begin, sitting up straight, placing your feet flat on the floor, allowing your eyes to close if this feels comfortable ... [Continue reciting the full Soles of the Feet routine (see "My Soles of the Feet Routine," Appendix 1D) as you practice with the student.]

PART III
Supplementary Materials

CHAPTER 14

Instructional Tips and Strategies

The previous chapters have detailed all the content for delivering Soles of the Feet (SoF) to classrooms and individual students. In our experience, when teachers and clinicians first begin to teach SoF, there are some common questions and problems that arise. In this chapter, we suggest solutions from our past experience with SoF that we've found helpful for addressing these questions. We would strongly encourage you to read through this entire chapter *before* you deliver SoF for the first time, as you will likely encounter at least some of these common challenges.

Please note that like anything else in life, the more you practice delivering SoF, the more fluent you will become. Although we've provided some suggestions and answers based on the questions we've received in the past, these answers are merely suggestions and are not meant to be exhaustive. As you become more skilled in this curriculum, it is likely that you will develop your own strategies for how to effectively teach mindfulness and SoF, and we would encourage you to trust your own judgment with the students whom you know best.

Enhancing Between-Session Practice

As you have probably noticed in your own personal mindfulness practice—which again we would strongly encourage you to develop prior to implementing SoF (see chapter 1 for details)—it can be difficult to practice mindfulness every day. Our daily lives are busy, there are many demands on our time, and it can be challenging to find time to practice even if we know it is important. However, in every mindfulness program, including SoF, we are asking those whom we are teaching to do just this. Now, considering that youth have a hard time starting any new behavior or following a routine, it is understandable (and likely!) that they may have a hard time practicing SoF between sessions. Here are a few suggestions for how to address this challenge. (Note that you can also apply these strategies to yourself to bolster your own mindfulness practice, so try it out!)

Underscore the importance of practice to meeting relevant goals. As detailed in Class 1 or Session 1, you should clearly identify the reasons for learning SoF. For most students, these include having the ability to stay calm *even when they are upset.* We suggest that this objective be revisited often to enhance motivation for practice, as this can remind students why they are doing this in the first place. We also recommend that you carefully assess whether the rationale provided is relevant to students. For some students, staying calm when upset may not be all that important, but perhaps not getting in trouble (which we know is related to getting upset) is more important. In this case, use this as the rationale and underscore that SoF can help them achieve their goal.

Tie practice to an existing routine. One of the easiest ways to change any behavior is to pair it with a behavior that you already do. For example, if you're a coffee drinker, it's a lot easier to remember taking a new medication every morning if you place the pill bottle next to your coffee machine, because you are already in the habit of going to that place for coffee every morning. Establishing a Soles of the Feet practice can be just as easy. If you are delivering SoF to a classroom, you could ask that SoF be practiced as a group immediately after morning announcements or some other established routine. For individual students, you can work with them to figure out one of their existing routines and yoke SoF practice to that. For example, we've had students practice SoF after they brush their teeth, after they shower, or after their morning prayers. The important thing is that students begin a habit of SoF that is linked to a previously established habit.

Use conspicuous reminders to help students' memories. A simple strategy to remind students to practice is to place a reminder on something they look at a lot. For example, in some of our studies, we distribute bright neon-orange stickers with pictures of a foot printed on them and tell students that this is their special Soles of the Feet reminder sticker, and when they see it they should remember to practice. These stickers can easily be created using 8.5"x11" label sheets, which can be inexpensively purchased at any office supply store. As an example, a sticker template document with a picture of a foot, formatted for two-inch circular labels, can be downloaded from the New Harbinger website (http://www.newharbinger.com/44741). Students can place these reminder stickers on their cell phones, school planners, bathroom mirrors, or anything else that they frequently see. The important elements are that you make explicit that this is a *special S* oF practice reminder sticker, and that this sticker should be placed somewhere where they will see it regularly (even better if they see it during a time they have identified to practice). Similarly, you can create "special" SoF bracelets, such as with colored rubber bands, for students to wear on their wrists. Telling students that these bracelets are specifically to remind them to practice may be helpful for students who can use an additional prompt to facilitate their memory.

Send daily reminders. This process requires a little more work on your end, but can be highly effective. In our studies, we've found different ways to send reminders to practice out to students. As one example, we send our high school students daily text messages reminding them to practice mindfulness that day, which has been highly effective. Students are increasingly used to receiving school reminders on their smartphones via text alerts, or from social media platforms (e.g., Facebook, Instagram, and Twitter), and these existing resources may be easily utilized as daily reminder prompts for students. Also, students frequently receive emails from their schools, so if your class has such a system of communication already in place, this could also be a potential means for sending reminders. Lastly, you can also have students set their own reminders if they have access to a cell phone or digital watch. Students simply set a recurring alarm during a specific time and are instructed that this is their special SoF alarm as a reminder to practice.

Create an action plan at the outset of Soles of the Feet. Action plans have been used for decades in cognitive-behavioral therapy and have recently begun to be investigated in the mindfulness literature as a viable strategy for enhancing home practice (see Galla, Baelen, Duckworth, & Baime, 2016). Creating an action plan for SoF would involve a few steps, which may be used together or separately to enhance practice. We recommend that this be conducted as a written exercise with students, so that they have a permanent record of this activity; however, it can be done without writing if necessary. First, students should *set their own practice goal* for using SoF. We suggest at least daily practice when students are learning SoF, but often challenge our students to practice more than once per day so that they can become more skilled at using SoF. Stating this as a *challenge* rather than a *demand* is important, as it enhances students' sense of autonomy or self-volition in the process. Just make sure the goals they set are attainable and realistic, as it will likely backfire if they set a goal that they fail to meet. Second, have students detail a *specific time and location* that they will practice SoF. General times and locations will be far less effective than something specific, and we strongly recommend that this be as detailed as possible. The third and fourth steps are intertwined: have students explicitly *state the greatest barriers to their goal*—work with your students to specifically identify a few of the biggest challenges and barriers that they anticipate getting in the way of practicing SoF—and then *problem-solve solutions to the identified barriers.* This can be done effectively in a group setting by having students support each other in developing solutions, and frequently the solutions they come up with are more applicable for each other than any you could create. For example, adolescents we've worked with have suggested forming a group-messaging board to remind each other to practice mindfulness using a popular smartphone app, a solution that we (who don't use social media) would have *never* considered! Concretely stating the problems and solutions as *if-then* statements can also be effective, as this is a format that students may be more accustomed to working with. (For example, *if* I can't practice because my sister is being too loud and bugging me, *then* I will move to a different room in the house.) Lastly, *writing out the steps to the action plan* can again create an effective permanent record (and reminder) for students.

Recruit peer support and feedback. A highly effective strategy for getting students to engage in mindfulness practice in group settings is to discuss what strategies students who are successful have used. In any given classroom, there will be some students who find strategies to remember to practice, and these students can oftentimes provide insightful feedback to the group. Students who are struggling to practice may resonate more with suggestions provided by their peers than suggestions provided by a teacher. Also, students may use strategies that you as an older adult are unaware of. For example, in some of our research, we provided students with their own personal digital music player that was preloaded with guided mindfulness practice tracks as a way to facilitate practice. To our surprise, students did not find this helpful at all, and instead much preferred to have these audio recordings available to them online as a streaming file. It can also be helpful to ask students what benefits they are noticing from SoF practice as a way of encouraging practice. Hearing peer students describe the benefits from practicing mindfulness skills such as SoF can be a highly impactful testimony for other students to hear, as their described experience will more closely resonate with them. Lastly, always make sure that sharing strategies is optional for students, because it can change the class climate if students feel pressured to provide this information or to describe an experience that they think that the teacher wants to hear (as opposed to what actually happened).

Provide praise and reinforcement for practice. Practicing mindfulness is challenging, and it is important to recognize when students are successful in doing this task. We always suggest discussing how practice allows students to develop new skills, which is no different than riding a bicycle for the first time or learning a new sport. When students do practice, be sure to praise them for this undertaking. Praise is most effective when it is *specific* (e.g., "I'm very impressed by the way you used your alarm on your smartphone to remember to practice, way to go!") and *timely* (e.g., praising a student immediately after they mention that they practiced between sessions, rather than later in the day). Teachers should also consider providing some other form of reinforcement for practice, such as by yoking between-session practice to an existing behavior plan. Similar to practice logs issued by music teachers, some find it helpful to provide a practice chart for students to complete as a way of tracking their practice, which may be initialed by their parent to provide some accountability at home.

Most importantly, if a student practices SoF during the school day to self-regulate their difficult feelings, it is *very* important that teachers recognize this and provide praise and any reinforcement possible. Using SoF when students need to stay calm is the whole point of this curriculum, and it cannot be stressed enough that this needs to be recognized and encouraged. If a student spends a significant amount of time with other teachers, it is well worth discussing with these teachers that your student is learning Soles of the Feet, and that if they ever witness the student practicing, that they should provide praise to encourage this practice.

Relate practice to other student activities. It is often helpful to have a conversation with students about how practice is the only way to get better at something, similar to other activities that students may be engaged in. For example, if a student has a favorite star athlete, it's worth taking the time to discuss how that athlete developed their skills. Using Socratic questioning and embodying genuine curiosity in this discussion can be very helpful (for example: "Hmm ... how do *you* think that they were able to get so good at basketball?"). It is also worth discussing how regular practice is needed to develop the SoF skill so that it can be used when it is needed most.

Students sometimes comment that they don't understand why they should practice SoF when they are feeling calm, because they thought it was a skill to use only when they feel upset. Again, relating this logic to an experience the student is familiar with can be helpful. For example, for students who are highly interested in basketball, we may discuss how a clutch free-throw shooter became so skilled. Posing to students the question: "Do you think that they *only* practice free-throw shooting in the final seconds of championship games?" can be effective in getting students to come to the realization that repeated practice of SoF in nonpressured situations (e.g., practicing it before they brush their teeth in the morning) can help them develop a fluent skill set that can be used under more demanding circumstances (e.g., using SoF when they receive a bad grade on a quiz).

Increasing Student Buy-In to Using Soles of the Feet

A common problem with students, and particularly adolescents, is that they don't see the need for learning another strategy. Often, students, particularly those with challenging behaviors, are told multiple times a day that they *should* use such-and-such a skill when they are upset. Because of this, SoF can be viewed and categorized as simply another strategy that adults are telling them to use. What often does not get recognized is the critical importance of students' own volition, self-identified goals, and internal motivation to use strategies such as SoF. We strongly recommend that at the outset of working with students or classrooms, teachers work with students to come up with a rationale for why learning SoF is important and then refer back to this rationale whenever students seem to be lacking the motivation or enthusiasm to continue.

Keep in mind that the kind of rationale you use really matters. For example, students may not feel motivated by the fact that they become dysregulated around adults; indeed, they may be very accustomed to being disruptive around adults. What they may be less aware of, however, are the social implications with peers for being dysregulated. Having conversations with your students on how they perceive their peers view them when they become disruptive can be highly motivating, as almost all youth have a desire to fit in with their peer group.

As another example, it may be worth asking students what it feels like for them when they are disruptive in the classroom. Some students may reply that it feels good. However, we would encourage you to kindly explore this and perhaps inquire further if this is really the case, as students may simply be posturing. In our clinical experience, we have never worked with any youth who genuinely like feeling dysregulated and the kind of intense unpleasant emotions that lead to disruptive behavior. Unpleasant feelings by their very definition are not pleasant, and it is natural that students would prefer to not feel this way. Giving students the space to describe how they don't like feeling these unpleasant emotions can be highly effective for motivating engagement with the curriculum, because SoF offers a concrete strategy for navigating these difficult emotional experiences.

Many students resonate with the idea that intense unpleasant emotions directly affect or "control" their behaviors, and that SoF is a way to regain their feelings of self-control. To be clear, as a mindfulness instructor, you must be aware that a central mindfulness practice is to let go of control, because attempting to control internal states can actually be counterproductive; however, it can be effective for students to use the language of "emotions controlling behavior" as a strategy for teaching them that SoF can be highly effective for self-regulating their emotions and behavior. Similarly, we've had success (particularly with adolescent populations) using a metaphor of unpleasant emotions "bullying" us into behaving in ways that get us in trouble in school. Simply posing the question: "Have you ever been so upset that you said or did something you regretted?" can be a way of starting this conversation, as every individual has had this experience at some point in time. The trick when working with students is to help them draw the connection between unpleasant emotions being causally related to disruptive behavior and help them realize that SoF is a highly effective practice for self-regulating these unpleasant feelings and thus preventing disruptive behavior.

Lastly, as a general rule for how to work with students to engage with SoF and use this program to self-regulate their unpleasant emotions (and, consequently, their disruptive behavior), we encourage you to remember this one fact: No student likes to be "out of control" and "get in trouble." In our experience, youth strongly desire autonomy and self-control over their day-to-day events (including their thoughts, feelings, and behaviors), as this is a normal part of growing up.

Children and adolescents frequently report enjoying SoF because they gain the ability to regulate themselves. We also believe that no student, even those with highly challenging behaviors, likes to be "in trouble." Getting scolded by adults or ostracized by peers or receiving office disciplinary referrals and detentions are by their very nature unpleasant. Individual students you are working with likely get in trouble often, or they wouldn't have been referred to you in the first place, so this will be a highly salient factor for them. Keeping these facts in mind can help you have a conversation with students around how to connect with the utility of SoF for these basic motivating factors in the lives of students.

How to Respond and Troubleshoot if Students Report Not Experiencing a Strong Emotion

Typically, when delivering SoF, the first class or session goes well without any major obstacles. Students enjoy the novelty of the curriculum, and the material is pretty straightforward. After this first class or session, however, many teachers experience the following scenario. Students are able to go through the focused attention activity of SoF and are able to report the details of a pleasant or unpleasant emotional event. Then, after running through an *in vivo* exercise where students imagine the described event and apply the SoF routine, the teacher inquires what the student's experience was during the exercise ... and the student reports that they *did not experience a strong emotion.* At this point, the teacher may feel a moment of panic, perhaps wondering what they themselves did wrong, or if something is flawed with this exercise or with this student. This scenario is not uncommon, and the following are strategies for how to proceed.

Be sure to embody mindfulness. Before considering how to work with students, first and foremost, practice mindfulness yourself and *be sure that you are embodying the qualities that you are trying to engender in the* *student.* No experience is invalid or "wrong," and it is very important to explicitly and implicitly give the student the message that whatever they experienced is okay simply as it is. Concretely, this means that in all further conversations, you should be careful to not convey the message that the student did anything wrong. Indeed, that is impossible, as you were simply asking them to tell you what their experience was like.

Probe for details. The first step is to gather more details on the event. Make sure you have highly detailed information about the event the student described. Sometimes the event isn't as detailed as you once thought, and getting this information can help you decide what to do next. You'll also want to know more details on what the student's experience was when they were trying to imagine the scenario. Could they actually imagine the described event? If not, what was happening during the exercise? It may be that the student was thinking of something else, or a distraction was interfering with their attention. If this is the case, you can work to eliminate these barriers and try repeating the exercise.

When to select a new event. After you've gathered information, you may notice that the event that the student selected was not ideal for this exercise. As this is a novel activity for most young people, it may be that the event they selected wasn't a good fit for this exercise. For example, sometimes students choose events that they remember in great detail and that were meaningful to them, but without a strong emotional experience associated with the event. If this is the case, then it's worth revisiting the psychoeducational elements of the class or session to make sure that students understand the feeling you are working on. If you are certain that students are clear on the feeling, then the next step is to probe to see if the event was *strongly* associated with that feeling. Differentiate between a powerful event and an event that was accompanied by a powerful emotion.

As another example, it may be that the event the student selected was associated with a strong emotional experience but the details of the event were less specific. Remember, the described memory of the event must be very detailed in order to recreate the experience for the student. If students are unable to provide many specific details concerning the event (who was there, what they were wearing, and so on) then this is an indication that the memory was not as strong as they thought. Revisit the criteria for the selection of the event to make sure that it is *both* an event associated with a strong emotional experience *and* an event that is highly detailed, in order to ensure that this *in vivo* exercise is a success.

Students Not Experiencing a Reduction in the Strong Emotion Following the Soles of the Feet Practice

Similar to the last section, it is common (particularly when working with a classroom of students) for a student to report that they were able to experience the strong emotional feeling during the *in vivo* exercise, but that when they practiced SoF, they didn't experience a reduction or elimination of the strong feeling. There are several reasons for why this may have occurred, and the following are a few strategies for how to proceed.

Be sure to embody mindfulness. As in the last example, it is extremely important to remember that no experience is invalid or "wrong," and that this message must be communicated implicitly and explicitly to the student. Similarly, you as the teacher are not doing a "bad" job at delivering the curriculum, this is just a problem to solve and work with, so go easy on yourself! Noticing and letting go of these natural tendencies to judge experience is critical to being a mindfulness instructor, and it is important to keep this at the forefront of all your interactions with the student.

Do *not* educate students on what they "should" have felt. Inherent to mindfulness practice is the concept of nonjudging and acceptance. This concept is taught to students via the teacher's perceived embodiment of mindfulness in their interaction with students. Thus, it is very important that teachers incorporate this foundational principle into their interactions with the student. The antithesis of mindful behavior is to impose what you as the teacher believe the student should be experiencing; this amounts to judging the student's response, which is counterproductive to teaching SoF and to establishing a trusting and positive relationship with the student. Thus, we strongly suggest that teachers refrain from sending any message, either directly or indirectly, that the student's experience is not okay exactly as it is. If the student did not experience what you, or this curriculum, expected them to experience, that is perfectly fine; and it may be an opportunity to troubleshoot the exercise and SoF practice.

Probe for details. It is important to begin the troubleshooting process by probing for details. First, make sure that the student actually experienced the strong emotion (see above). If they did, then begin to gently inquire about the details of the student's experience. Once you have these details, you can work to troubleshoot more precisely. Consider asking yourself this question as you gather these details: Is the student's inability to apply SoF to a strong emotion a "can't do" problem (i.e., a matter of skill acquisition) or a "won't do" problem (i.e., a matter of resistance or unwillingness to practice).

Student "can't" seem to use SoF to mitigate the strong feeling. The first thing to troubleshoot here is if the student is able to do the SoF routine at all. You may consider revisiting the previous materials to make sure that students are able to self-regulate their attention to their feet. If you have ascertained that the student is able to do the SoF routine but they just can't seem to do it during the *in vivo* experience of a strong feeling, then more practice with easier, less emotionally valanced exercises may be helpful. Ask the student about a recent neutral emotional experience (e.g., eating breakfast that morning). Walk the student through the memory just as you would have done for a strong emotional experience, and then practice

SoF. If the student is successful in this exercise, consider practicing the SoF with gradually more difficult memories, working your way up to a charged emotional event.

Student "won't" use SoF to mitigate the strong feeling. In this situation, the student is able to practice SoF, they can experience the intense emotion with the *in vivo* exercise, and they may have been able to apply the SoF routine to less intensive feelings, but they just don't seem to be able to use it while experiencing the strong emotional memory. Students sometimes have difficulty disengaging their attention from a strong memory and redirecting it to their feet. It may be that the strong emotional memory is something that the student wants to continue thinking about, such as reliving the pleasant emotional memory and not wanting to make the experience disappear or diminish via SoF. If this is the case, it may be helpful to gently remind the student that this is a time to practice so that they can develop the skill. Changing the pace of attention commands (so there is less time between statements) and repeated practice with different examples can often be a useful solution. Also, changing the tone of your voice to a sharper command when first beginning SoF may help students abruptly shift their attention away from the memory and to the somatic sensations of their feet. Sometimes students report that they are able to focus on the somatic experience of their feet for a few moments but then are "sucked" back into the memory. If this occurs, then additional practices with more scaffolded instructions (such as giving commands with less time in between) may be warranted. Alternatively, you might consider selecting a different event that the student may be more willing to work with. Lastly, developing fluency with the SoF routine through a few more practices without the associated *in vivo* memory may be warranted. Building some momentum with using this skill can often aid the student in successfully applying the routine.

Students Report Not Being Able to Feel Their Feet

Some students have difficulty experiencing the somatic experience of their feet. The first step in troubleshooting this comment is to go back to Class 1 (or Session 1) and make sure that they understand the vocabulary for parts of the feet. The next step is to make sure they can experience the somatic experience with some assistance, such as by gently pushing on these parts of the feet to elicit a sensation. You may also ask the student to describe, in their words, what they do feel when they pay attention to their feet. Modeling mindfulness in this process will be highly effective, allowing the student to convey their experience *in their words* as they feel it. In line with this inquiry, if the student reports feeling "nothing," then this is not an error. If this occurs, ask the student for more details on what "nothing" feels like for them. The absence of somatic sensation is not a void, and nothingness can be experienced just as much as "somethingness." Ask the student what nothing feels like for them, and then this becomes the focus of experience in the activity.

Creating Effective Class/Session Rules

To ensure a successful SoF experience, we strongly recommend that students be explicitly taught the expectations and boundaries for working together on this material. If you are in a school that already has effective rules and positive expectations set, then this is a simple process. At the onset of the curriculum, you simply revisit these existing rules and set the expectation that when you are with the students, these same expectations apply. However, it is sometimes the case that there are no clearly set rules in your school context, or the particular students with whom you are working require additional support. If this is the case, consider these following strategies.

Work together to set expectations. A highly effective

classroom or individual behavior-management strategy is to have the students be active participants in setting the expectations. Try starting the discussion with: "Since we'll be working together for the next few weeks, I'm curious if you have any ideas for rules that we should follow together." This will usually elicit most, if not all, of the rules that you would want in place. Students will feel a sense of ownership and buy-in if they are an active part of this process. If students do not mention all the rules that you would like them to specify after you ask them an open-ended question, consider using more leading questions to get at the rule you would like. For example, if you would like to set the expectation that only one student speaks at a time, you could ask: "I'm wondering if we should have some rule so that everyone gets a chance to speak, or so that we can all hear each other ... Does anyone have any ideas?" Again, having students come up with the rules will be more effective than you stating the expectations.

Frame the expectations positively. We typically find that when rules are framed from a positive perspective, the interpersonal qualities of the sessions become more positive as well. By this we mean that when setting rules and expectations, it will be most useful to frame them in terms of expected behavior and not in terms of what you do *not* want to see. Consider the following example. When asked what rules students would like in place, a student states that "I don't think everyone should talk at once or shout over each other, because then we can't hear each other." This is a good rule to have in place, but it can be easily reframed in a positive way, such as "That's a great idea! How about we have the rule that *only one person speaks at a time?*" Although a subtle differentiation, it can make a big difference for setting the tone of the classroom.

Create a safe and confidential environment. Particularly in group settings and with students who are being asked to share experiences that have strong unpleasant emotions associated with them, it is very important that a safe environment be set up. We encourage teachers to make sure the expectation is set that whatever is discussed during SoF groups or individual meetings is not shared outside of the group. You may want to hold a brief conversation about what it might feel like if students learned that something they shared during the class was being told to other students around school. Although you as the teacher can promise that you will not share any information outside of sessions (with the exceptions of mandated reporting standards and guidelines), confidentiality cannot be guaranteed when working in group settings. However, we find that by simply asking students to not share this information, most students will adhere to this expectation and protect each other's privacy.

No discussing examples that involve students or teachers whom others in the group know. It is worth stating that when discussing events in a classroom setting, students should *not* use and share examples that involve anyone else in the school (such as another student in the class) or in relation to anyone else in the school (such as a boyfriend of a student in a different classroom). This is a somewhat different topic than maintaining confidentiality. We set this expectation so that interpersonal conflicts do not arise as part of the class. Consider this example: A student is asked what event they have chosen that is associated with a strong unpleasant feeling, and they relay an experience of bullying with another student in the classroom. This can quickly become a challenging situation, but it can be prevented by establishing this expectation early in the curriculum.

Supporting Students' Use of Soles of the Feet When They Need It Most

Some students will be able to go through the entire SoF curriculum very successfully, including completely memorizing and being able to self-deliver the SoF routine and knowing when they should use it in their day-to-day lives; however, they do not seem to be able to actually use SoF when it is needed. In these situations, we recommend two effective strategies. First, gather information from the student to see if there is a simple barrier that you can problem-solve together. For example, some students may feel self-conscious about using the routine in front of peers. This misconception can be quickly addressed by reminding the student that SoF is a covert activity, and by demonstrating this in front of the student so that they can see that they can't tell when you as the teacher are using the strategy. If there are not readily identifiable barriers, you may consider *collaboratively establishing a way to remind the student to use Soles of the Feet.*

Sometimes, students become highly emotionally aroused and subsequently disruptive, and in the moment, they forget to use the routine. If this is the case, you can ask the student if they would like to be reminded to use SoF if you notice they are becoming dysregulated. If the student agrees that this would be helpful, then the next step is to work together to establish how the student would prefer to be reminded. Some students are perfectly fine with you telling them: "Now is a good time to use SoF." Other students find that this direct approach is embarrassing, and prefer a more subtle signal from the teacher, such as a tap on the desk or a special hand signal. A final strategy to consider is to *create a self-monitoring routine to enhance use of the SoF routine.* Asking students to track when they feel strong unpleasant emotions or become behaviorally dysregulated can help bring attention to these moments when SoF could be useful. Students can also track when they are using or practicing SoF. Both of these self-monitoring activities will help the students develop awareness of themselves, which may in turn boost the likelihood of their using the routine when they need it.

Supporting the Memorization of the Full Soles of the Feet Routine

Some students have difficulty remembering all of the steps in the SoF routine, particularly younger students or those with intellectual disabilities. If this is the case, there are a few strategies to consider. First, be sure that you are *consistent with your SoF routine script.* If you yourself are using different words and language when walking students through the routine, it is understandable that the student will have difficulty remembering the elements if they change from practice to practice! Be very careful about using consistent language to enhance memorization. Second, you should also *be mindful of using developmentally appropriate language.* Some students may have difficulty remembering longer words that they are unfamiliar with, or with memorizing seven or eight different steps in the SoF routine. Use your knowledge of the particular students and their developmental level to tailor your SoF routine script so that it is most accessible to them. Remember, the important thing is that students quickly shift their attention to the somatic experience of their feet and spend a few minutes being mindfully aware of this neutral part of the body. The language you use to engender this practice is not as important as the practice itself.

Also, consider *carefully scaffolding student's independence in self-deploying the SoF routine.* We have attempted to build scaffolded experiences of memorizing SoF into the curriculum, moving from entirely teacher-led practices to student-led practices. Sometimes students will need more gradual scaffolding, however, and it is your job as the teacher to deploy all your teaching strategies to create this. Be sure that students can successfully use a more highly scaffolded strategy (such as reading the steps on a piece of paper) before they are asked to practice SoF with less support (such as practicing without the piece of paper). In a classroom setting, using existing classroom strategies, such as choral reading or pairing more advanced students with less advanced students as "buddies," should be considered in your teaching. Lastly, be sure to *offer many opportunities to practice on a regular basis.* Remember that SoF should be practiced *at least once a day* during the curriculum and skill acquisition phase. Once a day, however, is the minimum that most students need in order to be successful; many students will require additional practice to memorize all the steps and gain fluency with the routine.

Creating In Vivo Emotional Experiences in Group Settings

One of the most challenging aspects of delivering SoF to groups is to make sure that all students are able to experience *in vivo* a strong pleasant or unpleasant feeling. This is much simpler at the individual level. When working with a single student, you can get many rich details to use in creating the memory with the student. In group settings, this is far more challenging, as you will not have the time to work with every single student one on one to get this much detail. Consider the following strategies and approaches.

Check with students about the *basic* details of their selected event. Although you typically will not have time to get into great detail with all students, you may have time to quickly go around the classroom to hear a one-sentence explanation of the event they selected for the exercise. This may give you enough time to troubleshoot with students before they actually are walked through their memory in the *in vivo* exercise. For example, if a student selects a birthday party that occurred five years ago as their pleasant event, this may be a poor choice since it's unlikely that they will be able to recall all the details of this older event as opposed to a birthday party that happened within the last few weeks. Quickly checking with students and giving brief feedback can help to make sure that students have selected an appropriate event.

Use the group to generate ideas. In addition to checking quickly with students, you can consider asking if there are any students who are willing to share more details of a specific event. If other students are able to hear this example from their peers, it might create ideas for events for themselves to select or details that they themselves have experienced—ideas and details that may be more relevant to them since they have come from a peer.

Be mindful of the group versus individual teaching time. If you have the time, it is of course totally appropriate to work with individual students who are having difficulty with any element of the SoF curriculum. However, you must also be mindful that you are using your time most efficiently when working in a group context. For example, if, in a class of fifteen students, only one student is unable to experience the *in vivo* unpleasant emotion, it may not be appropriate to spend a large portion of the group time working with this one student at the expense of the other fourteen. In this situation, you may consider validating the student's experience (for example: "It is totally normal that you are having trouble with this; I know many students who go through the same thing") and making a plan for how to support the student at another time (for example: "We have a lot more to get through today, so I'm wondering if you can just do your best for now and we can talk more after class").

Using Strong Emotions Other than "Happy" and "Angry"

The feelings of happiness (pleasant emotion) and anger (unpleasant emotion) are used in this curriculum as the examples of emotional experiences that are most familiar to students; however, you may choose a different feeling and modify the instructions accordingly.

As one example, the pleasant feeling "happy" may be replaced with a different strong positive feeling, such as joy or love, provided that the feeling is well defined and elicits a strong emotional response for the student. Be sure to elicit details about this alternative emotional word, such as what the student's body feels like and what thoughts they have when they are feeling that way. Similarly, if a student has another strong negative emotion that they connect more with than with anger (e.g., being frustrated, anxious, or upset), it is okay to substitute this affective label provided that it is a strong negative emotion for the student and is well defined and easily identifiable.

If you select a different emotion for the exercises, modifications will also need to include the behavioral manifestation of feeling that emotion. As an example, in some of our current research, we are experimenting with using test-taking anxiety as the target unpleasant feeling. Anxiety in any form is a strong unpleasant feeling, and SoF works very well for this in our clinical and research experience. However, we have found that focusing on a memory of a *past* event in which a student experienced test-anxiety was not nearly as effective as discussing a potential *future* event that the student was dreading. This is consistent with the emotion of anxiety, namely an apprehension of what could occur rather than feelings of worry about what has previously occurred (which is more often labeled as rumination and more commonly associated with depression). By creating an *in vivo* experience for students imagining all the details of an upcoming exam (e.g., where they will sit, who is there, sounds they may hear in the classroom), students reported feeling highly anxious and were able to practice SoF in this situation with good results. Any strong unpleasant emotion can be modified; what is important is that the students experience this emotion during practice. Similarly, disruptive behavior need not be physical or verbal aggression. For example, when targeting anxiety, a disruptive behavior can be not paying attention to the teacher during class and missing instructions or not being able to focus and do well on examinations. The SoF curriculum is a flexible strategy for coping with any unpleasant feeling and its associated behavior, and to make these modifications, teachers need only carefully consider how to tailor the procedure to best fit the specific needs of their students.

Critical Importance of Embodiment and Speaking from Experience

It is not an accident that we have repeated the importance of embodying mindfulness in this curriculum: it is just that important. Students will learn just as much from *how* you are teaching them (through seeing how you are mindfully practicing in the moment) as from *what* you are teaching them about mindfulness. Consider these specific situations when it is important to be a mindful teacher.

Validate all experiences. Remember, from a mindfulness theoretical viewpoint, nothing is good or bad (those terms reflect judgments). Whatever experience or behavior is occurring, it simply is, and labeling it as good or bad is not appropriate. What can be effective is bringing to mind the consequences of behavior. For example, when students become disruptive in the classroom, they may find that peers are afraid of them or that they get in trouble with their teachers. These consequences aren't good or bad, either; they are just what they are. Exploring all experiences with an intentional attitude of openness, curiosity, and kindness is one of the most effective strategies for teaching SoF. Lastly, be sure to apply this nonjudgmental attitude to yourself, being mindful to be accepting of your own experience, including when you are being judgmental (which is normal, and which can be treated with acceptance and nonjudgment) and when you are being nonjudgmental (which is normal and not a "good" thing either; it's simply a quality to embody that has outcomes that you are working to create).

Be particularly careful around your treatment of unpleasant feelings such as anger. Remember, the explicit message we are trying to convey to students is that *all feelings* are okay, including unpleasant ones such as anger; however, some reactions to anger (such as aggression) are not okay because of the harmful consequences of these behaviors. Given that SoF is intended to teach a skillful reaction to strong negative emotional experiences, be careful that these emotions are never invalidated or condemned!

Be mindful of your pace of instruction. Using a quicker pace of instruction can provide more scaffolding, particularly for students with shorter attention spans (e.g., leaving only a few seconds between the delivery of statements "Moving to your heels" and "Going to the arches of your feet"). However, delivering instructions too quickly can be confusing, or it may not give students enough time to fully place their attention on the soles of their feet and thus disrupt their escalating emotional difficulty. It is best to deliver commands at a pace that can keep the students' attention and then mindfully increase the gaps between the statements through sessions to stretch their attention to the point that they can keep attention on parts of their feet for 15–30 seconds between instructions.

You may find it useful to audiotape yourself and listen to your audio recording to hear how you sound as a way of developing your delivery of mindful instructions.

Give instructions as statements using the present participle rather than the imperative. A common strategy used by mindfulness instructors is to use the present participle of verbs rather than the imperative tense ("breathing" rather than "breathe") in order to avoid resistance to an authoritative command and to engender a mindful attitude of active engagement in the present moment. We similarly recommend getting into the habit of making statements using the present tense to use language to support students' awareness of their actions in the present moment.

Consider Avoiding the Following Words and

Phrases When Delivering Soles of the Feet

In our experience, the language used when delivering mindfulness curricula such as SoF can be an aid in a successful learning experience. Consider the following recommendations.

Avoid the phrase "deep breathing." We find that students are all too familiar with the instruction to breathe deeply, as this is the most common phrase when they are being examined by a physician. We recommend avoiding this phrase partially for this reason lest you inadvertently become associated with a trip to the doctor's office (which is not a pleasant experience for many students). Also, breathing deeply is not equivalent to breathing mindfully. In its truest form, mindful breathing is simply being aware of the breath, without restrictions or impositions, simply as it is.

In this curriculum, we find it helpful to provide some more explicit instructions with mindful breathing so that students breathe "low and slow" in order to emphasize that their awareness is on their lower abdomen, and to help slow down their breathing, which may help reduce physiological arousal when students are becoming behaviorally dysregulated. In this way, the instructions are more akin to diaphragmatic breathing, with the differences being how attention resources are being explicitly allocated in a mindful manner.

Do *not* use the word "homework"! Unfortunately, many students do not enjoy practicing academic skills and doing academic activities (homework) outside of school, and the word homework is therefore oftentimes associated with highly negatively charged feelings and thoughts. We thus strongly encourage you as a teacher to avoid using this word when assigning between-session SoF practice. Reminding students that repeated practice is crucial to getting better at things is of course important, and referring to the practices done outside of school (at home or with their peers) as simply "practice" is also important in this way. You don't hear athletic coaches giving homework to their players, they simply assign drills and practices so that students will improve, and this is the strategy that we suggest teachers adopt when teaching Soles of the Feet.

Be mindful of the word "trigger." In this curriculum, we use the word trigger to refer to events that are causally attributable to strong emotional experiences or emotions that can cause aggressive behaviors. The concept of trigger can be difficult for some students to grasp, especially young ones or those with cognitive impairments, since it requires an understanding of "before and after" as well as causality. Consider using metaphors and examples in your own life to illustrate and teach the concept of a trigger. For example, many students are familiar with video games, and can understand that pressing a button or *trigger* on a video game controller triggers an action of the video game character.

As one other point of caution, students who are exposed to or affected by gun violence may have a negative association with the word trigger. If this is the case with your students, consider substituting another noncharged word, such as "cause" or "antecedent" or "event," for the word "trigger." You can choose whatever word you like as long as it is explicitly defined and understood by your students.

Establish Rapport Before Beginning with the Soles of the Feet Curriculum

When teaching any curriculum to any student, it is important that the instruction occurs on the foundation of a positive, caring, and supportive relationship. We strongly recommend that you keep this in mind when working with your students and consider building this relationship prior to delving into the curriculum. You will find that the experience of teaching is more effective and pleasant when there is an established warm, positive relationship.

For many students, having a good relationship is important and beneficial for learning, but not necessarily critical. For some students, however, the relationship is absolutely critical to their learning process. As an example, we delivered SoF sessions to students in a residential facility for court-adjudicated youth. These students had been removed from their homes to this residential facility because of an unsafe home environment, which is of course by itself a traumatic experience. We learned that in this context it was necessary to spend at least a single 30-to 45-minute session building a trusting relationship with the student by playing games and learning about their interests before moving into the curriculum. Teachers should always be attentive to the individual needs of their students and pay special attention to the relationship when teaching, particularly with students who may require additional reassurance and work to forge this connection with an unknown adult.

Modifications for Alternatively Abled Students

SoF has been implemented and scientifically evaluated with many different individuals with different abilities. Although we cannot provide every possible suggestion for working with alternatively abled students, in what follows, we have provided a few suggestions based on our prior experience.

Use a team approach. When working with alternatively abled students, it is most effective to incorporate the entire educational team to support the students in all of their efforts, including their learning of SoF. Other professionals from different disciplines may have suggestions for how to modify or tailor the SoF protocol so that it will best meet the needs of your particular student or students. For example, you might contact all members of a student's IEP team, briefly describe your intentions to teach SoF to them, and ask if the team has any suggestions for how to make the experience a successful one.

Use modifications when appropriate. The core skill of SoF is learning to notice when you are becoming upset and then using the SoF routine to minimize the intense feelings and prevent escalating behavior. The materials provided are designed for students who are developmentally typical or neurotypical. When reading through the materials, if you realize that some of the practices may not be a good fit for your students, then you should make the appropriate accommodations and modifications so that they will fit into your specific context, bearing in mind important and critical elements of the SoF program. For example, we've worked with students with spinal injuries who had little or no sensation in their feet. It was not appropriate to ask such students to wiggle their toes, as they were not able to do this. However, the students were taught to focus their attention on what they could feel in their feet, including the sensations of very little or no feeling. In this way, an appropriate modification was made (striking the "wiggle your toes" part of the script) while maintaining the core feature of the practice (focusing attention on a neutral part of the body).

Students with trouble standing. Some students have difficulty standing upright or maintaining their balance. In this situation, it is entirely appropriate to conduct all of the practice with the student sitting. Remember, the crux of the curriculum is teaching self-awareness and a simple routine for redirecting attention; the physical posture is not that important.

Students with trouble sitting. Similarly, some students have difficulty remaining seated or find that staying seated is uncomfortable. In this situation, all of the exercises can be done while standing.

Students with difficulty writing. Some students have difficulty writing or find writing very aversive. In this situation, consider removing all of the writing elements of the task or writing for the student.

Students with difficulty reading or nonreaders. SoF can be delivered with fidelity even to those who cannot read. Again, the practices hinge on self-awareness and training attention, both of which are not contingent on any academic ability. For students with difficulty reading, consider using echo-reading, where you orient them to the passage or script you are reading, read it to them first, and then have them read it back to you. With enough repetition, they will eventually memorize the materials. If a student is a nonreader, consider developing nonverbal handouts that rely completely on pictorial examples of the SoF routine to scaffold their practice.

Enlisting and Facilitating Other Teachers or Staff Members in Soles of the Feet

We have found that, as with any other school-based intervention, SoF can be most successful if the students' educational team is aware of the practice and helps support the curriculum. As an example, when teaching SoF to students with severe disabilities, we have found it helpful to attend a team meeting with the staff before starting to work with the student. The team was given a brief overview of the curriculum followed by an experiential demonstration of the SoF routine. Following this, we worked as a team to discuss how best to support the individual student's use of the material. We arranged that each teacher would tell the student at the beginning of class that they were aware the student was learning SoF and would ask the student if they wanted to be reminded to practice during class when they needed it. We found this to be a highly successful strategy for facilitating practice and in helping support the student's use of the SoF routine when they needed to use it. We recommend educating the other team members about what SoF is and working together to discuss how best to support the student's practice and deployment of the skills they are developing.

Other teachers can also be a great resource for getting additional information about the student's challenging behavior. One useful piece of information would be specific examples of when the student becomes angry in the classroom. If this is appropriate, you can use these examples during sessions to practice applying SoF to a specific situation or trigger of a situation by introducing such examples. For example, if you know from a teacher that a student becomes emotionally and behaviorally dysregulated during physical education class, then you may consider in your work with the student asking if they felt that that class would be a good time to use SoF. Just be careful not to embarrass the student, as they may not feel comfortable with you knowing about their challenging behavior or the fact that teachers are sharing this information among themselves.

Other teachers and staff members can be useful in praising students for successfully using SoF. In addition to asking team members to help prompt the students for practice, we've found it highly successful to encourage other teachers to provide praise or rewards if they notice a student being successful with using the routine. Focusing on the student's successes with the material can be extremely effective.

For students who have behavior-support plans, teachers can help integrate SoF into the existing plan. For example, students may be able to earn additional behavioral points or classroom incentives if they use SoF during class when they become angry or frustrated. Ask teachers to try to notice the student using SoF and encourage them to prompt and reinforce.

Recommendations for Working with Students with Trauma, Anxiety, or Other Serious Emotional Problems

Given the co-occurrence of disruptive behavior with other psychological problems, it is not uncommon that the students you are teaching SoF to may have other behavioral and mental health concerns. Following are several recommendations to consider before and during your work with these students.

Mindfulness programs are not a panacea. Mindfulness programs are highly popular in contemporary society, and there are a lot of people who strongly believe that these approaches can help everyone. There is also mounting scientific evidence that mindfulness-based programs can be very useful for a wide range of populations and individuals. This is all true. However, mindfulness programs are not necessarily the most effective strategy for working with all types of kids and in all settings, and this applies to SoF as well. For example, some well-meaning teachers look to SoF as an effective strategy for improving their classroom's overall behavior. SoF may be helpful for supporting classrooms with high rates of disruptive behavior, but there are also many other effective classroom behavior management practices and interventions (many with very strong scientific supporting evidence) that can support classroom behavior. It is in the best interest of teachers and students to consider all available approaches when deciding on providing a classroom intervention and to be mindful of the balance between one's own personal interest in mindfulness programs and the best available technology for supporting students. Said differently, SoF is not a cure-all for classroom behavior problems, nor is it a good fit for all classrooms and all students. Several organizations have identified many other highly effective strategies for disruptive behavior with very strong evidence bases. A list of some of these repositories can be found in Appendix 4 ("Supplementary Resources").

Never instruct students that they must close their eyes. For students with a trauma history, being told to close their eyes can be a highly triggering experience. Thus, it is very important that you always *invite* students to close their eyes but never require it. Be sure to stress that it is perfectly acceptable and normal to not close one's eyes during the practices. If students would like to keep their eyes open, ask that they keep their gaze "soft," that is, that they not distract themselves by staring at any distracting content, as this will interfere with their ability to pay attention. We recommend a neutral visual target (such as the ground or a cleared desktop).

Monitor students during all exercises. While delivering all materials during SoF, it is very important that you remain vigilant of students' experiences while practicing. A common and recommended practice for those teaching mindfulness is to practice the mindfulness exercises with those whom you are instructing. However, during mindfulness exercises (such as mindful breathing or the SoF routine), the instructor should not close his or her own eyes, because then the instructor would not be able to monitor whether the student is having any adverse reactions to the practices. Adverse reactions to mindfulness exercises are not common, but they do occur. In our experience, the most common negative response by a student to mindfulness practice comes from the mindful breathing exercises. Students with a history of intense anxiety, panic attacks, or trauma sometimes focus their awareness on the sensations of breathing and become hyperaware of feelings of constriction in their chest, which causes them to become more anxious, leading to increased shallow breathing and constriction, which may ultimately trigger a panic attack. To be clear, this is unlikely to happen in your classroom. However, it is important that you as the instructor are monitoring for any negative responses to mindfulness practices in your students. If you notice behavioral indications of heightened discomfort, rapid breathing, or clear distress, you should stop the activity and check in with the student to make sure that they are okay. If a student does have a negative response to SoF or any mindfulness practice, consider directly communicating to the student that they have done nothing wrong and selecting a different intervention that may be a better fit for the student.

Working with Adolescents and Self-Conscious Students

In our experience, virtually every student who goes through the whole SoF curriculum reports that they enjoy learning the skill, find it to be helpful, and would recommend it to their peers. Nevertheless, some students report disliking certain elements of the curriculum or finding certain aspects of the material distracting. Following are a few scenarios that have come up in our experience for you to be aware of.

Be mindful of your word choices. Students may have unexpected responses to certain word choices. As previously mentioned, some students will hear the word "homework" and immediately feel negatively to whatever practice you are asking them to do, or hear the word "trigger" and think about gun violence. So you as the teacher should be mindful of your word choices. For example, adolescents sometimes hear the phrase "balls of your feet" and begin to laugh because in their vernacular, "balls" is commonly used to refer to testicles. In this situation, consider substituting a different word choice such as "foot pads" or "ball of feet." As another example, some students mistakenly hear the word "socks" as "sex" and become distracted. Taking steps to enunciate your words and monitor for their impact is important. Knowing your students and being proactive and vigilant of your word choices is thus highly recommended.

Self-conscious students. It is developmentally typical for adolescents, socially anxious students, and some more sensitive children to be highly self-conscious among their peers. They may thus be hesitant to use SoF if they feel it will draw attention to them. If you suspect that this is the case, then it is very important that you preemptively explain to students that SoF can be done covertly, as no one can tell if you are breathing slowly or paying attention to your toes. You can demonstrate using SoF in front of the student to emphasize this point. This may also require noting that SoF can be done with eyes open and without putting a hand on your stomach. However, it is best if the students become fluent with the activity first before removing these scaffold steps. In our experience, being explicit that SoF is entirely discrete and is a "ninja" strategy can actually make the practices more appealing, as students may be intrigued by the secrecy of the practice. As another example, whereas praising students is usually considered to be encouraging and a "reward" for students, some students do not like this attention from adults and find praise to be highly aversive. Be vigilant for this fact as well and consider offering some other form of encouragement.

APPENDIX 1

Worksheets and Handouts

The materials in this section are also available for download at http://www.newharbinger.com/44741.

APPENDIX 1A

Handout—Knowing Your Feet

Directions: Look at the shaded areas to learn about the different parts of your feet. The entire bottom of your feet is called the ***sole*** of the feet.

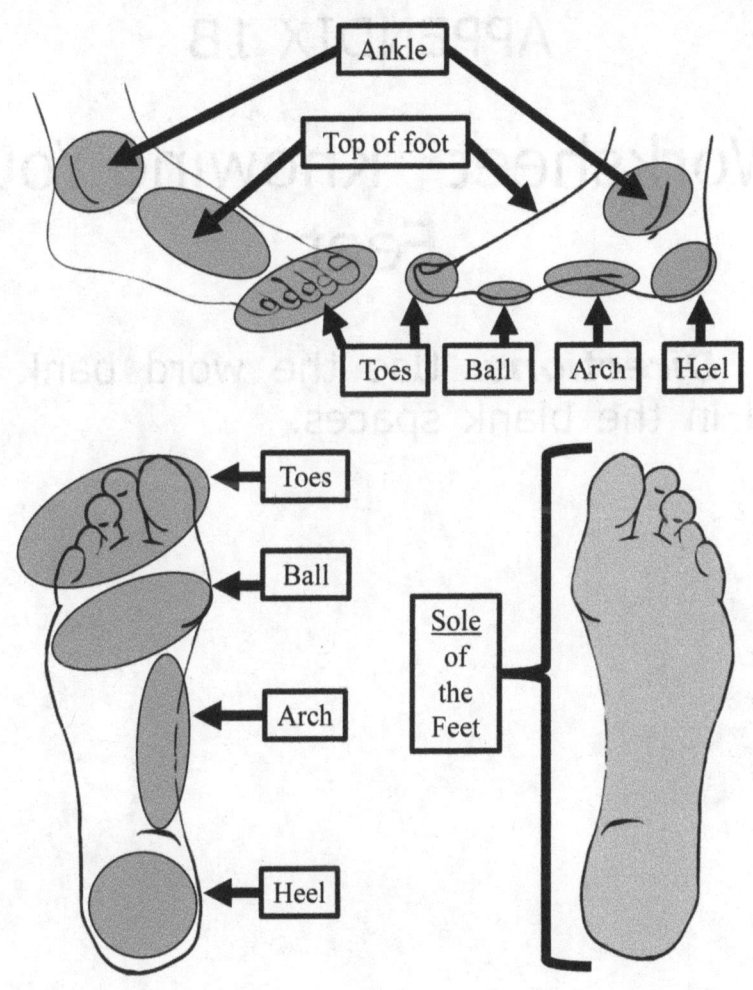

APPENDIX 1B

Worksheet—Knowing Your Feet

Directions: Use the word bank to fill in the blank spaces.

379

Word Bank
Ankle   Arch
Ball   Heel
Toes   Sole
Top of foot

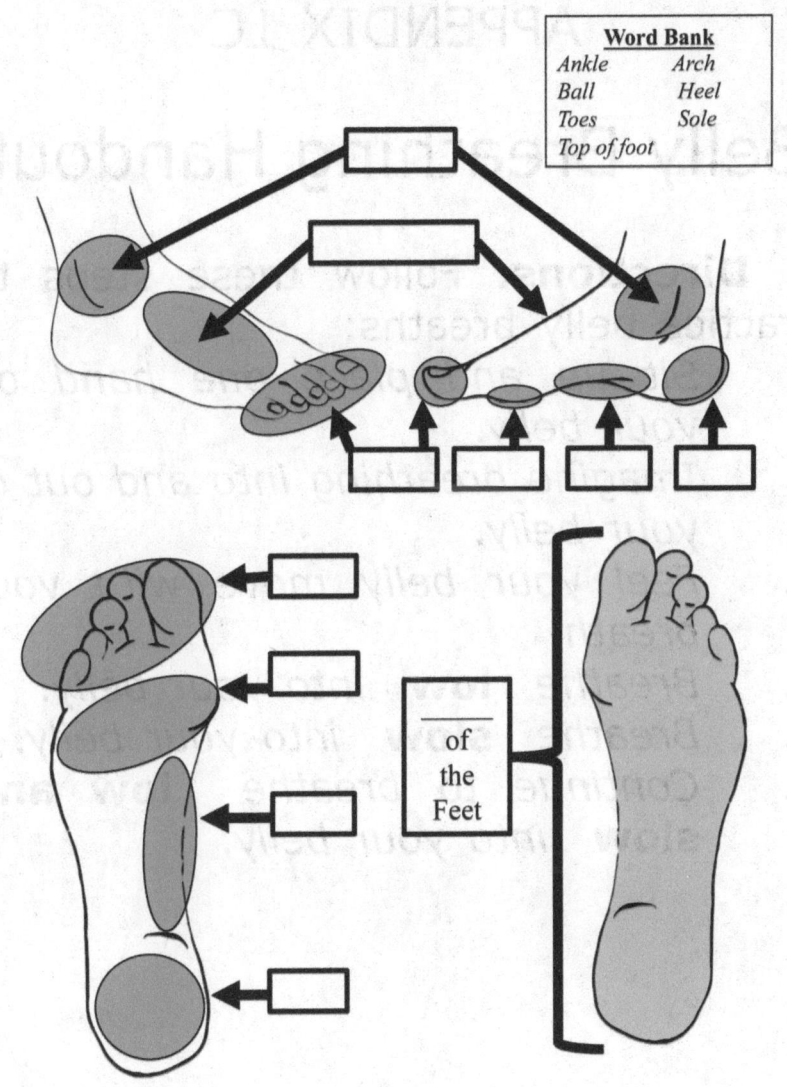

of the Feet

APPENDIX 1C

Belly Breathing Handout

Directions: Follow these steps to practice belly breaths:
1. *Sit up and place one hand on your belly.*
2. *Imagine breathing into and out of your belly.*
3. *Feel your belly move with your breath.*
4. *Breathe* **low** *into your belly.*
5. *Breathe* **slow** *into your belly.*
6. *Continue to breathe* **low and slow** *into your belly.*

APPENDIX 1D

My Soles of the Feet Routine

1. *To begin, sitting up straight, placing your feet flat on the floor, allowing your eyes to close if this feels comfortable...*
2. *Placing one hand on your belly, and beginning to pay attention to your breath coming into and out of your belly ... Noticing your breathing ... Noticing your belly moving with your breath ... Breathing low and slow into your belly...*
3. *Now, quickly shift the focus of your attention to your feet...*
4. *All of your attention is on your feet...*
5. *Wiggling and noticing your toes...*
6. *Putting attention on the ball of your feet...*
7. *Focusing on the arches of your feet...*
8. *Going to the heel of your feet...*

9. *Putting your attention on the soles of your feet...*
10. *Feeling the entire foot...*
11. *Continuing to stay in your feet just by wiggling your toes and noticing your feet...*
12. *Now, slowly opening your eyes, and returning to your class...*

APPENDIX 1E

Eliciting Emotions Support Sheet

Directions: To trigger a strong emotion in response to remembering a past event, it is very useful to incorporate multiple sensory modalities to elicit a detailed memory. Use this sheet to help record feedback from students as they recall an experience that you will use to practice Soles of the Feet on. This sheet can be helpful to record certain pieces of information when reciting the experience back to students, or for practice using this type of questioning. Keep your questions to pure fact-finding and pose them in a neutral manner—you are only looking for specific details that you can use later on, not conducting a psychotherapy session. Remember to record the student's verbatim response whenever possible.

Overview of memory

Basics of the event (What was happening generally? Where did this happen? When?)

What happened that made the student feel a strong emotion?

Persons attending (Who was there at the event? What did they say?)

What was the moment they remember feeling *the most?*

Details of memory

Sight (What do they remember seeing? What clothes were people wearing?)

Smells (What smells do they remember?)

Sounds (What sounds do they remember? Talking, laughing, yelling? What did people say?)

Touch (What was the weather like? Hot or cold temperature?)

Taste (If food was involved, what did they eat?)

Mind (Do they remember any specific thoughts? Any feelings or emotions?)

APPENDIX 1F

Identifying Triggers Worksheet

A trigger is anything that happens *before* an event that *causes* an event to happen. Use this worksheet to identify specific triggers for the student's unpleasant emotions. After creating this list, discuss with the student the most powerful and frequently occurring triggers that will then become the focus for their practice. Remember to be as specific as possible.

External Triggers

Other person's action or speech:
Situation with friends:
Situation with teachers:
Situation with family:
Other events:

Internal Triggers

Thoughts:
Feelings:

Physical sensations:
Memories:
Other experiences:

My Biggest Triggers are...

(1)
(2)
(3)

APPENDIX 1G

Using Soles of the Feet in Daily Life

My Biggest Triggers

(1)
(2)
(3)

Situations where SoF can be useful

In school

When?
Where?
With whom?

At home

When?
Where?
With whom?

Other

When?
Where?
With whom?

These are the best times for me to use Soles of the Feet:

	Trigger (Internal and external)	Situation (When? Where? With whom?)
1		
2		
3		

APPENDIX 2

Soles of the Feet–Fidelity Monitoring Forms

Name of rater:
Date:
Start time:
End time:

Directions: Record student's score as either **0, 1,** or **2** across fidelity elements in the shaded box to the right of each column. Tally student's score at the bottom of the sheet. Higher scores indicate better fidelity.

Structural—Procedural			
	0 Not at all or very little. <10%	**1** Somewhat or moderately. 10% to 90%	**2** Fully or very much. >90%
Reviewed previous session (n/a Session 1)	This element was not implemented in any substantive way.	This element was partially implemented; some aspect was not covered.	This element was fully implemented; followed program completely or nearly completely.
Reviewed between-session practice (n/a Session 1)	This element was not implemented in any substantive way.	This element was partially implemented; some aspect was not covered.	This element was fully implemented; followed program completely or nearly completely.
Introduced session	This element was not implemented in any substantive way.	This element was partially implemented; some aspect was not covered.	This element was fully implemented; followed program completely or nearly completely.
Delivered main session content: *Session 1* Introduced mindful breathing and somatic foot exercises. *Session 2* In vivo exposure and practice with pleasant experience. *Session 3* In vivo exposure and practice with unpleasant experience. *Session 4* In vivo exposure and practice with antecedent to unpleasant experience. *Session 5* Made plan for future SoF practice.	Main session content was not delivered in a substantive way.	Main session content was somewhat delivered; some aspect of this element was not covered.	Main session content was delivered fully; followed program completely or nearly completely.
Closed by reviewing session content.	This element was not implemented in any substantive way.	This element was partially implemented; some aspect was not covered.	This element was fully implemented; followed program completely or nearly completely.
Made a plan for between-session practice.	No plan was made or mentioned for between-session practice.	A poorly defined plan was mentioned for between-session practice; not concrete (e.g., only said to "practice SoF" without specifications).	A clear plan was made for between-session practice; followed program completely or nearly completely.
Distributed and utilized handouts.	Handouts were not distributed or utilized.	Handouts were distributed but not utilized and/or discussed.	Handouts were distributed and utilized and/or discussed.
Practiced SoF routine at least twice during session.	SoF routine was not practiced.	SoF routine was practiced once.	SoF routine was practiced twice or more.

Structural Total (out of 16)

	Instructional—Pedagogical		
	0 Not at all or very little. <10%	**1** Somewhat or moderately. 10% to 90%	**2** Fully or very much. >90%
Engaged students in learning through providing examples of applying material to instructors' own lives and/or that of student(s).	Provided no example.	Provided one example.	Provided two or more examples.
Managed classroom behavior by redirecting negative behavior and reinforcing on-task behavior.	Instructor did not redirect negative behavior or reinforce on-task behavior.	Only once did instructor redirect negative behavior or reinforce on-task behavior.	Instructor redirected negative behavior or reinforced on-task behavior more than once.
Modeled mindful qualities by treating human experiences (both instructor's and student's) with accepting and nonjudgmental attitude.	Responded to reported experiences more than once with nonacceptance or judgment, for example by labeling experience as correct/incorrect, as right/wrong, as good/bad, or as something that should or should not have happened.	Responded to reported experiences once with nonacceptance or judgment, for example by labeling experience as correct/incorrect, as right/wrong, as good/bad, or as something that should or should not have happened.	Never responded to reported experiences with nonacceptance or judgment, for example by labeling experience as correct/incorrect, as right/wrong, as good/bad, or as something that should or should not have happened.
Instructor checked for understanding of material.	Did not stop to check for understanding during session.	Cursory check for understanding or assessed for understanding with a closed question such as "Do you understand this?"	Thoroughly checked for understanding using open-ended questions, by having subject demonstrate procedure, or by facilitating dialogue to ensure understanding.
	Instructional—Engagement		
Student(s) participated in activities.	Student(s) did not seem to be engaged in activity; student (or in group, most students) appeared to not practice during sessions.	Student(s) somewhat engaged in activity; student (or in group, about half of students) appeared to not practice during sessions.	Student(s) highly engaged in activity; student (or in group, most students) appeared to practice during sessions.
Student(s) participated in discussion.	Student (in a group, only one or two students) very reluctantly (or not at all) answered questions or engaged in discussion.	Student (or in a group, about half of students) only some of the time answered questions or engaged in discussion.	Student (or in a group, most students) answered questions or engaged in discussion during majority of session.
Student(s) practiced between sessions.	Student did not practice between session. Few among the group (50%) practiced between sessions.	Student practiced during some days (50%) between sessions.	Student practiced most days (>50%) between sessions. Most of the group (>75%) practiced most days (>50%) between sessions.

Instructional Total (out of 14)

Observational Notes/Comments:

APPENDIX 3

Soles of the Feet Research

With the advent of the seminal program Mindfulness-Based Stress Reduction (MBSR; Kabat-Zinn, 1990), research on the effectiveness of mindfulness-based programs generally has grown exponentially. Most of this research has assessed the utility of MBSR or Mindfulness-Based Cognitive Therapy (MBCT; Segal, Williams, & Teasdale, 2002) in their original form across different adult participant groups and settings, but more recent research has focused on either adaptations of these two programs or on new programs that have their genesis in these programs. In adult populations, there is good evidence to suggest that mindfulness-based programs (MBPs) are moderately effective in reducing psychological and emotional distress (Khoury et al., 2013). Bearing in mind the methodological limitations of current studies, MBPs appear to be effective in mitigating depression, anxiety, and stress, and in enhancing several aspects of quality of life (Eberth & Sedlmeier, 2012). Furthermore, they are effective in ameliorating physical health conditions, including chronic pain, immune system functioning, and several disease-specific physical health variables (Creswell, 2017).

The application of MBPs with children and youth is in the early stages of research (Zack, Saekow, Kelly, & Radke, 2014). Some early studies have adapted MBSR and MBCT for children and youth (such as Biegel, Brown, Shapiro, & Schubert, 2009; Semple, Reid, & Miller, 2005), but others have reported on a diversity of mindfulness programs for children and youth. Examples include such programs as "Learning to BREATHE" (Broderick & Metz, 2009) and "the .b curriculum" (Kuyken et al., 2013). These programs were developed from slightly different theoretical orientations, but they share overlapping mindfulness component practices, such as breath awareness, attention training, body scan, and emotion regulation, and are typically presented in a group format (Zenner, Herrnleben-Kurz, & Walach, 2014). These programs were designed to be developmentally appropriate to the age of the participants, for example, having shorter sessions than those with adults, being offered in small groups, typically with more than one therapist or teacher, having shorter home practice exercises, and being contextualized with games, pictures, and videos.

In general, although the research has methodological shortcomings, meta-analyses have reported small to moderate effects for a number of variables, such as cognitive performance, anxiety, depression, stress, attention, resilience, and mindfulness (Borquist-Conlon, Maynard, Brendel, & Farina, 2017; Kallapiran, Koo, Kirubakaran, & Hancock, 2015; Klingbeil et al., 2017; Zenner et al., 2014; Zoogman, Goldberg, Hoyt, & Miller, 2015). Clinically, research with youth suggests that mindfulness-based programs may have an impact on symptoms of attention deficit/hyperactivity disorder, such as hyperactivity, impulsivity, and inattention (Cairncross & Miller, in press). Other research indicates that adolescents with behavior disorders show reductions in externalizing symptoms, higher levels of perceived attention, and enhanced attentional task scores (Bogels, Hoogstad, van Dun, Schutter, & Restifo, 2008). Mindfulness-based programs have been promising in terms of adolescents being able to better manage their hyperactivity, impulsivity, and verbal and physical aggression (Van Vliet et al., 2017).

We also conducted our own systematic review of the existing school-based mindfulness intervention literature and drew similar conclusions (Felver, Celis-de Hoyos, Tezanos, & Singh, 2016). We found that mindfulness programs do seem to be beneficial across a wide array of outcomes, similar to results in the adult literature. However, there were some notable limitations in the field, and based on these limitations, we provided several targeted recommendations for future research. One recommendation is that researchers replicate mindfulness protocols. Without replication, by which we mean repeating a study protocol using the same intervention, it is hard to definitively conclude that a specific intervention is effective, as any results obtained from a single study may have been due to chance. Another recommendation is that MBPs be delivered to students with disabilities, as this was rarely done at the time. A final recommendation worth noting is that researchers examine outcomes that are most relevant to schools. Most researchers used, and continue to use, self-report psychological questionnaires to study MBPs (e.g., a form providing a checklist of symptoms for stress). While this is an important methodology, it does not actually assess for things that are directly relevant to school systems, such as academic behavior and grades.

SoF stands out in the field of MBPs in school settings because it addresses many of the limitations in the field noted by ourselves and other peer research scientists. SoF is notable for being one of the few MBPs that has been used with students with disabilities. We believe that the simplicity of SoF is what allows it to be so effective even with students with significant behavioral and cognitive limitations. SoF is also unusual in the field of MBI literature as being one of the only interventions that has demonstrated effects on student academic behavior as measured via direct observation (as opposed to a questionnaire about what one thinks about student behavior). Direct observation measures are the exact tools that schools use when conducting school-based evaluations of student behavior (such as Functional Behavioral Assessments), and, therefore, we believe our findings are highly relevant to school systems.

SoF has been replicated more times in the scientific literature than most other MBPs, and to our knowledge, has been replicated more times than any other MBP that is used in school settings. With every replication, we can more definitively conclude that this intervention is effective. Replicating studies is one of the most important considerations—perhaps*the* most important—when scientifically assessing the effectiveness of an intervention. What these replications mean is that across multiple studies, with multiple researchers, and multiple different populations, SoF has demonstrated utility to reduce disruptive behavior and support individuals in various contexts. To quantify this, we have aggregated the existing research findings using a statistical approach called a meta-analysis (Clawson, Martens, Wang, & Felver, in preparation). This meta-analysis examined the effects of SoF across 14 single-case research experiments among participants whose ages ranged from 9 to 49 and included participants from diverse settings (including schools, inpatient units, and community settings) and diverse disability statuses (Autism Spectrum Disorder, depressions, intellectual disability, no disability, and so on). This study concluded that the SoF program is effective for reducing disruptive behavior (Tau-U effect size = -0.75; CI95 = -0.81 to -0.68), regardless of the individuals' age and disability status. This finding provides the strongest evidence to date that SoF can support individuals with challenging behaviors.

To illustrate SoF further, it is worth describing in greater detail some of the studies that went into the aforementioned meta-analysis, as this will highlight how this protocol has been refined over the years. In the earliest published study, Singh, Wahler, Adkins, and Myers (2003) reported the case of a young man with mental illness and developmental disabilities who had a revolving-door entry to a psychiatric hospital whenever he was aggressive in the community. After several psychiatric readmissions during which he was on behavior intervention plans and psychotropic medications for his aggressive behavior, he was taught the SoF practice so that he could be successfully reintegrated in the community without further readmissions. He achieved self-control of his aggressive behavior at the psychiatric hospital, followed by a six-month period of no aggressive behavior, and was then discharged to community housing without any further readmission. During the following year in the community, he did not engage in physical or verbal aggression, he showed self-control during incidents that previously would have resulted in aggressive behavior, he no longer required the use of psychotropic medications for his aggressive behavior, and he engaged in socially and physically integrated activities in his community, including regular paid employment. He did so well that he was able to teach the SoF practice to his peers in the community who were having anger and aggression management problems (Singh, Lancioni, Winton, Singh, Singh, et al., 2011A), indicating how a practitioner can easily teach another person based on personal experience of the SoF practice.

In a multiple-baseline study, three adolescent students with conduct disorder learned to use SoF to manage their aggressive or bullying behavior and to track their self-reported collateral behaviors, including fire setting, cruelty to animals, and noncompliance with teacher requests in the classroom (Singh, Lancioni, Joy, et al., 2007a). In four sessions, a therapist taught the students individually to use the SoF practice for self-management of aggressive behavior. Teachers recorded all incidents of aggressive behavior at school, and the students recorded their own collateral behaviors. Results showed that all three adolescents were able to substantially reduce their aggressive behavior to levels acceptable to the school system. The levels of change were mixed for the nontargeted collateral behaviors, with fire setting being reduced by 50%, cruelty to animals being reduced by 18%, and only a 4% reduction in noncompliance with teacher requests. The data suggested that the adolescents developed inhibitory responses only to aggressive behavior because its escalation would have resulted in their expulsion from school, but chose not to inhibit the non-targeted collateral behaviors. This study suggested that adolescents with conduct disorder can selectively use SoF to self-manage their socially undesirable behaviors.

Individuals who function at moderate levels of intellectual disability are often at risk for losing their community placement due to aggressive and disruptive behaviors. In a multiple-baseline design, Singh, Lancioni, Winton, Adkins, Singh, et al. (2007b) taught three such adults the SoF practice to self-manage their aggressive behavior. All three individuals evidenced some difficulty in being able to learn the SoF practice, especially the task of visualizing past anger-producing situations or past instances during which they were angry and physically aggressive. Procedural changes were made to help them to overcome this problem. "Recreating the scene" (Van Houten & Rolider, 1988), a mediational procedure that enables the trainer to recreate behavioral sequences of an individual's past behaviors so that consequences can be delivered following the simulation, was added to enable the individuals to develop their SoF practice following an anger-producing situation. Adding this component enabled the three adults to learn the SoF practice and to use it to reduce and eventually eliminate their aggressive behavior, to maintain the behavioral change during the two-year follow-up period, and to not lose their community placement.

This study showed how people with seriously compromised cognitive capacity can learn to use the SoF procedure through simple adaptations of complementary learning-based procedures.

Individuals with severe and persistent mental illness often evince aggressive behaviors. They are usually prescribed several psychotropic medications for their mental illness as well as for physical aggression. In addition, aggressive behavior sometimes emerges as an unintended effect of these medications. Singh, Lancioni, Winton, Adkins, Wahler, et al. (2007c) explored the possibility of teaching three adults with severe and persistent mental illness and aggressive behavior to use the SoF program for the self-management of their aggressive behavior. Training was initiated at the psychiatric hospital where the three adults were inpatients. They learned to use the SoF program and were able to stop being physically aggressive, with very low levels of verbal aggression. Upon discharge to the community, they were able to maintain their behavioral gains during the four-year follow-up period. This study showed that people with mental illness are capable of managing aggressive behavior if they are given training in a simple and effective method for controlling their own behavior.

Adult offenders who function at mild levels of intellectual disability sometimes engage in aggressive behavior. In a multiple baseline study, Singh, Lancioni, Winton, Singh, Adkins, et al. (2008a) taught six such adult offenders to use SoF for their aggressive behaviors. Results showed that all six were able to use the SoF program to control their aggressive behaviors. In addition, the study assessed cost-benefit during the 12-month period before and 12 months after teaching these six adult offenders the SoF practice. In terms of additional costs incurred by the agency due to the aggressive behavior of these adults, it was $51,508 before when compared to $2,244 after SoF training. This study suggests that the benefits of SoF may have clinical, social, and cost-benefit advantages over other interventions.

As people age, some develop Alzheimer's disease. One common adverse effect of that disease is that some people begin to exhibit verbal and physical aggression toward their loved ones and professional caregivers. Singh, Lancioni, Medvedev, Sreenivas, Myers, and Hwang (2019) explored the utility of teaching people in the early stages of Alzheimer's disease to use SoF to self-manage their anger and aggression. What they found was that people with early stage Alzheimer's disease were indeed able to manage their anger and aggression. However, they lose this skill as the disease progresses. This study shows that people's quality of life can be improved for a time even when they have a progressive disease that will eventually overwhelm their cognitive system. SoF provides a simple means of doing this.

Most of the research on SoF has used single-subject experimental research design to evaluate its internal validity. Singh, Lancioni, Karazsia, et al. (2013) reported a randomized trial using a waitlist control condition to assess the effects and external validity of SoF with adults who functioned at a mild level of intellectual disability. Results showed the adults were able to significantly reduce their physical and verbal aggression due to SoF when compared to the waitlist control condition. Similar findings were reported for the waitlist control group when they were taught SoF as well. This study suggests it is likely that many individuals who function at a mild level of intellectual disability may benefit from learning the SoF program for controlling their aggressive and destructive behaviors.

In these studies, SoF was used as a single intervention. In other studies, SoF has been used adjunctively to enhance the potency of other interventions. For example, in work with individuals with Prader-Willi syndrome (PWS), SoF has been used as a default self-control practice against the urge to eat between meals. Individuals with PWS, a genetic disorder, often exhibit multiple symptoms, the most debilitating of which include hyperphagia and obesity. The hyperphagia is thought to produce a delayed satiation response, which leads individuals with PWS to continue eating even when they are full, thus resulting in gross obesity. There are no effective treatments for obesity in this population, but a mindfulness-based approach appears to show some promise. In a proof-of-concept study, Singh, Lancioni, Singh, Winton, Singh, McAleavey, et al. (2008b) reported significant reduction in weight due to a lifestyle Mindfulness-Based Health Wellness (MBHW) program that was maintained during a three-year follow-up period. The components of this program include physical exercise, food awareness, mindful eating to manage rapid eating, visualizing and labeling hunger, and SoF to reduce the urge to eat between meals. Using a changing-criterion design, Singh, Lancioni, Singh, Winton, Singh, and Singh (2011B) reported the use of the MBHW program by three individuals with PWS. These individuals were able to make lifestyle changes through this program and reach their desired body weight and maintain their body mass index (BMI) within the average healthy range (20 to 25) during the three-year follow-up period.

Recently, Myers et al. (2018) replicated these findings with a large sample of individuals with intellectual and developmental disabilities.

Elementary school students often engage in off-task behavior that reduces their academic engagement. What teachers need is a simple, portable, and effective intervention that may affect both of these behaviors. Felver and colleagues (2014) evaluated the effectiveness, acceptability, and feasibility of the SoF practice in doing just this. In a multiple baseline design, they observed three elementary school students for both behaviors during baseline, training on the SoF, and follow-up. They reported reductions in the students' off-task behaviors and increases in their academic engagement as a consequence of the children learning to use the SoF practice. The participating students and their teachers rated SoF as a socially valid, feasible, and acceptable intervention for use in public schools. In a subsequent study, Felver et al. (2017) systematically replicated their initial study but with special-education students. Both studies reported similar findings, suggesting the robustness of the SoF practice in decreasing disruptive off-task behaviors and increasing academic engagement regardless of the students' ability status. These school-based studies also incorporated several minor adaptations (such as the creation of worksheets) so that SoF was delivered in a format that students and teachers were most familiar with.

In some of our current work, we are exploring the utility of SoF when delivered to classrooms of students. In one clinical trial, college freshmen with heightened levels of test-taking anxiety were recruited for a randomized clinical trial of SoF. We used a group protocol that is described in this book and that was initially developed for classrooms of students with severe psychiatric disabilities. Results of this research are forthcoming, but the preliminary analyses we've conducted have provided some very exciting results. SoF appears to reduce feelings of test-taking anxiety at similar levels to an active control condition (cognitive-behavioral therapy); however, students who use SoF during test-taking situations (including high-stakes final examinations) evidenced improved scores on their tests. In addition, we are actively researching the degree to which classroom-administered SoF can support the behavior of groups of students in special-education settings.

APPENDIX 4

Supplementary Resources

This book explores a mindfulness-based program, Soles of the Feet. The utility of this program is that it is brief and, compared to other interventions, relatively simple. It is designed to teach students a single mindfulness practice to support their day-to-day lives, and we believe that this book contains all of the necessary instructions and details to teach the curriculum thoroughly.

That being said, Soles of the Feet as a mini-curriculum does not exist in a vacuum. It needs to be delivered by a teacher or school-based professional who is skilled at working with children in general, and with children with behavioral problems in particular. It is also delivered in the context of a complex school ecosystem, which includes other professionals, students, and existing practices.

It is well beyond the scope of this (or any!) book to detail all the prerequisite instructor qualifications that make one competent to teach students with disruptive behavioral problems. It is also beyond the scope of this book to enumerate the school-based practices that might exist in public school settings. This being said, we do believe it is worth providing some additional *targeted* resources that you as a teacher may find useful in your delivery of Soles of the Feet.

In this appendix, we provide a list of supplementary resources that you may find useful for developing skills in mindfulness practice or for supporting students who are struggling with disruptive behavior problems. This list of resources is not exhaustive and we are certain that there are many other fine resources that are not included here. It is simply a list of external resources that we have used and found useful in our own work. We provide it to you as a teacher with the intention that it may be supportive of your work with students. This list is explicitly provided as references and does not represent any official endorsement.

Resources for Mindfulness Practice

Mindfulness-Based Stress Reduction (MBSR; Kabat-Zinn, 1990) is a foundational secular mindfulness training curriculum. Searching for this program will likely yield trainings in your local area. MBSR is the most evidence-based mindfulness training program available, and it is a recommended curriculum to develop a foundational mindfulness practice.

Cultivating Awareness and Resilience in Education is a mindfulness training program developed specifically for teachers. Details on trainings can be found on their website, https://createforeducation.org/.

Nonsecular mindfulness training is also frequently provided by Buddhist groups across the world. It is worth noting that many people have found that Buddhist practices do not conflict with core spiritual or religious traditions. In fact, some Buddhist centers offer retreats and mindfulness trainings specifically for other religious communities. However, as in any spiritual traditions, some sects of Buddhism are more secular than others, and some also are more acculturated to Western culture. The Insight Meditation Society in Massachusetts (https://www.dharma.org/) and the affiliated Spirit Rock Insight Meditation Center in California (https://www.spiritrock.org/) are two examples of Buddhist-affiliated centers that offer a range of trainings and programs, including fully secular and nonsecular programs, that you might consider exploring.

Resources for Mindfulness Research

American Mindfulness Research Association (https://goamra.org/) offers a wealth of resources related to mindfulness research, including a well-developed list of training and research centers across the world.

Mindfulness (https://link.springer.com/journal/12671) is the preeminent peer-reviewed scientific journal for research related to mindfulness practices.

The Journal of Contemplative Inquiry (https://www.contemplativemind.org/journal) is a peer-reviewed journal focused on contemplative practices (such as mindfulness) in higher education.

Mindfulness Research and Training Centers

Below is a list of some of the largest research centers in the world. Again, this list is not exhaustive, and there are many other organizations that do excellent work that are not listed here. Many research centers provide mindfulness training, opportunities for collaboration, and additional resources that you may find very useful (such as guided mindfulness practice recordings).

Bangor University Centre for Mindfulness Research and Practice (https://www.bangor.ac.uk/mindfulness/).

Mind and Life Institute (https://centerhealthyminds.org/).

Brown University Mindfulness Center (https://www.brown.edu/public-health/mindfulness/node/1).
University of Oxford Mindfulness Centre (http://oxfordmindfulness.org/).
University of California Los Angeles Mindful Awareness Research Center (https://www.uclahealth.org/marc/).
University of California San Diego Center for Mindfulness (https://medschool.ucsd.edu/som/fmph/research/mindfulness/pages/default.aspx).
University of Massachusetts Medical School Center for Mindfulness (https://www.umassmed.edu/cfm/).
University of Virginia Contemplative Sciences Center (https://csc.virginia.edu/).
University of Wisconsin Madison Center for Healthy Minds (https://centerhealthyminds.org/).

Resources for Other Evidence-Based Programs

Soles of the Feet is an effective intervention to reduce disruptive behavior in educational and noneducational settings. We and our colleagues have conducted years of research on Soles of the Feet and have provided compelling evidence that this curriculum is effective for many individuals. This being said, there are also other interventions that are effective and that have strong scientific support for reducing behavioral problems in school settings. Following are a list of resources that you can use to identify other evidence-based interventions to support classrooms or individual students.

Institute of Education Sciences What Works Clearinghouse (https://ies.ed.gov/ncee/wwc/).

PracticeWise (https://www.practicewise.com/).

University of Missouri Evidence Based Intervention Network (http://ebi.missouri.edu/).

U.S. Department of Education's Technical Assistance Center on Positive Behavioral Interventions & Supports (https://www.pbis.org/).

References

Baer, R.A. (2003). Mindfulness training as a clinical intervention: A conceptual and empirical review. *Clinical Psychology: Science and Practice, 10,* 125-143.

Biegel, G.M., Brown, K.W., Shapiro, S.L., & Schubert, C.M. (2009). Mindfulness-based stress reduction for the treatment of adolescent psychiatric outpatients: A randomized clinical trial. *Journal of Consulting and Clinical Psychology, 77(5),* 855.

Bishop, S.R., Lau, M., Shapiro, S., Carlson, L., Anderson, N.D., Carmody, J., et al. (2004). Mindfulness: A proposed operational definition. *Clinical Psychology: Science and Practice, 11(3),* 2 30-241.

Bogels, S., Hoogstad, B., van Dun, L., de Schutter, S., & Restifo, K. (2008). Mindfulness training for adolescents with externalizing disorders and their parents. *Behavioural and Cognitive Psychotherapy, 36(2),* 193–209.

Borquist-Conlon, D.S., Maynard, B.R., Brendel, K.E., & Farina, A.S.J. (2017). Mindfulness-based interventions for youth with anxiety: A systematic review and meta-analysis. *Research on Social Work Practice, 29(2),* 195–205.

Broderick, P.C., & Metz, S. (2009). Learning to BREATHE: A pilot trial of a mindfulness curriculum for adolescents. *Advances in School Mental Health Promotion, 2,* 35–46.

Brown, K.W., Ryan, R.M., & Creswell, J.D. (2007). Mindfulness: Theoretical foundations and evidence for its salutary effects. *Psychological Inquiry, 18,* 211–237.

Cairncross, M., & Miller, C.J. (in press). The effectiveness of mindfulness-based therapies for ADHS: A meta-analytic review. *Journal of Attention Disorders.*

Century, J., Rudnick, M., & Freeman, C. (2010). A framework for measuring fidelity of implementation: A foundation for shared language and accumulation of knowledge. *American Journal of Evaluation, 31(2)*, 199–218.

Chiesa, A., & Serretti, A. (2013). Are mindfulness-based interventions effective for substance use disorders? A systematic review of the evidence. *Substance Use & Misuse, 49(5)*, 492–512.

Clawson, A.J., Martens, B., Wang, Q., & Felver, J.C. (in preparation). A meta-analysis of Soles of the Feet mindfulness intervention single case research studies.

Creswell, D.J. (2017). Mindfulness interventions. *Annual Review of Psychology, 68*, 491–516.

Eberth, J., & Sedlmeier, P. (2012). The effects of mindfulness meditation: A meta-analysis. *Mindfulness, 3*, 174–189.

Feagans Gould, L., Dariotis, J.K., Greenberg, M.T., & Mendelson, T. (2016). Assessing fidelity of implementation (FOI) for school-based mindfulness and yoga interventions: A systematic review. *Mindfulness, 7*(1), 5–33.

Felver, J.C., Celis-de Hoyos, C.E., Tezanos, K., & Singh, N.N. (2016). A systematic review of mindfulness-based interventions for youth in school settings. *Mindfulness, 7,* 34–45.

Felver, J.C., Felver, S.L., Margolis, K.L., Ravitch, N.K., Romer, N., & Horner, R.H. (2017) Effectiveness and social validity of the Soles of the Feet mindfulness-based intervention with special education students. *Contemporary School Psychology, 21,* 358–368.

Felver, J.C., Frank, J.L., & McEachern, A.D. (2014). Effectiveness, acceptability, and feasibility of the Soles of the Feet mindfulness-based intervention with elementary school students. *Mindfulness, 5,* 589–597.

Felver, J.C., & Jennings, P.A. (2016). Applications of mindfulness-based interventions in school settings. *Mindfulness, 7(1)*, 1–29.

Galla, B.M., Baelen, R.N., Duckworth, A.L., & Baime, M. (2016). Mindfulness, meet self-regulation: Boosting out-of-class meditation practice with brief action plans. *Motivation Science, 2*, 220–237.

Hölzel, B.K., Lazar, S.W., Gard, T., Schuman-Olivier, Z., Vago, D.R., & Ott, U. (2011). How does mindfulness meditation work? Proposing mechanisms of action from a conceptual and neural perspective. *Perspectives on Psychological Science, 6*, 537–559.

Kabat-Zinn, J. (1990). *Full catastrophe living: Using the wisdom of your body and mind to face stress, pain, and illness.* New York: Delta.

Kallapiran, K., Koo, S., Kirubakaran, R., & Hancock, K. (2015). Review: Effectiveness of mindfulness in improving mental health symptoms of children and adolescents: A meta-analysis. *Child and Adolescent Mental Health, 20,* 182–194.

Jennings, P.A. (2019). *The mindful school: Transforming school culture through mindfulness and compassion.* New York: Guilford.

Khoury, B., Lecomte, T., Fortin, G., Masse, M., Therien, P., Bouchard, V., et al. (2013). Mindfulness-based therapy: A comprehensive meta-analysis. *Clinical Psychology Review, 33(6),* 763–771.

Khoury, B., Sharma, M., Rush, S.E., & Fournier, C. (2015). Mindfulness-based stress reduction for healthy individuals: A meta-analysis. *Journal of Psychosomatic Research, 78,* 519–528.

Klingbeil, D.A., Renshaw, T.L., Willenbrink, J.B., Copek, R.A., Chan, K.T., Haddock, A., et al. (2017). Mindfulness-based interventions with youth: A comprehensive meta-analysis of group-design studies. *Journal of School Psychology, 63,* 77–103.

Kuyken, W., Weare, K., Ukoumunne, O.C., Vicary, R., Motton, N., Burnett, R., et al. (2013). Effectiveness of the Mindfulness in Schools Programme: Non-randomized controlled feasibility study. *British Journal of Psychiatry, 203(2),* 126–131.

Myers, R.E., Karazsia, B.T., Kim, E., Jackman, M.M., McPherson, C.L., & Singh, N.N. (2018). A telehealth parent-mediated mindfulness-based health wellness intervention for adolescents and young adults with intellectual and developmental disabilities. *Advances in Neurodevelopmental Disabilities, 2,* 241–252.

Renshaw, T.L., & Cook, C.R. (2017). Introduction to the special issue: mindfulness in the schools—Historical roots, current status, and future directions. *Psychology in the Schools, 54(1),* 5–12. https://doi.org/10.1002/pits.21978

Schonert-Reichl, K.A., & Roeser, R.W. (2016). *Handbook of mindfulness in education: Integrating theory and research into practice.* New York: Springer.

Segal, Z.V., Williams, J.M.G., & Teasdale, J.D. (2002). *Mindfulness-based cognitive therapy for depression.* New York: Guilford.

Semple, R.J., Reid, E.F., & Miller, L. (2005). Treating anxiety with mindfulness: An open trial of mindfulness training for anxious children. *Journal of Cognitive Psychotherapy, 19(4),* 379.

Singh, N.N., Lancioni, G.E., Joy, S.D.S., Winton, A.S.W., Sabaawi, M., Wahler, R.G., et al. (2007a). Adolescents with conduct disorder can be mindful of their aggressive behavior. *Journal of Emotional and Behavioral Disorders, 15,* 56–63.

Singh, N.N., Lancioni, G.E., Karazsia, B.T., Winton, A.S.W., Myers, R.E., Singh, A.N.A., et al. (2013). Mindfulness-based treatment of aggression in individuals with intellectual disabilities: A waiting list control study. *Mindfulness, 4,* 158–167.

Singh, N.N., Lancioni, G.E., Medvedev, O.N., Sreenivas, S., Myers, R.E., & Hwang, Y-S. (2019). Meditation on the Soles of the Feet practice provides some control of aggression for individuals with Alzheimer's disease. *Mindfulness,* 10(7), 1232–1242.

Singh, N.N., Lancioni, G.E., Singh, A.N.A., Winton, A.S.W., Singh, A.D.A., & Singh, J. (2011B). A mindfulness-based health wellness program for individuals with Prader-Willi syndrome. *Journal of Mental Health Research in Intellectual Disabilities,* 4, 90–106.

Singh, N.N., Lancioni, G.E., Singh, A.N., Winton, A.S.W., Singh, J., McAleavey, K.M., et al. (2008b). A mindfulness-based health wellness program for managing obesity. *Clinical Case Studies, 7,* 327–339.

Singh, N.N., Lancioni, G.E., Winton, A.S.W., Adkins, A.D., Singh, J., &

Singh, A. (2007b). Mindfulness training assists individuals with moderate mental retardation to maintain their community placements. *Behavior Modification, 31,* 800–814.

Singh, N.N., Lancioni, G.E., Winton, A.S.W., Adkins, A.D., Wahler, R.G., Sabaawi, M., et al. (2007c). Individuals with mental illness can control their aggressive behavior through mindfulness training. *Behavior Modification, 31,* 313–328.

Singh, N.N., Lancioni, G.E., Winton, A.S.W., Singh, A.N., Adkins, A.D., & Singh, J. (2008a). Clinical and benefit-cost outcomes of teaching a mindfulness-based procedure to adult offenders with intellectual disabilities. *Behavior Modification, 32,* 622–637.

Singh, N.N., Lancioni, G.E., Winton, A.S.W., Singh, J., Singh, A.N.A., & Singh, A.D.A. (2011A). Peer with intellectual disabilities as a mindfulness-based anger and aggression management therapist. *Research in*

Developmental Disabilities, 32, 2690-2696.

Singh, N.N., Wahler, R.G., Adkins, A.D., & Myers, R.E. (2003). Soles of the Feet: A mindfulness-based self-control intervention for aggression by an individual with mild mental retardation and mental illness. *Research in Developmental Disabilities, 24,* 158-169.

Tang, Y.Y., Hölzel, B.K., & Posner, M.I. (2015). The neuroscience of mindfulness meditation. *Nature Reviews Neuroscience, 16(4),* 213-215.

Van Houten, R., & Rolider, A. (1988). Recreating the scene: An effective way to provide delayed punishment for inappropriate motor behavior. *Journal of Applied Behavior Analysis, 21,* 187-192.

Van Vliet, K.J., Foskett, A.J., Williams, J.L., Singhal, A., Dolcos, F., & Vohra, S. (2017). Impact of a mindfulness-based stress reduction program from the perspective of adolescents with serious mental health concerns. *Child & Adolescent Mental Health, 22(1),* 16–22.

Zack, S., Saekow, J., Kelly, M., & Radke, A. (2014). Mindfulness based interventions for youth. *Journal of Rational-Emotive & Cognitive-Behavior Therapy, 32(1),* 44–56.

Zenner, C., Herrnleben-Kurz, S., & Walach, H. (2014). Mindfulness-based interventions in schools—A systematic review and meta-analysis. *Frontiers in Psychology, 5,* 603.

Zoogman, S., Goldberg, S.B., Hoyt, W.T., & Miller, L. (2015). Mindfulness interventions with youth: A meta-analysis. *Mindfulness, 6,* 290–302.

Joshua C. Felver, PhD, ABPP, is assistant professor of psychology at Syracuse University, and director of clinical training in the school psychology program. Felver teaches courses in child development, child and family interventions, and school-based mental health. His research broadly focuses on the development, implementation, and study of mindfulness-based programming in school and community settings. He directs the Mind Body Laboratory which studies how mindfulness-based programming implemented in schools can support academic functioning and classroom behavior, and investigates the neurobiological mechanisms of contemplative practices.

Nirbhay N. Singh, PhD, BCBA-D, is clinical professor of psychiatry and health behavior at the Medical College of Georgia, Augusta University, certified behavior analyst, and developer of the Mindfulness-Based Positive Behavior Support (MBPBS) and Soles of the Feet programs. His research focuses on assistive technology, health and wellness interventions, and mindfulness-based programs across the life span that reduce suffering and enhance quality of life. He is editor in chief of *Mindfulness* and *Advances in Neurodevelopmental Disorders.*

Foreword writer **Robert Horner, PhD,** is professor emeritus of special education at the University of Oregon. His history of research, grants management, and systems change efforts related to school reform and positive behavior support include helping schools and school administrators develop systems for positive behavior support.

Real change is possible

For more than forty-five years, New Harbinger has published proven-effective self-help books and pioneering workbooks to help readers of all ages and backgrounds improve mental health and well-being, and achieve lasting personal growth. In addition, our spirituality books offer profound guidance for deepening awareness and cultivating healing, self-discovery, and fulfillment.

Founded by psychologist Matthew McKay and Patrick Fanning, New Harbinger is proud to be an independent, employee-owned company. Our books reflect our core values of integrity, innovation, commitment, sustainability, compassion, and trust. Written by leaders in the field and recommended by therapists worldwide, New Harbinger books are practical, accessible, and provide real tools for real change.

 new**harbinger**publications

MORE BOOKS from NEW HARBINGER PUBLICATIONS

LEARNING TO BREATHE
A Mindfulness Curriculum for Adolescents to Cultivate Emotion Regulation, Attention, & Performance

A STILL QUIET PLACE
A Mindfulness Program for Teaching Children & Adolescents to Ease Stress & Difficult Emotions

THE GRIT GUIDE FOR TEENS
A Workbook to Help You Build Perseverance, Self-Control & a Growth Mindset

MASTER OF MINDFULNESS
How to Be Your Own Superhero in Times of Stress

SUPERHERO THERAPY
Mindfulness Skills to Help Teens & Young Adults Deal with Anxiety, Depression & Trauma

THE EXECUTIVE FUNCTIONING WORKBOOK FOR TEENS
Help for Unprepared, Late & Scattered Teens

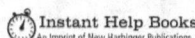

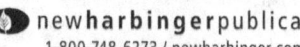

1-800-748-6273 / newharbinger.com

(VISA, MC, AMEX / prices subject to change without notice)

Follow Us

Don't miss out on new books in the subjects that interest you.
Sign up for our **Book Alerts** at **newharbinger.com/bookalerts**

Register your **new harbinger** titles for additional benefits!

When you register your **new harbinger** title—purchased in any format, from any source—you get access to benefits like the following:

- Downloadable accessories like printable worksheets and extra content
- Instructional videos and audio files
- Information about updates, corrections, and new editions

Not every title has accessories, but we're adding new material all the time.

Access free accessories in 3 easy steps:

1. Sign in at NewHarbinger.com (or **register** to create an account).

2. Click on **register a book**. Search for your title and click the **register** button when it appears.

3. Click on the **book cover or title** to go to its details page. Click on **accessories** to view and access files.

That's all there is to it!

If you need help, visit:

NewHarbinger.com/accessories

new harbinger
CELEBRATING
40 YEARS

Back Cover Material

A Groundbreaking Mindfulness Resource for Teachers and Educators

As a teacher, you understand that some children need extra help staying focused in the classroom. However, when disruptive behavior leads to less learning time for everyone, you may also need support. Whether kids are suffering from stress, a behavior disorder, or emotional issues—the good news is there are real tools you can use now to help children manage their feelings, stay on task, and reach their full potential. This book provides an innovative mindfulness solution to help kids be their very best.

Based on the popular Soles of the Feet program, this groundbreaking guide for teachers offers a proven-effective, mindfulness-based intervention to reduce disruptive behavior in the classroom—so everyone can get back to learning. In the book, you'll find strategies for helping kids deal with difficult emotions, as well as in-class exercises and printable worksheets to help increase focus and academic engagement. In addition to improving productivity in the classroom, the Soles of the Feet program will help children experiencing behavior challenges learn important skills to help them thrive—beyond school and well into adulthood.

"**Full of practical wisdom, *Mindfulness in the Classroom* offers a well-researched way to help students cultivate self-regulation skills.**"—Patricia C. Broderick, PhD, author of *Learning to Breathe* and *Mindfulness in the Secondary Classroom*

JOSHUA C. FELVER, PHD, ABPP, is assistant professor of psychology at Syracuse University, and director of clinical training in the school psychology program. His research focuses on the implementation of mindfulness-based interventions in school and community settings.

NIRBHAY N. SINGH, PhD, BCBA-D, is clinical professor of psychiatry and health behavior at the Medical College of Georgia, Augusta

University, certified behavior analyst, and developer of the Mindfulness-Based Positive Behavior Support (MBPBS) and Soles of the Feet programs.

Index

A

action plans, *317, 320*
adolescents: recommendations for working with, *374*
 See also students,
aggressive behavior, *97, 232*
alarm reminders, *317*
alternatively abled students, *363, 365*
anger: aggression related to, *97, 232*
 identifying the feeling of, *94, 97, 161, 229, 232, 295*
 recalling a recent event of, *97, 99, 232, 234*
 Soles of the Feet applied to, *99, 102, 234, 237*
 triggers of, *119, 122, 125, 164, 166, 254, 257, 260, 297, 299, 302*
ankles, identifying, *47, 187*
antecedent-based strategies,
anxiety, SoF for, *352, 371*
arch of the foot, *47, 187*

B

ball of the foot, *47, 184*
behavioral expectations: classroom curriculum, *39, 42*
 individual program, *179, 182*
belly breathing instruction: classroom curriculum, *44*
 individual program, *184*

between-session practice strategies, *311, 315, 317, 320, 323*
  creating an action plan, *317, 320*
  enhancing motivation to achieve goals, *311, 315*
  placing reminder stickers to aid memory, *315*
  providing praise and reinforcement, *320, 323*
  recruiting peer support and feedback, *320*
  relating practice to other activities, *323*
  sending daily practice reminders, *317*
  tying practice to existing routines, *315*

booster class, *151, 153, 155, 158, 161, 164, 166, 169, 171, 172*
  between-class practice review, *158*
  class content reviews, *161, 164*
  closure and practice, *171, 172*
  outline and materials, *153*
  plan for future practice, *169, 171*
  post-practice discussion, *166, 169*
  reviewing the purpose of SoF, *158*
  Soles of the Feet practice, *155, 164, 166, 172*
  understanding check, *155, 158, 161, 164, 169, 171*

booster session, *284, 287, 289, 292, 295, 297, 299, 302, 304, 306*

between-session practice review, *292*
closure and practice, *306*
outline and materials, *287*
plan for future practice, *304*
post-practice discussion, *302*
reviewing the purpose of SoF, *292*
session content reviews, *295, 297*
Soles of the Feet practice, *289, 299, 302, 306*
understanding check, *289, 292, 297, 299, 304, 306*
bracelets, reminder, *315*
breathing instruction: classroom curriculum, *44*
'deep breathing' phrase avoided in, *358*
individual program, *184*

C

children and youth: research on MBPs with,
working with adolescents, *374*
See also students,
Class 1: Introducing Soles of the Feet, *36, 39, 42, 44, 47, 49, 51, 53, 56, 57*
between-class practice assignment, *56, 57*
class review and closure, *56*
defining behavioral expectations, *39, 42*
introducing students to SoF, *39*

learning about the foot, *44, 47*
mindful breathing instruction, *44*
outline and materials, *36*
paying attention to the feet, *47, 49, 51*
posture instruction, *42, 44*
Soles of the Feet practice, *51, 53, 57*
understanding check, *53*

Class 2: Practicing with a Pleasant Feeling, *59, 62, 65, 67, 71, 74, 77, 79, 82*
    between-class practice assignment, *79, 82*
    booster class content review, *161*
    class review and closure, *79*
    identifying the feeling of happiness, *67, 71*
    introducing the class, *65, 67*
    outline and materials, *59*
    post-practice discussion, *77, 79*
    recalling a happy event, *71*
    review of previous class and assignment, *62, 65*
    Soles of the Feet practice, *62, 74, 82*
    understanding check, *65, 79*

Class 3: Practicing with an Unpleasant Feeling, *85, 87, 90, 94, 97, 99, 102, 105, 107, 109*
    between-class practice assignment, *107, 109*
    booster class content review, *161*
    class review and closure, *107*

identifying the feeling of anger, *94, 97*
introducing the class, *94*
outline and materials, *85*
post-practice discussion, *102, 105*
recalling an angry event, *97, 99*
review of previous class and assignment, *87, 90*
Soles of the Feet practice, *87, 99, 102, 109*
understanding check, *94, 105*

Class 4: Practicing with the Triggers to an Unpleasant Feeling, *111, 114, 116, 119, 122, 125, 127, 130, 131*
between-class practice assignment, *130*
booster class content review, *164, 297*
class review and closure, *127, 130*
identifying the triggers of anger, *119, 122*
introducing the class, *119*
outline and materials, *111*
post-practice discussion, *125, 127*
review of previous class and assignment, *114, 116*
Soles of the Feet practice, *114, 122, 125, 131*
understanding check, *116, 127*

Class 5: Planning to Use Soles of the Feet in Daily Life, *133, 136, 139, 141, 144, 147, 149*
curriculum review and closure, *141, 149*

importance of practice discussion, *141, 144*
introducing the class, *139, 141*
mastery check, *147, 149*
outline and materials, *133*
plan for future practice, *144, 147*
review of previous class and assignment, *136, 139*
Soles of the Feet practice, *136, 149*
understanding check, *139, 149*
See also booster class
class/session rules,,
classroom curriculum,
   See specific classes,
classrooms: creating in vivo emotional experiences in, *349, 352*
   identifying support needed in, *18*
   logistics of delivering SoF in, *24*
confidential environment, *340, 343*
control, letting go of, *326*
covert behavior, *56, 196, 374*

D

daily life use of SoF: classroom curriculum, *133, 136, 139, 141, 144, 147, 149*
   individual program, *267, 270, 273, 275, 278, 281, 283*
daily reminders, *315, 317*
'deep breathing', avoiding the phrase, *358*

developmental considerations, *346*
disruptive behavior: active off-task behaviors as,
  anxiety as form of, *352*
  effective strategies for, *371*

E

email reminders, *317*
emotional problems, *369, 371, 374*
emotions:
behaviors controlled by, *326*
  identifying angry, *94, 97, 161, 229, 232, 295*
  identifying happy, *67, 71, 161, 208, 295*
  reviewing class content on, *161, 295*
  Soles of the Feet practice and, *74, 77, 79, 210, 213*
  substituting different, *352, 355*
troubleshooting with students, *329, 331, 335, 337*
  See also feelings, everyday use of SoF,
  See daily life use of SoF,
expectations, setting and framing, *340*
experiences, validating all, *355*
eyes, consideration on closing, *371*

F

feelings: practicing with pleasant, *59, 62, 65, 67, 71, 74, 77, 79, 82, 199, 202, 205, 208, 210, 213, 216, 218*
  practicing with unpleasant, *85, 87, 90, 94, 97, 99, 102, 105, 107, 109, 221, 223, 226, 229, 232, 234, 237, 239, 242, 244*
  substituting different, *352, 355*

troubleshooting with students, *329, 331, 335, 337*
See also emotions,
feet: difficulty feeling, *337*
learning about, *44, 47, 184, 187*
shifting attention to, *51, 191*
somatic experiencing of, *47, 49, 51, 187, 189, 191*
fidelity of implementation, *27*
follow-up class or session,
See booster class; booster session,
See also handouts; worksheets,
framing expectations, *340*
functional behavioral assessment (FBA), *21*

G
goal achievement, *311, 315*
group settings: creating in vivo emotional experiences in, *349, 352*
See also classrooms,
group-messaging board, *317*
See also worksheets,

H
happiness: identifying the feeling of, *67, 161, 208, 295*
recalling a recent event of, *71, 208, 210*
Soles of the Feet applied to, *74, 210, 213*
heel of the foot, *47, 184*

'homework', avoiding the word, *358, 360*

I

if-then statements, *317*

in vivo emotional experiences, *4*
  creating in group settings, *349, 352*
  memories related to, *122, 164, 257, 299*
  pleasant feelings and, *59, 199*
  unpleasant feelings and, *85, 221*

individual program sessions,
  See specific sessions,

instructional tips and strategies, *311, 315, 317, 320, 323, 326, 329, 331, 335, 337, 340, 343, 346, 349, 352, 355, 358, 360, 363, 365, 369, 371, 374*
  for adolescents, *374*
  for alternatively abled students, *363, 365*
  class/session rules creation, *337, 340, 343*
  creating in vivo experiences in groups, *349, 352*
  embodying mindfulness, *355, 358*
  enhancing between-session practice, *311, 315, 317, 320, 323*
  enlisting other teachers or staff members, *365, 369*
  establishing rapport with students, *360, 363*
  increasing student buy-in, *323, 326, 329*
  reminding students to use SoF, *343, 346*
  for self-conscious students, *374*

for students with emotional problems, *369, 371, 374*
supporting memorization of SoF routine, *346, 349*
troubleshooting student issues with SoF, *329, 331, 335, 337*
words and phrases to avoid, *358, 360, 374*
working with different emotions, *352, 355*

M

mastery check: classroom curriculum, *147, 149*
  individual program, *281, 283*
memorizing the SoF routine, *346, 349*
mindful breathing instruction: classroom curriculum, *44*
  'deep breathing' phrase avoided in, *358*
  individual program, *184*
mindfulness:
cautions on use of, *18, 369, 371, 374*
  embodying, *329, 331, 355*
  introducing into public schools, *12, 15*
  modeling the qualities of, *77, 102, 213, 237, 337*
  nonjudgment in, *27, 67, 77, 355*
  peer support for practicing, *320*
  training in, *7, 10*
mindfulness-based programs (MBPs), *18*
monitoring students, *371, 374*

motivation enhancement, *311, 315*
movement activities:
classroom curriculum, *44, 47*
  individual program, *184, 187*
Multi-Tiered System of Support (MTSS), *15*

N

nonjudgment, *27, 67, 77, 355*

P

pace of instruction, *355, 358*
peer support and feedback, *320*
plan for future SoF practice: classroom curriculum, *144, 147, 169, 171*
  individual program, *278, 281, 304*

pleasant feelings: class on practicing with, *59, 62, 65, 67, 71, 74, 77, 79, 82*
  individual session on practicing with, *199, 202, 205, 208, 210, 213, 216, 218*
  substituting alternative, *352*
  See also happiness,
Positive Behavior Interventions and Supports (PBIS), *15*
posture instruction: classroom curriculum, *42, 44*
  individual program, *182*
praising students, *320, 323, 374*
present tense statements, *358*
probing for details, *329, 335*
process fidelity, *27*
psychological problems, *369, 371, 374*

R

rapport, establishing, *360, 363*
reading difficulties, *365*
refresher class or session,
   See booster class; booster session, reinforcement, *320, 323*
reminder stickers, *56, 196, 315*
Response to Intervention (RTI), *15*
routines: My Soles of the Feet Routine handout,
   tying practice to existing, *315*
rules for classes/sessions, *337, 340, 343*

S

safe environment, *340, 343*
scaffolding: providing across SoF sessions, *30, 31*
   student self-deployment of SoF routine, *346*
schools: behavior supports in, *15, 18*
   introducing mindfulness into, *12, 15*
   logistics of delivering SoF in, *24*
   preparing for SoF program, *12, 15, 18, 21, 24*
   recruiting staff for SoF support in, *21, 365, 369*
self-conscious students, *374*
self-monitoring activities, *346*
self-regulation skills, *v, vi, 326*

Session 1: Introducing Soles of the Feet, *176, 179, 182, 184, 187, 189, 191, 193, 196, 197*
  between-session practice assignment, *196*
  defining behavioral expectations, *179, 182*
  introducing students to SoF, *179*
  learning about the foot, *184, 187*
  mindful breathing instruction, *184*
  outline and materials, *176*
  paying attention to the feet, *187, 189, 191*
  posture instruction, *182*
  session review and closure, *193*
  Soles of the Feet practice, *191, 193, 197*
  understanding check, *193*

Session 2: Practicing with a Pleasant Feeling, *199, 202, 205, 208, 210, 213, 216, 218*
  between-session practice assignment, *218*
  booster class content review, *295*
  identifying the feeling of happiness, *208*
  introducing the session, *205, 208*
  outline and materials, *199*
  post-practice discussion, *213, 216*
  recalling a happy event, *208, 210*
  review of previous session and assignment, *202, 205*
  session review and closure, *216, 218*

Soles of the Feet practice, *202, 210, 213, 218*
understanding check, *205, 216*
Session 3: Practicing with an Unpleasant Feeling, *221, 223, 226, 229, 232, 234, 237, 239, 242, 244*
  between-session practice assignment, *242, 244*
  booster class content review, *295*
  identifying the feeling of anger, *229, 232*
  introducing the session, *229*
  outline and materials, *221*
  post-practice discussion, *237, 239*
  recalling an angry event, *232, 234*
  review of previous session and assignment, *223, 226*
  session review and closure, *242*
  Soles of the Feet practice, *223, 234, 237, 244*
  understanding check, *229, 239*
Session 4: Practicing with the Triggers to an Unpleasant Feeling, *246, 249, 252, 254, 257, 260, 262, 265*
  between-session practice assignment, *265*
  booster class content review, *297*
  identifying the triggers of anger, *254, 257*
  introducing the session, *252, 254*
  outline and materials, *246*

post-practice discussion, *260, 262*
review of previous session and assignment, *249, 252*
session review and closure, *262, 265*
Soles of the Feet practice, *249, 257, 260, 265*
understanding check, *252, 262*
Session 5: Planning to Use Soles of the Feet in Daily Life, *267, 270, 273, 275, 278, 281, 283*
   curriculum review and closure, *275, 283*
   importance of practice discussion, *275, 278*
   introducing the session, *273, 275*
   mastery check, *281, 283*
   outline and materials, *267*
   plan for future practice, *278, 281*
   review of previous session and assignment, *270, 273*
   Soles of the Feet practice, *270, 283*
   understanding check, *273, 283*
   See also booster session,
session/class rules, *337, 340, 343*
setting expectations, *340*
sitting difficulties, *365*
skill development, *323*
Socratic questioning, *323*
sole of the foot, *47, 187*
Soles of the Feet (SoF): action plan for, *317, 320*
   daily life use of, *133, 136, 139, 141, 144, 147, 149, 267, 270, 273, 275, 278, 281, 283*

emotions and, *74, 77, 79, 210, 213*
enhancing between-session practice of, *311, 315, 317, 320, 323*
fidelity of implementing, *27*
importance of practicing, *141, 144, 275, 278*
increasing student buy-in for, *323, 326, 329*
instructional tips and strategies, *311, 315, 317, 320, 323, 326, 329, 331, 335, 337, 340, 343, 346, 349, 352, 355, 358, 360, 363, 365, 369, 371, 374*
introducing to students, *39, 179*
logistics for delivering, *24*
mastery check for, *147, 149, 281, 283*
memorizing the routine for, *346, 349*
mindfulness instruction in, *369, 371*
modifications for alternatively abled students, *363, 365*
overview description of, *4, 7*
planning for future practice of, *144, 147, 278, 281*
practicing for the first time, *51, 53, 191, 193*
preparing yourself to use, *7, 10, 12*
reminder sticker for, *56, 196*
reviewing the purpose of, *158, 292*
scaffolding across sessions of, *30, 31*
school preparations for using, *12, 15, 18, 21, 24*
structure and process of, *24, 27, 30*

supporting student use of, *343, 346*
team approach to using, *363, 365, 369*
somatic experience of feet: classroom curriculum, *47, 49, 51*
  individual program, *187, 189, 191*
  student difficulty with, *337*
standing difficulties, *363, 365*
stickers, reminder, *56, 196, 315*
structural fidelity, *27*
students:
alternatively abled, *363, 365*
  emotional problems in, *369, 371, 374*
  enhancing between-session practice in, *311, 315, 317, 320, 323*
  establishing rapport with, *360, 363*
  identifying support needed by, *18, 21, 24*
  increasing SoF buy-in among, *323, 326, 329*
  introducing SoF curriculum to, *39, 179*
  monitoring during exercises, *371, 374*
  praising and encouraging, *320, 323, 374*
  self-consciousness in, *374*
  supporting SoF use by, *343, 346*
supplementary resources, *See* resources,

T

teaching strategies,

See instructional tips and strategies,
team approach to SoF, *363, 365, 369*
text message reminders, *317*
toes, identifying, *47, 187*
top of the foot, *47, 187*
trauma, students with, *371*
  identifying for anger, *119, 122, 164, 254, 257, 297*
  introducing the concept of, *119, 252, 254*
  mindful use of word, *360, 374*
  reviewing class content on, *164, 297*
  Soles of the Feet applied to, *122, 125, 164, 166, 257, 260, 299, 302*

U

unpleasant feelings: class on practicing with, *85, 87, 90, 94, 97, 99, 102, 105, 107, 109*
individual session on practicing with, *221, 223, 226, 229, 232, 234, 237, 239, 242, 244*
relating to disruptive behaviors, *326*
substituting alternative, *352, 355*
See also anger,

W

word choices, *358, 360, 374*
  See also handouts,
writing difficulties, *365*

Y

youth,
  See children and youth,

www.ingramcontent.com/pod-product-compliance
Lightning Source LLC
Chambersburg PA
CBHW011721220426
43664CB00021B/2885